Personal
copy
E Kay Canterbury

The Exhaustion of the Dollar

The Exhaustion of the Dollar

Its Implications for Global Prosperity

H. Peter Gray
*Professor emeritus of international economics and business,
Rutgers – the State University of New Jersey and
Rensselaer Polytechnic Institute*

First published 2004 by
PALGRAVE MACMILLAN
Houndmills, Basingstoke, Hampshire RG21 6XS and
175 Fifth Avenue, New York, N.Y. 10010
Companies and representatives throughout the world

PALGRAVE MACMILLAN is the global academic imprint of the Palgrave Macmillan division of St. Martin's Press, LLC and of Palgrave Macmillan Ltd. Macmillan® is a registered trademark in the United States, United Kingdom and other countries. Palgrave is a registered trademark in the European Union and other countries.

ISBN 1–4039–1885–6

This book is printed on paper suitable for recycling and made from fully managed and sustained forest sources.

A catalogue record for this book is available from the British Library.

Library of Congress Cataloging-in-Publication Data
Gray, H. Peter.
    The exhaustion of the dollar : its implications for global prosperity / H. Peter Gray.
      p. cm.
    Includes bibliographical references and index.
    ISBN 1–4039–1885–6
      1. Financial crises. 2. International finance. 3. Dollar, American.
    4. Currency crises. I. Title.

HB3722.G73 2004
332'.042—dc22
                                        2004042733

10 9 8 7 6 5 4 3 2 1
13 12 11 10 09 08 07 06 05 04

Printed and bound in Great Britain by
Antony Rowe Ltd, Chippenham and Eastbourne

To Cassandra of Troy

Contents

List of Tables

List of Figures

Preface

When a person has been working in an area of economics for over thirty years, he will have acquired intellectual debts. It is important then that I acknowledge some friends and colleagues whose wisdom and lore have helped me get some understanding of balance-of-payments adjustment and the international financial system. Many of these colleagues are people who are dissatisfied with some aspects, frequently the irrelevance, of mainstream economics.

In this venture, Robert G. Hawkins played an important rôle because he encouraged me and gave valuable constructive comments on an ambitious attempt to create an article-length version of this monograph. This proved impossible but I carried Bob's insights over to the longer version although I doubt greatly if either of us could identify them in this version. Two people, both associated with The Jerome Levy Economics Institute of Bard College, played key conceptual rôles. Foremost, is the late Hyman P. Minsky, who more than anyone else, instilled into me the importance of financial stability and the danger of instability. Many years ago Hyman edited a book entitled "Can it Happen Again?" This monograph would, without implying inevitability, answer "yes" and the source of the instability will be the international financial system. Wynne Godley created a new and valuable model of the "real" sector and used it to identify several unsustainable processes. The macroeconomic incompatibilities within the US economy allowed him (and his colleagues) to identify the serious implications of the chronic current-account deficits and the threat of instability in the real sector. Others who have contributed to my work in the past and/or to aspects of this monograph are: E. Ray Canterbery, Paul Davidson, Jean Gray, Jan Kregel, Will Milberg, Terutomo Ozawa, Scheherazade Rehman and Ingo Walter as well as many ex-students and other members of the International Trade and Finance Association.

The rôle of two other people, Bernard and Lisa Cooke, must be acknowledged because they were the ones who convinced me that I should give up leisure and go to work to write this monograph. They were and are working hard and saw no need for me to continue to lead an easy life of retirement. They should have convinced me earlier because someone writing this kind of book lives in dread that the forecast phenomenon will precede publication. The data get worse every year and strengthen the empirical support for Proposition One (the exhaustion of the dollar and its demise as the global key currency).

With this monograph, I have resumed a partnership with Macmillan Press (now Palgrave). The original editor who shepherded me through three books in five years, Tim Farmiloe, is now retired and, I hope, happily so. The friendly support for authors has not changed.

H. PETER GRAY
March, 2004

Part I
Introduction

1
The Purpose and Three Propositions

I The focus of the monograph

To function efficiently, the global economy must both ensure the absence of major financial crisis and maintain adequate aggregate demand at the global level. There is substantial evidence that the existing system is vulnerable in both the financial and the "real" sectors. This systemic vulnerability and its potentially very large adverse consequences for global macrofinancial efficiency are the foci of this monograph.

There are two basic weaknesses. First, there is a danger that the key-currency nation or hegemon, the United States, will exhaust the ability of its currency to retain the confidence of foreign holders of dollar-denominated assets. Second, domestic concerns with chronic current-account deficits (and consequent weaknesses in the rate of domestic capacity utilization and in the domestic labor market) will lead to a renunciation of the duties of being the global locomotive economy (providing the global economy with needed aggregate demand). The two triggers of financial crisis and serious global recession are closely interwoven so that the occurrence of either will automatically trigger the second and mutual interaction will aggravate the degree of inefficiency.[1] Renunciation of these responsibilities by the United States would create a serious void in the international macrofinancial architecture.[2] In addition to examining the minimization of the direct costs of exhaustion, the analysis must, therefore, address the ways in which the transition to a replacement system can be accomplished with minimal disruptions.

The capability of the United States to continue as the hegemon and to continue to assume both of the major responsibilities of that rôle has, with the acceptance of some minor institutional changes, been taken for

3

granted for over fifty years. There are, therefore, many aspects of the international financial system based on a key-currency, which have not, insofar as they relate to the performance of the key-currency nation, been as fully analyzed and documented as is now necessary.

The four chapters in Parts I and II lay the basis for the subject matter of the monograph. Chapter 1 lays out three propositions, one main and two derivative, which relate to the phenomenon of a weak hegemon. Chapters 2, 3 and 4 focus on the specific constraints on and linkages which characterize the existing, dollar-reliant global financial system and which define the rôle of the hegemon. They provide the background needed for an assessment of the three propositions as they apply to the leading financial power (the hegemon) in the modern, highly interdependent, globalized world. These chapters also identify the way in which a global system differs from a national system in its institutional architecture and in the complexity of eliminating or preventing a malfunction.

At the end of the Second World War, the United States accepted the task of being the global financial leader with the responsibility of caring for the efficient functioning of the global financial/economic system. This rôle involves both benefits and duties. The benefit, which attracts major attention, is international seigniorage but over a long period, the cost of the duties outweigh the benefits (Grubel, 1964). The major duties include allowing the US dollar to be used as the so-called "key currency," which serves as the international reference norm for the value of national currencies, the main means of payment for international transactions (especially in those basic commodities which have a worldwide market) and the main currency of denomination for the international reserves of other nations. To fulfil this task, the key currency must be both freely available and a reliable store of value through time for official and private non-residents. The latter entails maintaining its strength in foreign exchange markets. The second major responsibility is to act as the Keynesian locomotive for the global economy. In this rôle, the US dollar and the US economy have become vital contributors to the efficiency of the global economy by allowing the US current balance to fluctuate, to supply the net aggregate demand needed by the global system.[3]

Almost sixty years later, the United States has come close to losing the international financial strength necessary for the dollar to have the qualities needed for the key currency. In fulfilling the locomotive rôle, the US economy has been "living beyond its income" since 1983 thereby weakening the international financial strength of the US dollar (see Table 1.1). In the last four years, 1999 through 2002, the country

Table 1.1 US net international investment position (1983–2002) (with direct investments at current cost)[a] ($ billions at end of year)

Periods/years	1983–87[b]	1988–92[b]	1993–97[b]	1998	1999	2000	2001	2002r
INW (end of prior period or year)	+329.0	−80.0	−431.2	−833.2	−918.7	−797.6	−1,387.7	−1,978.9
Current account balance[c]	−559.1	−344.5	−552.7	−204.7	−290.8	−411.5	−393.7	−480.9
	(−111.8)	(−68.9)	(−110.5)					
Total adjustments	+79.2	+31.8	+252.7	+10.5	+352.8	−134.5	−176.7	+118.5
Statistical discrepancy	+70.9	−38.5	−102.0	+129.7	+59.1	−44.1	−20.8	−45.9
INW at end of period/year	−80.0	−431.2	−833.2	−918.7	−797.6	−1,387.7	−1,978.9	−2,387.2
Memorandum								
With direct investments at market	+50.5	−452.3	−835.2	−1,094.1	−1,053.6	−1,583.2	−2,309.1	−2,605.2

Notes

[a] Gold is valued at year end market price. INW at market valuations is given in the memorandum. For details on the sources and construction, see below, pp 94–8. "Total Adjustments" includes value changes of both real and financial assets in US dollars. This number is clearly sensitive to changes in exchange rates. "Statistical Discrepancy," when positive, shows "unexplained credits" in the international accounts (and vice versa).

[b] Rows, 2, 3 and 4, current account balance, total adjustments and statistical discrepancy are cumulative totals for the five-year periods. For year-to-year detail, see Table 4.1. Average values of the current deficit are given here in parentheses.

[c] The total current deficit in the 20 years was $2.757 trillion. There was a negligible current surplus in 1991 resulting from transfers received by the US government from noncombattant allies in the Gulf War. The sum of the statistical discrepancies was + $55.6 billion. The sum of the "total adjustments" is +$606.9 billion (see Table 5.3).

r = revised

Source: Survey of Current Business, July, 2002, pp. 18–19 and 50–51. For methodological details, see Landefeld and Lawson (1991).

has increased its *net* liabilities to foreigners by more than one and a half trillion dollars. This is the amount by which its purchases of goods and services from foreign suppliers have exceeded revenues from the sale of goods and services to foreign customers. Such excesses of outgo over income must be financed either by drawing down (selling) assets to or by incurring liabilities with ("borrowing" from) non-residents. In the same four years, the shortfall on current transactions has averaged just under 4 percent (3.98) of gross domestic product (GDP). As yet this weakening has not triggered either an unwillingness by creditors to hold assets in dollar-denominated securities or a resolve by the US economic authorities to confront the latent problem.[4]

During the 1960s, there was also much concern over a growing loss of foreign confidence in the US dollar. There is a major distinction between then and the first decade of the twenty-first century. In the 1960s, Despres, Kindleberger and Salant (1966) were able to argue that short-term (liquid) liabilities of the United States were merely a part of an international intermediation process and to confront the problem on that premise. In the mid-1960s, the US dollar was strong in the sense that the country was running a current surplus. The essential problem was that the country's residents, largely multinational corporations, were acquiring assets abroad at a rate in excess of the current surplus so that the ratio of short-term foreign claims to US reserves was increasing. *Then, as now, there was no means by which US corporations and citizens, who own assets in foreign countries, could be required to repatriate foreign assets to bolster the strength of the dollar.*

The possibility that the US dollar will not be able to continue to serve as the key-currency warrants an investigation of the implications of this *exhaustion* for the future prosperity of both the hegemon *and* the rest of the globalized economy. The second area of investigation is the way in which the global economy will accomplish the transformation from a "worn-out" international financial system to a new viable system.[5] It should be explicit that our purpose is to investigate the three propositions. It is not our purpose to allocate blame at either the level of nations or individuals. Rather we seek to identify measures, which will reduce the costs of adjustment, and to identify the need for large-scale international co-operation if the economic and social costs are to be kept within bounds. It is an old truism that the best environment for economic development is for the industrialized or affluent nations to preserve their prosperity (and their willingness to import from the developing countries). This concern and recognition of the social costs of large-scale unemployment in the industrialized countries lie at the heart of the need for keeping the dislocation and the costs of adjustment in resource allocation and levels of living, as small as possible.[6]

II The three propositions

The analysis can be seen as comprising an assessment of each of three related propositions. The propositions are laid out immediately below and the following pages in this section provide some amplification of the need for concern. The propositions are:

1. that the United States will be forced by the exhaustion of its capability to perform the macrofinancial duties of the key-currency country, to relinquish that rôle. In consequence the global economy, as it has existed and evolved over the past fifty plus years, will have to confront major structural change within an unknowable but relatively brief period of time;
2. that attention must be given immediately to the problem of financing the chronic international dissaving by the key-currency country in order to avoid major crisis during the time needed for remedial policy measures to take hold. This need will be greater the larger are the ongoing current deficit and the volume of easily-encashable assets in the hands of non-residents;
3. that the world's financial powers must recognize the need quickly to begin to collaborate in designing a replacement set of institutions to take the place of the existing dollar-reliant global financial system.

The three propositions are closely intertwined. They are of major importance because the efficiency of the international macrofinancial system impinges directly on the general global prosperity and on the rates of capacity utilization and economic growth of the constituent national economies. The first, the exhaustion proposition, addresses the loss of reserve strength on the part of the dollar and its consequent vulnerability to substantial depreciation.[7] Substantial depreciation of the dollar vis-à-vis foreign currencies will lead, at a minimum, to reduced willingness on the part of non-residents to provide the credits needed for the dollar to continue to run deficits on current account. These deficits contribute directly to the level of aggregate demand in the other $n - 1$ countries (the "rest of the world"). In all probability, fear of a substantial depreciation will engender a reversal of past investments in dollar-denominated assets: existing holdings of non-residents will be encashed and transferred out of dollars. The dollar will lose its acceptance as being *the* reliable currency in the global economy and that image of reliability will not be susceptible to instantaneous recovery. The United States will simultaneously lose its power to serve as the global locomotive. Exhaustion can come about for either of two reasons: the loss of confidence on the part of foreign lenders and their unwillingness to continue to hold or to increase their holdings of dollar-denominated assets; and, second, economic and political pressures in the United States that derive from the burden on the domestic economy of the duties of being the global locomotive (injecting aggregate demand into the global system by running current deficits, thereby reducing aggregate demand for domestic capacity), may become intolerable (Godley, 1999) and (Godley and Izurieta, 2002). The mechanisms underlying both triggers and their interdependence are developed in Chapter 5.

The second proposition examines how the eradication of the current-account deficit will get more difficult, more costly and more likely to trigger a crisis as both the flow of international dissaving and the stock of the "net indebtedness" of the United States continue to increase.

The third proposition addresses the need for a reconstitution of the "architecture" of the international macrofinancial system, which came into being at the end of the Second World War and which, despite evolution, continues to rely essentially on the economy of the United States and its dollar. Once a key currency has lost global confidence in its integrity (as a store of value), it cannot quickly re-establish confidence. Failure to replace the hegemon will aggravate the already serious costs of adjustment in the short- and medium-term as the allocation of resources and levels of living adapt to the new conditions. In the long run, the absence of a hegemon will drastically reduce the overall macroeconomic efficiency of the global system.

The exhaustion of the capability (and/or of the will) of the United States to continue to play the rôle and perform the "duties" of the key-currency nation or "global financial hegemon" is hypothesized to derive from the series of large deficits on current account run by the United States in recent years. This string of deficits shows no sign of spontaneously decreasing to manageable proportions.[8] As noted, current-account deficits (shortfalls of revenues from current transactions with non-residents over US expenditures on current transactions with non-residents[9]) have to be financed by a reduction of US claims on foreigners and/or by an increase in the value of claims of non-residents on US residents.[10] Current-account deficits therefore involve *international dissaving* (by the residents of the deficit country vis-à-vis residents of the rest of the world) or, to use the terminology developed below, they reduce the international net worth (INW) of the deficit country. If, as some economists believe, the inflow of foreign saving adds directly to capital formation in the capital-importing country, the country's total net worth (the sum of domestic assets and its INW) is unchanged.[11] In the United States in 2003, the Bush Administration has, in its first three years, continued the indifference to the sign and the size of the current-account balance, which characterized the second Clinton Administration (1997–2001). All four secretaries of the US Treasury involved[12] seem to have regarded the current deficit as nothing more than the measure of the degree to which foreign residents wanted to invest in the United States (in excess of acquisitions of foreign assets by US residents). A similar passivity was registered by Chairman Alan Greenspan in the question and answer period following his testimony before the Joint Economic Committee of the US Congress on November 13, 2002.[13]

There has been an evolutionary change in the global Northian institutions (North, 1990, ch. 1) whereby freedom of capital movements and the existence of a large mass of assets denominated in currencies other than the functional currency of the asset owner, have limited the freedom of nations to set an independent monetary policy out of fear of a flight from their currency.

The implications of the ongoing string of US current-account deficits have not gone completely unnoticed. The three most incisive commentaries, the Bank for International Settlements (2002, pp. 29–31), Godley (1999), and Mann (1999), were all written before data on the size of the US deficits showed the substantial increases that began in 1999 and which continued through 2003 (Figure 1.1 and Table 1.1). These concerns were, therefore, written without knowledge of the full force of the problem. Godley refers to the deficit as "unsustainable" and Mann estimates the future magnitudes of current deficits will exceed anything ever supported by a major nation without engendering a collapse. Experience in the years (2000 through 2002) has validated the order of magnitude of Mann's estimates. In September, 2002, many directors of the International Monetary Fund saw "the persistently high current account deficit and the still high [strong] US dollar as posing some risk of an abrupt and disruptive adjustment." The Bank for International Settlements returned to the issue in its 73rd Annual Report (The Bank for International Settlements, 2003). The problem is summarized in the "Overview" of its Annual Report (p. 1–5):

A final issue is the widening of current account imbalances observed in recent years. This has reflected major shifts in the position of

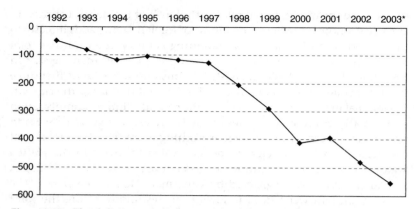

Figure 1.1a   The deficits on current account of the United States (1992–2003)

* Estimated by doubling the seasonally adjusted preliminary datum for the first two quarters of the year. Preliminary data for the balance on goods and services for 2003 (−\$489.4 billion) are consistent with the estimated value of the current deficit shown.

Source: Table 5.3.

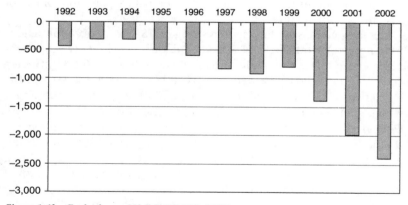

Figure 1.1b   End-of-year US INW (1992–2002)

Source: Table 5.3.

countries or regions as the suppliers or users of saving. While lower fiscal deficits in the medium term would be helpful, a sustainable reduction in the U.S. current account deficit may also need to be associated with a higher household saving rate in the United States and higher levels of demand in other countries.[14]

It is not possible to know exactly when the exhaustion of capability (i.e. the loss by the dollar of the degree of confidence needed for successful key-currency status) will take place because the actual timing will depend on the occurrence of an adverse exogenous shock *and/or* on the spontaneous triggering of a widespread loss of confidence. The timing of the renunciation of the rôle of locomotive as a result of domestic political concerns with the rate of unemployment and/or capacity utilization, is equally unknown (Godley and Izurieta, 2002). Current trends suggest that, as a working hypothesis, exhaustion will occur within the first decade of the twenty-first century. As confidence in the dollar erodes and expectations of substantial depreciation of the dollar strengthen,[15] both non-residents and residents of the United States who own easily encashable dollar-denominated assets, will seek to hold their wealth in assets denominated in stronger currencies (those expected to appreciate relative to the dollar). If the problem is aggravated by a creditor country having to draw a substantial amount from its credit balance, the exhaustion is likely to occur that much sooner.

The usual assumption in economic analysis is that any system can be subject to an exogenous shock but that the effects of the shock are unplanned. The modern world that exists since the attacks on New York and Washington on September 11, 2001, can be characterized as having major diplomatic antagonisms and/or veiled or open hostility. Joffe (2001) itemizes the ways in which the United States has steadily alienated erstwhile allies and the electorates in those countries – one might argue that the United States has been running a deficit on the public relations front for several years (in addition to its financial dissaving). An adverse shock can be conjured up deliberately by foreign organizations (including governments), which own sizeable amounts of easily-encashable dollar-denominated assets, as a political tactic to embarrass the United States by simultaneously weakening both the reputation of its currency and its economy.[16] Such an action, if it is large enough to trigger a self-reinforcing mechanism of withdrawals of assets from the United States and an induced self-reinforcing depreciation of the dollar (see Chapter 4), will leave no time for anticipatory policies to limit the destructive impact of the exhaustion of the dollar.

The first proposition rests on the presumption that the length of time needed to arrange and implement constructive policies to rid the dollar of the perception of vulnerability, will exceed the period over which the dollar can, unaided, retain the degree of confidence needed by a key-currency. In the unlikely event that policymakers in all of the major financial powers were to combine to give the matter a high priority and to reduce, through some bold support mechanism, the uncertainty surrounding the future value of dollar-denominated assets in foreign currencies, the dollar's effectiveness as the key currency could, perhaps, be extended. There is a "catch-22" problem here: when a group of major national authorities take publicized steps to address the issue, they inevitably draw serious attention to the fundamental problem and could, in the process, trigger the lack of confidence needed to precipitate a crisis.

The success of the United States in avoiding large-scale withdrawals of assets from dollar-denominated securities through October, 2003, must be attributed mainly to the inherited belief in the huge strength of the US economy and, by extension, in its currency.[17] The weaknesses of the economies of the main alternative currencies, the yen and the euro, in 2003 also contribute to the continuing willingness to hold dollar-denominated assets.

The United States assumed the rôle of the key-currency nation at the end of the Second World War after the Bretton Woods Conference. The country has been the hegemon and the US dollar has been the global key currency for the working lifetime of most if not all professionally active people.[18] There is an inevitable lag in perceiving a major change when the change contradicts the inherited wisdom. The elimination of what has been a fixed point in the international financial firmament for over fifty years will require serious changes in the existing set of institutions, which will, in turn, call for accommodating changes in the mindset of the involved professionals and policymakers. These changes will not be easily achieved (Tversky and Kahneman, 1982).

It is useful to view the second and third propositions as following directly from the first. The first proposition can be termed "the exhaustion hypothesis"; the second, "the crisis-avoidance and adjustment problems"; and the third, "the institutional restructuring problem." *The purpose of this monograph is to draw together the evidence on the potential exhaustion and to confront the implications of that event for future global prosperity.* While the essential problem is economic, the arguments must be comprehensible to policymakers and political scientists.

The second proposition emphasizes the process of adjustment to the change in conditions (the elimination of the chronic international dissaving by the key-currency country) with the goal of avoiding serious instability on foreign exchange markets. A more formal way of stating proposition 2, is to identify what measures must be taken to ease any currency crisis that the dollar will encounter when the United States relinquishes the duties of the key-currency nation. The goal must be to "manage" the rate of the inevitable depreciation of the dollar (and the loss of value in foreign currencies of dollar-denominated assets) during the period of adjustment. In the absence of such financing arrangements, the probability that the global economy will be afflicted with a major financial crisis involving a flight from the dollar and severe losses in the value of financial assets, will increase substantially. If crisis is not avoided, the social and economic costs of re-establishing a prosperous global economy will be much higher and the process of adjustment to the new conditions will take much longer.

The need for pre-arranged plans to finance the process of adjustment[19] derives from the fact that financial instability will, almost inevitably, have large adverse effects on the efficiency (rates of capacity utilization) of economic systems (Crockett, 1997).[20] Financial (capital) markets can change much more rapidly than markets for real goods and services can reallocate resources and impose, even with policy support, the needed adjustments in levels of living (Tobin, 1978). A currency crisis impacts on the real economy of the currency's domain. The domain of the key currency incorporates both the global financial system and the global macroeconomy.

Special local and temporal factors may have increased the absolute value of recent US current deficits. These factors weakened the ability of some important nations to engender adequate demand for their own domestic value-added so that the United States, by running current deficits and adding to aggregate demand for production in other countries, played a constructive role for the world economy in line with its duties as the key-currency nation.[21] However, such deficits cumulate and no country can serve as the "Keynesian locomotive" for the global economy for a long time without some breathing space and an opportunity to run current surpluses to restore its reserves or to diminish its liabilities (Table 1.1). The string of US current deficits has resulted in (and been partially generated by) a large accumulation of easily-encashable, foreign-owned dollar-denominated liabilities during the years 1983 through 2002 and particularly so in the last five years (see Tables 1.1 and 5.3). The international net worth (INW) (or the net international investment position)[22] of the United States peaked in 1982 at plus $329 billion (12 percent of GDP).[23] It has now become a large negative number, minus $2,387 billion (almost 23 percent of GDP at the end of 2002) (Table 1.1).[24] Gross dollar-denominated financial assets owned by private non-residents amounted to $5.9 trillion at the end of 2002.[25] During its period of global financial leadership, the United States has been transformed from "super-creditor" to "super-debtor" but US economic/financial policymakers have neither countenanced nor seriously confronted this transition.[26]

The third proposition, like the second, derives from the first proposition. It deals with the question of how to establish a new global macrofinancial system. In such negotiations, as Galbraith (2002) notes, the United States as a major debtor nation will be, at best, an important but not a dominant force. Once a key currency has lost global confidence in its integrity (as a store of value), it cannot quickly re-establish confidence. Failure to create an alternative to a national hegemon will aggravate the already serious costs of adjustment in the short- and medium-term as resources and levels of living adapt to the new conditions. In the long run, the absence of a hegemon will drastically reduce the overall macroeconomic efficiency of the global system. The collaboration must also identify and accommodate all of the other changes that will necessarily follow from the development of a new institutional régime.

All three problems embodied in the propositions must be addressed quickly.[27] The longer the existing pattern (of chronic US dissaving vis-à-vis residents of other nations and the concomitant reduction in INW) continues, the greater will be the global social and economic costs of economic adjustment (the reduction in the standard of living of US residents and the reallocation of labor and other resources among industries throughout the world). Equally, the longer the period of chronic international dissaving, the harder will it be to resolve the problem of a vulnerable dollar without the dollar being subjected to major pressures in the foreign exchange markets with induced strain on the performance of national economies. The greater the stock of net indebtedness of the United States and the greater its rate or annual flow of international dissaving, the greater will be the depreciation of the dollar required to return the US economy to international financial self-sufficiency.[28] The greater the necessary degree of dollar depreciation perceived by non-resident owners of easily-encashable dollar-denominated assets, the greater will be their incentive to change the currency of denomination of those assets and the greater the probability (and the magnitude) of crisis in foreign exchange markets. Finding a means of financing to buy time for the United States to adjust its economy away from the heavy burden of chronic international dissaving (and accumulated "debt"), and bringing the global financial leadership of the United States to an end, will facilitate arranging the conversion to the new system as well as the remodeling of the international financial architecture.

III   The institutional environment

When considering the exhaustion of the US capability to continue as hegemon, it is necessary to remember that the years of US hegemony have been far more successful than any of the delegates at the 1944 conference in Bretton Woods would have dared to expect (if only because of their depression-oriented mindset). Indeed, the arrant existing overvaluation of the dollar (testified to by the very large deficits on current account) began only in 1998 (Table 1.1), but the five years from 1998 through 2002 have resulted in cumulative dissaving vis-à-vis foreign nations in the amount of $1.7 trillion. There is no end in sight. Policymakers in Washington have disregarded the downside of current policy and the "costs of currency overvaluation" on domestic economic performance and strength.[29] In addition to all of these pessimistic auguries, the costs of occupation of Iraq must be recognized as aggravating the current deficit.

The governments of the major powers have no experience in replacing an exhausted financial leader and, possibly because of the success of the dollar's reign as key currency, the problems of a badly functioning hegemonic system have received little analytic attention. Many of economic policies of the last quarter of a century might have benefitted from consideration of their potential effects on the strength and continued viability of the hegemon. The question to be confronted was "How best to allocate the dissipation of the great international reserves of the United States over time?" Had this question been explicitly posed, it is possible but by no means certain, that the leading nations would have recognized the temporary viability of the international financial architecture. The result will necessarily be that when the negotiators from the major financial powers come to address the creation of a substitute set of international financial institutions (proposition 3), they will be starting from pretty much where the Bretton Woods conference concluded in 1944 but having knowledge of the institutional evolution, which has taken place in the, roughly, sixty years of US hegemony. The negotiators will face a far harder task than the negotiators at Bretton Woods in 1944. At that conference there was an obvious candidate for the position of financial leader (Harrod, 1951) (Triffin, 1961, ch. 1). Currently, there exists no single country (or currency) that has both the commitment required for the task and the economic strength to play the role of global financial leader. Failure to recognize the need for redesign threatens seriously to reduce the macrofinancial efficiency of the global economy as well as substantially to increase the length of the system's exposure to financial crisis.[30]

The word "hegemon," while frequently used to describe the world's leading economic/financial power, is less than fully appropriate because "hegemon" implies a dominant force, usually of one nation state over another (its client). This is not an exact description of the world's economic/financial superpower, which is as much a servant to the global economy as its master.[31] The hegemon supplies to the global economy what Kindleberger, in his presidential address to the American Economic Association (1986), called "*international public goods.*" Very briefly, the major component services are: the provision of a key currency which serves as an international currency and storehouse for the international reserves of other nations;[32] and a willingness to accept responsibility that increases in key currency-denominated assets of other nations (saving) do not generate avoidably low levels of global aggregate demand.[33] Both of these responsibilities impose, over a period of years, costs on the hegemon leading, in context, to the United States running deficits on current transactions (international dissaving), which, in turn, lead to a reduction in the country's INW. The replacement system must be designed so that it is capable of providing these international public goods without, at the same time, weakening its long-run capacity to serve as hegemon. Since a national currency must sooner or later approach exhaustion, the new system will need to have the power to create liquidity (or international money): in this it will resemble the so-called Keynes Plan proposed by the British delegation at Bretton Woods. Tying global liquidity and aggregate demand to a national money supply was the primary (very long-run) weakness in the international financial architecture generated by the Bretton Woods Conference. However, in the early post-war years there was no alternative.

Because the hegemon's national currency is also the key currency of the global economy, it must be "above suspicion" so that it may fulfil its roles as a transaction medium and, in a world of liberal conditions governing international capital mobility, a store of both international reserves of governments and of assets of individual, wealth-seeking firms and families.[34] As the foreign-exchange costs of its hegemonic duties erode the *net* international assets of the hegemon (its INW), recognition of the potential need for a depreciation of the key currency (see Chapter 3) makes that currency vulnerable to a loss of confidence: private parties owning encashable dollar-denominated assets (as distinct from real assets) will be motivated to transfer that portion of their wealth into assets denominated in a different currency. The sale of dollar-denominated assets can become self-reinforcing as sales of dollars force down the value of the dollar in foreign exchange markets and both reinforce and deepen expectations of further depreciation (see Chapter 4).[35] At the same time, the burden on the hegemon's domestic economy can begin to engender domestic dissatisfaction with the country's role. Godley (1999) singled out the effect of the international deficits on domestic aggregate demand and employment as a cause of the non-sustainability of the seemingly chronic deficits. Since Godley made that identification, the rate of international dissaving has increased substantially (Table 1.1) and, because the net inflow of foreign capital unduly strengthens the dollar, the effects will be concentrated in marginally competitive industries and the unemployment issue will become very powerful (Blecker, 2002).

These stresses are, in brief, the potential causes of the United States having to lay down its rôle as hegemon within the foreseeable future and the global economy must either accept the non-existence of a hegemon at no small cost to its own macrofinancial efficiency or create a replacement system. Because there exists, at the present time, no single country (or currency), which can realistically take on the rôle of hegemon,[36] some sort of co-operative institution will be needed (Gray, 1996). Further, recent changes in the regulation of capital markets and in the freedom of international capital transactions (Herring and Litan, 1994, ch. 2) have allowed private gain-seeking parties to invest internationally in "easily-encashable" assets:[37] a loss of confidence in the dollar could, therefore, lead to an exodus of funds to the "home nation" of the asset-owner (or to some alternative currency of denomination). Private asset-holders will not be willing to sacrifice their own interests for an uncertain and possibly illusory global financial stability but will seek to protect their own wealth as best they can. The possibility of flight from the dollar does *not* apply to the physical assets of foreign multinational enterprise (MNE), which are illiquid. The sale of real assets would involve substantial transaction costs, but MNEs are able and are ideally equipped to adjust their payments flows (working capital positions) according to their own self interest. Extant political stresses, differences in values and philosophies and antagonisms between the United States and other developed nations (Kissinger, 2001) (Joffe, 2001) and concern by incumbent politicians with the electoral repercussions of policies of economic retrenchment, suggest that the development of a replacement system faces severe obstacles. As noted above, the difficulties of financing the US dissaving and the threat of a financial crisis are very likely to grow more severe as the world clings to its nearly exhausted, existing system despite the change in the underlying conditions.[38]

The world has had two economic/financial superpowers but it has never faced the problem of replacing an exhausted hegemon. The first aspect of the "replacement problem" is that *the exhausted hegemon must recognize its own limitations*. The United Kingdom was hegemon in the late nineteenth and early twentieth century, but its capability to continue in that rôle was waning when First World War broke out.[39]

By November, 1918, the strains and the costs of war had removed any possibility that the United Kingdom could continue in that role. This fact was not recognized by the Cunliffe Committee (The Committee on Currency) in 1918. The Cunliffe Committee strongly recommended returning to gold at the pre-war parity. Giving an idealized description of the workings of the gold standard, the Committee failed completely to see the distinction between the efficiency of a system in maintaining an effective system under relatively tranquil circumstances and its efficiency in correcting an extant major dislocation without collapsing under the stress. The policymaking élite of Great Britain generally supported this policy and a return to gold became the mainstay of the UK post-war economic policy which, when accomplished, would have re-established the pre-war exchange rate of \$4.86 = £1 and full convertibility (Winch, 1969, ch. 5). At this sterling/dollar exchange rate, sterling was severely overvalued.[40] During the war, British wholesale prices had risen by 200 percent (tripled), while in the United States, wholesale prices had only doubled. Thus, the United Kingdom had to force its domestic price level down by one third in order to restore the inflation-adjusted (or "real") pre-war exchange rate (the pre-war terms of trade) between sterling and the dollar. Allowing for the difference in inflationary experience would have set the post-war rate at (approximately) (\$3.24 = £1). Such a "computation" obviously neglects the effects of the war on the British economy other than differences in past relative rates of inflation. The age and wartime wear-and-tear on the stock of capital goods reduced the competitiveness of British industry in international markets and wartime sales of assets had seriously reduced British INW and its net income from foreign assets. The post-war rate of exchange consistent with balanced current accounts at satisfactory levels of global output must have exchanged sterling for dollars at a rate significantly below the rate consistent with a constant inflation-adjusted exchange-rate (£1 = \$3.24) if the United Kingdom was not to have deliberately to depress its economy through tight money to retain and attract foreign financial deposits.[41] The result was the depression of basic British industries as a result of both the overvaluation of sterling and the consequent severity of price competition from foreign suppliers as well as by the difficulties and costs of renewing and updating the capital stock brought about by low profit rates and the high interest rates needed to retain foreign deposits in sterling.[42] The severe depression in Great Britain coincided with the recession in the German economy, which had been deliberately created as a contribution to the problem of German reparations payments, that is, Germany had to have reduced standard of living of the German people so that resources would be available for the export surplus needed to pay the reparations (the budgetary problem) (Johnson, 1958). The depression of two major European economies (coupled with an undervalued French franc, which the French transformed into a huge surplus on current account which they hoarded and, in this way, destroyed much of the extant global aggregate demand) contributed in a substantial way to the malfunction of the international economy between the two wars. Countries with masses of unemployed workers were unwilling to aggravate their domestic problems by running deficits on international current account and chose to impede imports. Germany was denied the ability to use her idle resources to manufacture exports to earn the money to pay the reparations (the transfer problem) (Johnson, 1958). The magnitude of the postwar disequilibrium of stocks and flows exceeded the capacity of the gold standard and of national economies for smooth adjustment. Misaligned currencies and protective tariffs caused asset values to collapse and forced Europe and the world into a slough of economic despond (Gray, 1990). Small wonder that Winston S. Churchill, Chancellor of the Exchequer in the United Kingdom in 1925, when the decision to revert to the full gold standard (full convertibility) was undertaken, regarded this as the greatest mistake of his life (Winch, 1969, p. 75).

The subject matter of this book could be seen to resemble that of *The Economic Consequences of the Peace* (Keynes, 1919) after the First World War. The subject matter of both books identifies sets of developments and conditions capable both of adversely affecting the capacity of the hegemon and of diminishing the efficiency of operation of the international economic and financial systems as well as those of their constituent economies. Both books attempt to encourage international understanding, co-operation and collective policy measures to reduce the serious impending economic dislocation.[43]

In the years immediately after the First World War, a burst of isolationist sentiment in the United States and its Congress prevented the United States from assuming the rôle of hegemon, a task for which it was much better equipped than the United Kingdom. No-one can know whether the British would have continued in their vain attempt to resume the duties of the hegemon if the United States had not turned inward but the concept of exhaustion does not come easily to those used to playing leading roles in a global system. The history of the inter-war years is well known and it is not clear that economists and statesmen knew enough then to avoid the terrible economic aftermath of the 1914–18 war even if the United States had accepted the rôle of hegemon.

IV   The severity of the adjustment

The first two propositions set out at the beginning of this chapter effectively allow for the exhaustion of the United States's capability to continue to provide the needed international public goods to the global economy. This exhaustion can have outcomes which cover a range of severity. Two terms have come to be commonly used to indicate the severity of the effect of the elimination of the US current deficits on the US economy and, by extension, on the global economy: a "soft landing" and a "hard landing." These terms have not been defined in a way that has led to general acceptance although one group of commissioners of the US Trade Deficit Review Commission (2000, p. xviii) defined a "hard landing" as one that would generate two consecutive quarters of negative real growth in the country's inflation-adjusted gross domestic product (GDP). By inference, then, a "soft landing" is, then, one which does not generate a recession. Modern conditions, with the rate of international dissaving of about 4.6 percent of US GDP, suggest that a "soft landing" is a highly unrealistic and excessively optimistic target.[44] A hard landing could cover a broad range of severity of macrofinancial inefficiency in the adjustment process and a crisis-induced, serious dislocation would lead to large increases in unemployment rates in the United States and elsewhere. A hard landing would also be likely to bring about a financial crisis in foreign-exchange markets with substantial repercussions in equity and bond markets in major financial centres as massive international shifts of funds take place. The aeronautical metaphor could be extended to include a "crash landing" in which financial stress would bring about a major, worldwide collapse of asset prices (Gray, 1990). If foreign-exchange markets were severely disrupted, serious disruption of national capital markets and stock and bond exchanges would be an almost inevitable consequence. While this volume does not address this very pessimistic possibility in great depth, the outer range of severity covered by the concept of a "hard landing," a "crash landing," could encompass developments that would inflict upon large parts of the industrialized world, conditions, which have not been faced since the 1930s.

The exhaustion of the United States's ability to continue as hegemon is virtually certain (Table 5.3 and Chapter 6) but there is no way of knowing *ex ante* how big or how pervasive the ramifications of the adjustment process would be. Preventing such a situation from devolving into a major financial crisis must be the major goal of collective economic policy in the foreseeable future if only because no-one can know the extent of the damage, which such a crisis might wreak.[45] This view underlies the second proposition that the reversal of existing patterns must be financed so that a serious dislocation is prevented. The task of the conferees at any international conference organized to address the potential internal stresses of the international financial system will have two secondary purposes: the first is to allow the existing imbalance in stocks as well as flows to be resolved by relatively gradual economic adjustments in both deficit and surplus nations;[46] and the second, less immediate problem,[47] is to design a permanent replacement system to provide the services of the hegemon (proposition three). These problems will not be independent of each other and will call for new insights and solutions, which can only be implemented on a collaborative basis.

It is important that diplomats, policymakers, readers and elected politicians realize that the costs of adjustment will not devolve wholly upon the United States. Those countries with currencies destined to appreciate against the dollar will also undergo seriously disruptive changes in inter-sectoral resource allocation, changes in absolute and relative financial values (in their home currency) and, as a result of both the strengthening of their currencies and the inevitable decrease in global aggregate demand, the loss of foreign markets in their export sector.

There are many difficulties to overcome even if the problem receives prompt attention. Five may be identified here. *First*, the international financial system has been seen as one in which there exists a dominant country (the hegemon) capable of countering any weaknesses which the system may develop. The possibility of instability in the international financial system must be confronted. Mainstream economic analysis generally disregards the possibility of financial instability in its search to identify the conditions that will generate optimum resource allocation. There are two subareas of economics, which do address financial instability: the adequacy of equity capital in financial institutions (commercial banks); and studies of financial crisis in nation states, which cannot meet both minimum standards of living for their population *and* service their foreign debt obligations. *Second*, the possibility of instability in the dominant country has not been seriously addressed. Very little analysis has been committed to the task and the problems of hegemony because the fifty-plus years of US hegemony have been, on the whole, very successful.[48] Only when the system was suffering minor "hiccups" was any attention given to the problems of a hegemonic system (operating within a fixed-rate system). *Third*, nearly all active economists have led their entire professional lives in a world in which there existed a satisfactory hegemon providing, albeit with a couple of hiccups, the requisite international public goods. *Fourth*, modern economists, in an unusual disregard for what can go wrong, seem to have rejected both Thomas Carlyle's description of their discipline as "dismal" and what Yergin and Stanislaw (1998, p. 124) call Thatcher's Law. ("The unexpected happens. You had better prepare for it.") Economists have assumed, usually implicitly, that market systems are stable to the point of invulnerability and that the provision of the international public goods by the United States can continue *sine die* irrespective of the negative INW of the United States. A *fifth* contributory factor may be that modeling the task of the hegemon has both stock (balance-sheet) and flow dimensions so that it does not lend itself to formal analysis unless the stock/flow interaction is fully specified.[49] Since the United States has acquired many dollar-denominated liabilities, which can be easily withdrawn from their dollar-denomination, the problem is analogous to the question of the capital adequacy of financial intermediaries (see Table 5.2). This is a notoriously difficult concept to operationalize since reserve adequacy is sensitive to, among other things, the herd (or stampede) instinct of operators in financial markets. The potential problem faced by the dollar can be cast in terms of a run on a commercial bank. A solvent bank can be subjected to a run when depositors believe that quick withdrawals are the only defense against serious loss. This message can be easily communicated when depositors are all in close geographic proximity (the same town) so that they react to the same news and to word of mouth. The potential herd movement can also be generated when large numbers of depositors or asset holders read the same data, use the same analytic framework and form the same expectation with regard to the future value of a currency.[50] Major instability can depend on a number of specific values and institutions, whose characteristics are likely to change, possibly abruptly, through time. Possibly because formal modeling is very much in vogue in economics at the beginning of the twenty-first century, potential financial instability at the hegemonic level has escaped major attention.[51] Such attention to instability in international markets as exists, has focused mainly on instability in individual countries and the loss of the ability of a *national* financial system to meet its scheduled debt payments to foreigners and/or to counter a flight from its currency (Irwin and Vines, 2001).

The international financial system can usefully be seen as comprising three layers of institutions and to have the shape of an inverted pyramid. The top layer can be identified as the 150 (the $n - 1$ countries) or so national economic authorities with their individual currencies.[52] The second layer consists of supranational institutions such as the Bretton Woods institutions (the World Bank and the International Monetary Fund) and The Bank for International Settlements. The bottom unit, the hegemon, bears the weight of the whole system (see Figure 1.2): the hegemon provides the required international public goods to the global financial and economic systems. There are, of course, both horizontal and vertical interactions among the layers: national crises in the top layer can spread the costs of adjustment from one sovereign state to another (contagion)[53] and can weaken both of the lower levels. Moreover, some national countries have tied their currencies to those of another member or members of the top layer.[54] Misconceived policies by second-layer institutions can create havoc in the top layer of national economies (witness the collapse of the Thai baht in July, 1997) (Shelburne, 2002).[55] The focus of this book, weakness at the bottom level, can drastically reduce the macrofinancial efficiency of the global economy in terms of both allocative efficiency and the rate of global capacity utilization. Thus, redesign of the international financial architecture because of structural weakness in the weight-bearing hegemon, will be likely to involve substantial redesign of the second level of (supranational) institutions as well as the provision of a different institutional environment in which national economic authorities will operate. The emphasis here is, then, quite different from such analyses of instability as have recently been conducted. It confronts the

Figure 1.2 The inverted pyramid of the international financial system

Note: The horizontal distances can be conceived as measuring what Mundell (2003) terms "monetary mass" or, alternatively, the size of the financial sector. The hegemon is shown as having substantially less breadth than the top layer of independent financial system. It will be "broadened" by the efficiency- enhancing capabilities of the supranational intermediaries.

In context, the breadth or the hegemon could be seen as shrinking as "top-level" nations increase their international reserves because of greater international involvement and as the hegemon's strength and foreign confidence in its resilience weaken. The system becomes increasingly precarious (i.e. "top heavy").

At the end of the Second World War, the global system was an ordinary pyramid because of the great strength of both the economy and the international asset position of the hegemon. The shape changed slowly towards that of an inverted hegemon as the United States ran current deficits and as the economic competitiveness of other nations increased.

likelihood that the *hegemon* will not be able to retain the strength needed to perform its duties because of the magnitude of its net foreign liabilities and of the weakening of confidence of non-resident asset-holders. Residents of the hegemon anticipating a loss of value of the dollar against foreign currencies are quite capable of seeking a capital gain by substituting assets denominated in foreign currencies for home-country assets. Here the multinational corporations with their continuous supervision of working capital costs, are likely to play a key rôle as they rearrange the currency composition of short-term assets and liabilities.

In 1999, the US Congress created a Commission, which was to investigate the causes and sustainability of the country's trade deficits. The Commission was also to make recommendations as to policy. At first blush, it would appear that the charge of the Congressional Commission and the foci of this book would overlap. The US trade deficits were the focus of the Commission's inquiries. Their close relative, the balances on current transactions (international saving or dissaving) are the central features of this book. The two approaches are quite different (see Appendix 1).

At this point, the study has identified three problems, represented by the propositions. It has suggested, subject to confirmation in Chapter 6, that the validity of the first proposition can, in the absence of a large miracle, be accepted as a working hypothesis. The remedial policy issues are the minimization of the disruptive effects of the renunciation of its key-currency duties by the United States and the rapid creation of an efficient replacement system.

Another, secondary proposition underlies the argument of this book. This proposition strikes at the heart of the reigning financial/economic philosophy: that a system of perfectly free markets, financial as well as for goods and services, in a globally integrated world comprising independent self-seeking régimes (or countries) can be sustained *sine die* (Buch, 1999). Here an important aspect of the problem is a weakness in modern democracies that, in a world of zero-sum constraints, policymakers may see political gain in postponing corrective actions so that potential crises are allowed to fester. A serious possibility of failures in political decision-making is not irrelevant to economic analysis. The loss of the capability of the key-currency nation to play its stabilizing rôle effectively implies that there exist sets of conditions which are capable, over time, of destroying the stability of global free markets unless there be a set of institutions which will build in increases in liquidity needed to finance economic growth. The existing hegemon has performed in that rôle for almost sixty years, but its original massive reserves of financial strength have been whittled away over that time and the implications of the loss of strength of the key-currency nation have been largely ignored.[56] The benefits that have resulted in terms of additions to aggregate demand in the $n - 1$ countries other than the hegemon, have been recognized – particularly the Marshall Plan, and the benefits to Asian economies during the Korean and Vietnam wars (Fetherston and Gray, 1998).

Yergin and Stanislaw (1998, pp. 9–17) entitled their overview of post-war political economy *Commanding Heights*. The major theme was the replacement of government intervention by market forces as the long-run characteristic of the era. It is possible to think of the era as beginning with a fundamental distrust of markets after the inter-war experience and, in a well-behaved (tranquil) world blessed by the supply of international public goods, a recognition of both the virtues of a market system and the potential fallibility and the ponderous nature of government intervention. However, there was one serious omission in this evolution: this was the failure to identify the degree to which the innate stability efficiency or resilience inherited after the Second World War, was transient. This monograph can be seen as focusing on the danger of over-reliance on the market system because of a failure to recognize the steady using-up of a finite stock of resilience in an international context.

V   The layout of the study

The monograph contains five parts. Part I, consists of this chapter's description of the problems to be confronted in the monograph. Part II is devoted to supplying some theoretical and institutional background for the policy-oriented parts to follow. Chapter 2 provides background for some basic analytic and institutional issues, which relate the close integration of the modern world to the vitality of the hegemon's economy. Crucial is the relationship of equation 2.6, which examines the world as a closed economy. Readers must be familiar with these linkages. Chapter 3 examines the problem of balance-of-payments adjustment from the point of view of the hegemon (as distinct from that of a "top-layer," national economy to which the standard version of the absorption theory is addressed). The distinction, largely one of the size of the domain of the key currency and the sheer amount of debt that a hegemon, whose currency is deemed "above suspicion," can generate. Chapter 4 provides a model of instability in asset markets which serves as a point of departure for the analysis of the phenomena, which will contribute to or moderate the severity of the adjustment process.

Chapter 5 opens Part III by providing and describing the data needed to confront the first proposition and then develops the important point that the two potential triggers of exhaustion are closely interdependent so that the probability of exhaustion is the sum of the two probabilities that one trigger will be activated. The data lay the basis for the contention that a lack of confidence is inevitable in the foreseeable future by virtue of the steady deterioration of the INW of the United States and ease of encashability of such a large volume of foreign-owned financial assets. These data together with the effect of the current deficits on the performance of the US economy constitute the basis for the support, in Chapter 6, of the "exhaustion" proposition and the high probability of a hard landing. Recognition of the interaction of the two dimensions is vital. The data also set the stage for assessing the second and third propositions of Chapter 1.

While the reader must always bear in mind the difficulties of generating precise aggregate data of the kind necessarily relied upon here,[57] Chapter 6 examines the data in terms of the models presented in Part II. It is important to note that the approach to critical conditions does not *require* some external or exogenous adverse shock but can, instead, derive from a continuing series of current deficits of the type already being experienced by the United States in its role as hegemon. When there is no adverse economic shock, recognition of the vulnerability of the dollar will grow with the rate of international dissaving and/or the negative INW of the key-currency nation. At some point, it will precipitate a change in investor psychology. Chapter 7 considers the possibility that built-in measures can aggravate the costs of adjustment and enhance the likelihood of some financial malfunction. It is also possible that the continuing weakening of the innate resilience of foreign exchange markets does make the system more vulnerable to some seemingly exogenous adverse shock. Even more troublesome is the possibility that a shock could be created as a result of international stress and animosity. The gradual erosion of such resilience as exists is crucial to a full understanding of the problem: here the inquiry addresses discrepancies between the changes in real and financial values of assets. Chapter 8 summarizes Part II by considering the limits of unilateral initiatives by the United States and, in the process, by addressing Proposition Two.

Part IV ventures into the problem of design of a replacement hegemon whose capability does not rely on a single nation and national currency. Part IV is, necessarily, exploratory: the design of the new institutional set will, like the outcome of the Bretton Woods conference, be path- and personality-dependent. Because of the interaction between the degree of dislocation, which prompts confrontation of the problem and the total costs of adjustment and institutional reform, the design of the new international financial architecture will depend importantly on the speed with which the existing condition of chronic international dissaving is confronted. In addition the outcome will be determined significantly by the way in which the negotiations develop. Given the much larger number of influential players destined to take part in such a conference, path-dependency is likely to assume major importance. One possible approach is offered in Chapter 10. Chapter 11 provides a retrospective summary.

There exists a severe problem to generating constructive economic policies to address the problem of exhaustion. It can be traced to the equivalent in political decision-making of the agency problem. The agency problem exists when managers, the agents of stockholders, operate in their own rather than the stockholders' interest (Jensen and Meckling, 1976) and (Fama, 1980). Even in the setting of a profit-maximizing entity, agency behavior is not always easy to identify. Its political equivalent exists when elected representatives (agents) are motivated to defer necessary unpopular measures in the hopes of avoiding defeat in a forthcoming election and the delay in introducing the policy increases the ultimate costs of adjustment to be borne by the electorate (principals). Such delays can be continued until crisis dominates. If exhaustion does come about, the policy reaction must put the long-run global welfare over short-run national concerns – something that did not prove feasible at Versailles.

The reader should be given one final *caveat*. This monograph was written after the attacks on New York and Washington on September 11, 2001. Much of the underlying thought was developed earlier (Gray, 1969, 1974, 1992 and 1996). No one can know, with any precision, what the long-run effects of the attacks will be – psychological or economic – but it seems unlikely that the attacks will contribute to any reduction in the severity of the basic problem addressed in this book (neither annual data for 2002 nor preliminary data for the first half of 2003 showed a reduction in the rate of dissaving).[58] One obvious danger is that preoccupation with terrorism or with the invasion and the rebuilding of Iraq will cause or *allow* the potential international economic malfunctions to be suppressed rather than addressed. If so, the fragility of the system will increase more rapidly as the dollar's resources become stretched even further. Tensions over Iraq have further estranged major allies whose co-operation will be vital when collaboration to minimize the costs of exhaustion and negotiations over the new international financial system are required.[59]

Appendix

The "Report" of the US Trade Deficit Review Commission

In 1999, the U. S. Congress created a Commission to analyze the causes and consequences of the ongoing U.S. trade deficits. This inquiry involves an apparent overlap with the subject matter of this monograph. The differences in the purposes and analytic approaches of the Commission and this monograph are identified in this appendix. The US Trade Deficit Review Commission published *The U.S. Trade Deficit: Causes, Consequences and Recommendations for Action* in November 2000.[60] The Commission's task was to investigate the trade deficits from the point of view of a national economy, that is, as if the United States were simply an economy in the top layer of the inverted pyramid (Figure 1.2, p. 23). There was no instruction to extend the analysis to examine the relationship between the chronic deficits, the status of the key-currency nation and the well-being of the international financial system.

The Commission was concerned with the sustainability of the trade deficit (defined essentially as the ability of the United States to continue to attract the needed foreign capital to offset its international dissaving) and with the causes underlying the existence of chronic deficits. The Commission considered as possible causes: shortcomings in US international trade policy, and what may be called "structural characteristics" such as inequality of impediments to international trade and, following Mann (1999), the large disparity between the marginal propensity to import of the United States and that of the "Rest of the World" to import from the United States.[61] The Commission's *Report* emphasized so-called real factors and neglected the rôle of the financial sector (and the ongoing strengthening of the US dollar despite producing Figure A1.1). Much of its analysis was locked into an earlier world and neither the members of the Commission nor many of its witnesses took into account the increased interdependence and the evolution of (Northian) institutions in the world economy in the last quarter of the twentieth century (i.e. globalization) including, most importantly, the responsiveness of exchange rates to the flows of funds and the huge increase in the mobility of portfolio capital. As a result of this methodological approach, the Commission inherited the view that the dollar was preordained to continue as the key currency and any unsustainability of the admitted large and chronic current deficits, would prove temporary and inflict (bearable) adjustment pains on the US economy. When the magnitude of the deficits increased substantially during the life of the Commission, its members seemed to find difficulty in adjusting their analytic viewpoints to the new realities.[62]

The first concern of this volume is the ability of the financial system to generate, without serious disequilibrium or instability, the necessary adjustments as and when they are forced upon it. The second consideration is the possibility that the strength of the dollar will prove intolerable for the goal of high employment in the United States so that the United States will, in effect, resign from the position of hegemon and a replacement system will need to be developed.

The tendency by the Commission to emphasize real activities and to de-emphasize the financial dimensions of the string of deficits accords with the doctrinal development of international trade theory and the derivative argument for free trade. The theory of international trade has always focused on equilibrium solutions with balanced exports and imports so that the ratio of export prices to import prices in a common numeraire (the net barter terms of trade) is assumed to be consonant, in equilibrium, with the extant rates of exchange given price levels in individual countries. The traditional approach assumes that the levels of prices in individual countries are determined outside of the analytic system. *The Report* (p. 140) introduces some rough computation about the total saving of the world (less that of the United States) and computes the percentage of that flow of saving which needs to be attracted to the United States if the ongoing deficits are to be financed. In the process, the problem of retaining the foreign savings already attracted to the United States and gauging their sensitivity to a depreciation of the dollar was glossed over (effectively assuming either that such assets are not easily encashable or that they would not be encashed). One witness seemed locked into an earlier set of conditions in which the composition of foreign assets in the United States comprised mainly either direct investments or official reserves rather than easily encashable financial assets of private non-residents with different functional currencies (US TDRC, p. 24):

> the current account [deficit] is as high as it is, and growing, because ... foreigners want to invest in America – in stocks, bonds, real estate, industrial plant and other assets. Investments in America are viewed favorably around the world, and for good reason: the US economy is a good, steady performer, less sluggish than Europe and Japan and less volatile than emerging markets, inflows of investment funds push up the dollar and make foreign goods more competitive.

The willingness of non-residents to invest in dollar-denominated *financial* assets is sensitive to expectations about the rate of exchange of the dollar and a country with a steadily increasing negative INW cannot expect to be permanently viewed

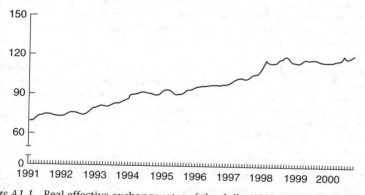

Figure A1.1   Real effective exchange rates of the dollar 1991–2000

Source: US Trade Deficit Review Commission (2000, p. 24). Data taken from Federal Reserve Board, Broad Index. For a *caveat* on the dangers of overreliance on indexes of "real effective exchange rates", see Box 7.1, Chapter 7.

as a "good, steady performer" when its currency comes to be perceived as vulnerable.

In formal models of international trade, flows of international capital were not and are not introduced. The world has evolved so that the assumptions of international trade theory seriously constrain its realism: international capital movements are now quantitatively important and direct investments serve as conduits through which proprietary and other technology and managerial knowhow are transferred internationally (Gray, 1999). Net capital flows affect exchange rates and, therefore, the price competitiveness of the goods of one country relative to those of its trading partners. The assumption of balanced trade (or balanced current account) is, as the charge of the Commission and existing conditions make clear, both heroic and illusory. Moreover, this assumption precludes concerns with financial instability except in country-level studies in which exceptional conditions are explicitly recognized.

In the 1990s, the deficit increased again after some recovery from the stresses of the mid-1980s (Yergin and Stanislaw, 1998, 334–5) as the US economy grew more quickly than those of its trading partners so that foreign capital was spontaneously attracted to the United States in the form of both inward net direct and portfolio investments – the latter contributing to "the irrational exuberance" of the New York Stock Exchange in the mid-1990s. The dollar strengthened against trading-partner currencies (after adjustment for changes in price levels) (Figure A1.1).[63] The price-competitiveness of US output with foreign production was thereby reduced again and the economy ultimately incurred the very large current deficits of the four years (1999 to 2002).[64] A current deficit will, in a world in which exchange rates are determined by net flows of funds and capital movements are negligible, tend to be self-correcting because a deficit implies less demand for the home currency than for foreign currencies so that *a chronic deficit must be financed by spontaneous inflows of capital if it is not to be steadily reduced by a decline in aggregate demand in and a depreciation of the currency of the deficit country.* This constraint does not automatically apply to a hegemon.

The Report in its focus on the sustainability of the deficits relies heavily on the earlier study by Catherine L. Mann (1999). Mann's focus was the length of time for which US deficits will not generate any self-destructive characteristics. Mann's definition of "sustainability" is precise and formal:[65]

> A sustainable external balance is one in which the feedback relationships between the external balance and the exchange rates and interest rates are relatively weak in comparison to other macroeconomic forces that affect these asset prices. For example, a large current deficit may make investors worry that they might not be repaid. They might then decide to sell some assets. Which would generate upward pressure on interest rates or depreciation pressure on the exchange rate. In this case, the current account deficit would not be sustainable by this definition. (Mann,1999, p. 151)

Mann's study confronts the possibility of a serious shock to the US economy when the current deficits grow to exceed what can be financed by accommodating capital imports out of current foreign saving. Her study, then, depends upon estimating the magnitude of future current deficits and assessing whether or not they will not feed back on exchange rates and the interest rates . Mann's study does not explicitly confront the possibility of instability in foreign exchange markets or confront the possibility that the accumulation of foreign claims lodged in dollar-denominated financial assets will be withdrawn but her definition of non-sustainability is fully compatible with such an occurrence. Going beyond mere abstract argument, Mann developed a model (1999, p. 158) that enables her to generate estimates of US current account deficits in future years under varying sets of circumstances. The model does not introduce the (real) rate of exchange but allows for the historical excess of the marginal propensity to import of the United States over that of trading partner nations so that its results are sensitive to the relative rates of growth in the United States and other countries. Mann, with rare attention to detail, also allows for the carrying costs of the net international indebtedness as an annual cost of the negative international net worth and as a component of the current deficit. Except for attention paid to the net balance on international assets, the base case scenario relies wholly on forecast rates of economic growth and the asymmetric marginal propensities to import in its estimates of the trade deficits. This approach provides estimates that give some idea of the magnitude of the problem in both its flow and its stock dimensions. According to her computations, the US current deficit in 2005 is estimated to be approximately $600 billion (about − 5 percent of GDP) and, if the model is carried forward to 2010, the estimate of the current account deficit attains $1 trillion. Both estimates are, as the author notes, well beyond any recorded experience for an industrialized country and they therefore strongly suggest that the deficits will become unsustainable. There is no explicit indication of the way in which the unsustainability will impinge on the national or the global economy. Stock concerns are introduced by estimates of the net international investment position (or INW) of the United States : the estimated US INW in 2005 is −$4.4 trillion (−39 percent of projected gross domestic product) and in 2010, is −$8.5 trillion (−58 percent of projected GDP).[66] The INW at the end of 2005, if financed at Mann's cost estimate of 4 percent, will generate annual negative income on international assets equal to $176 billion (with the probable escalation of significant domestic political discontent).[67] Mann (2000) remarks on the need for recognition of the implications of the size of the deficits, their magnitude and, by implication, the probability of a (very) hard landing.

One reason for the small attention given to financial factors in addition to the traditional approach of the theory of international trade, could be that mainstream balance-of-payments and national income accounting models, developed in the 1950s, do not allow for spontaneous international capital flows of serious magnitude and allocate such flows to additional capital formation. The idea that current deficits are allocated completely to additional capital formation is *"comforting"*[68] since this implies that the total net worth (INW plus the change in the stock of capital) is independent of the current account. By extension, then, the rate of domestic saving is independent of the current account and, under a system of flexible exchange rates, of the rate of exchange. The basic identity that the deficit on current account $(M−X)$ is, *given balanced government account*, equal to domestic investment (I) less domestic saving (S) derives from a Keynesian model of flows of expenditure in which all flows were independent of the rate of exchange (which was deemed to be fixed). "Investment" measures "net capital formation" so that if a country is operating at full capacity and undergoing a surge of investment demand, its rate of investment will be constrained in a closed economy, by domestic saving or, in an open economy, by the ability to supplement domestic saving by "borrowing" from abroad: The latter strategy implies spending the proceeds on imports (of capital goods) to generate a current deficit equal to the "loan." This model was developed during the days when international capital flows were items of secondary importance and almost inevitably involved loans to developing countries to increase their capital stock or direct investments by multinational corporations, which resulted in "greenfield" investments. *Provided that the deficit were, in fact, wholly devoted to increasing capital formation with no spillover effects, the "accounting identity" would hold* and capital formation would increase net by the current deficit.

Recently, large international capital flows have taken place to acquire existing assets (acquisitions and mergers of operating firms by multinational corporations and portfolio investments in bonds and equities by non-resident individuals and families).[69] Such transactions do not directly affect the rate of domestic investment as measured in the national income accounts but they do, through their effect on the rate of exchange, affect the current balance (and INW).[70] The strengthening of the currency, which accompanies the inflow of portfolio capital cheapens imports and reduces the price-competitiveness of export industries. To the extent that the capital inflows reduce the cost of capital in the deficit country and, through this, increase the rate of capital formation, the original model would hold.[71] But it is difficult to imagine that a currency, which has strengthened as much as the US dollar, has not affected the saving function (see Figure A1.1). *If household saving decreases as the currency strengthens , then the comforting idea that a deficit leaves total net worth unchanged is spurious.* Presumably as a response to net inflows of capital, the real (inflation-adjusted) rate of exchange of the dollar has appreciated steadily, though not monotonically, between 1991 and 2000 by roughly 50 percent (Figure A1.1).[72]

In a short passage of *The Report* (pp. 134–6),[73] the question of a hard landing is broached and a gloomy scenario of deep global recession is offered. Two excerpts (p. 136) approach the focus of this volume.

> If the current deficit continues to grow, at some point in the near future we are likely to reach the limit of our ability to borrow abroad in order to finance trade deficits. This could force the United States to reduce the deficit quickly and risk a "hard landing," or abrupt correction, with the clear possibility of triggering a recession. This would have serious repercussions not only for the United States, but also for the world economy.

> For these reasons, we strongly advise policymakers to develop contingency plans that can be implemented if a crisis develops to ensure stable financial markets and continued economic prosperity.[74]

Part II

How a Hegemonic System Works

2
Background Concepts and Relationships in a Globalized World

The United States has, historically, enjoyed a large degree of self-sufficiency in international economic affairs so that the ratio of exports and imports to gross domestic product is extremely low in comparison with smaller countries such as those in western Europe and in East Asia. There is, therefore, a tendency for US-trained economists and economic policymakers to downplay international phenomena in much of their thinking and to focus on closed-economy models. The ratio of exports and imports to gross domestic product in the United States has increased in recent years and the value of international financial transactions has also grown. There are many reasons. They include the liberalization of international trade, the greater freedom of international transfers of funds, the growth of foreign direct investments by multinational corporations and the end of approximate self-sufficiency in petroleum and other sources of energy. The word "globalization" has come to signify the greater *interdependence* of national economies. Some relationships must be spelled out. In addition, some of the issues of major concern to the subject matter of this volume are not a part of the mainstream of modern economic thought. Because the apparatus to be used will rely on little-used concepts and relationships that are not generally emphasized, it is useful, at this juncture, to provide some conceptual and definitional background before beginning to consider the subject of balance-of-payments adjustment by a hegemon under modern conditions in Chapter 3. Clearly, readers will only read those topic sections with which they are not familiar. A list of the topics is as follows:

1. Capital flows, the rate of exchange and the current balance.
2. The relationship between a country's current deficit or surplus and its INW.

3. The world as a closed economic system (*global* financial and economic constraints).
4. The costs of adjustment after a major financial shock.
5. Asset positions and functional currencies.
6. The burdens of hegemony.
7. Enlarging the burdens of hegemony: the American experience.
8. Regulation of financial markets and allocative efficiency.
9. Recent years: a retrospective.

I   Capital flows, the rate of exchange and the current balance

The rate of exchange is determined by the international flows of funds. The presumption is that capital flows are relatively immune to current rates of exchange (but certainly not completely so). Speculative flows will frequently be largely covered by other offsetting transactions and long-term capital flows will have a pronounced lead time so the assets which are acquired by capital flows with a long-term horizon will be relatively immune to small and/or short-lived variations in the rate of exchange. This simple model is illustrated in Figure 2.1. The implications are that the lion's share of net capital flows is reflected, with the opposite sign, in the current balance (and by the reported statistical discrepancy). The recipient country's currency (the dollar) generates credits earned largely through the sale of goods and services plus the net capital inflow (K). The cheaper the currency, the more willing are foreign nations to spend increasing amounts of foreign currencies on goods made in the United States. When there are no capital movements, the rate of exchange is marked at r_0 and the current account is balanced (current credits equal current debits). When there exist net capital inflows into the United States, the dollar is strengthened to r_1 by the net inflow of funds and, since capital movements are relatively insensitive to the existing rate of exchange, the US current account will run a deficit large enough to offset the main part of the net capital inflow.[1] In this simple model, the capital movements, through their effect on the rate of exchange, generate the net exports (international saving) needed to pay for the acquisition of the assets. The electorate of the investing country is presumably sufficiently docile to allow the reduction in the standard of living brought about by the weakening of their home currency.

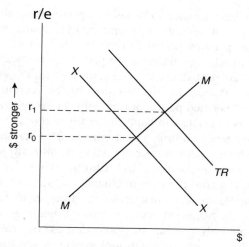

Figure 2.1   Capital flows and the exchange rate

Notes: The diagram measures the strength of the home currency (the dollar) as the number of units of foreign currency which the dollar purchases so the dollar strengthens with height. The downward-sloping schedule measures the home country's revenues from current transactions (*XX*) and the upward-sloping schedule (*MM*) shows expenditures on imports of goods and services. Trade is balanced at exchange rate r_0. When there is a net inflow of capital that does not affect the demand for exports or imports of either nation, revenues increase at all rates of exchange. The total revenues (*TR*) is parallel to *XX* and to its right. The rate of exchange that will clear the market is shown by r_1. The home currency is strengthened by virtue of the inflow of capital. The deficit at r_1 is equal to the net inflow of capital. The difference in the two exchange rates depends on the size of the capital inflow and to the joint sensitivity of *XX* and *MM* to the rate of exchange.

If the inflow of capital affected current transactions, the net inflow would be smaller than the gross inflow: some of the inflow would be dissipated on imports. If the inflow took the form of a direct investment, it might be expected to result in additional imports of capital goods and the strengthening of the host country's currency would be less. The interaction between the capital inflow and its use in the host currency becomes crucial when the inflow is portfolio or direct investment. (Note that if the current transactions are affected by the capital transaction, the *MM* schedule moves to the right.)

II   The relationship between the current balance and net asset position[2]

Tables 1.1 and 5.3 require that it be possible to knit together a flow of current transactions, which takes place over a period of time (usually a year), and stock ("balance-sheet") positions which exist at a moment of time (at the beginning or end of a calendar year). This section employs

a flow-of-funds approach to balance-of-payments analysis and accounting to this end. A net imbalance on current transactions of an economic
unit over a specified period of time (a flow) automatically involves a
compensating change in the end-of-period asset (stock) position. In sim-
plest terms, any imbalance in current flows of funds (sources and uses or
revenues and disbursements) deriving from an economic unit's transactions over a specified period of time must be recognized by adjustment
of the stocks of assets and liabilities at the end of that period (whether
the unit be a family, a firm, a government or a national economy[3]). It is
this fact which relates current transactions (annual flows) to the year-
end stocks of financial assets and liabilities (Gray and Gray, 1988–89):[4]
in context, it relates the current balance to the change in international
net worth. Figure 2.2 illustrates this linkage. In terms of national
economies, the balance on current account measures the net inflows (or
outflows) of funds from (to) foreign countries on current transactions; it
measures the current international saving (a surplus) or dissaving (a
deficit) of the residents of one country vis-à-vis the residents of the rest
of the world. Current dissaving must be financed either by "borrowing"
(acquiring liabilities) or the drawing down (sale) of claims against foreign residents: the net international investment position (the country's
international net worth or INW[5]) then decreases. The financing transactions are the capital flows. Notationally, the balance on current account
in a year, as denoted in equation (2.1) in terms of the balance on goods
$(X-M)$, equals international saving (>0) or dissaving (<0) vis-à-vis non-
residents and changes in the country's INW.

$$(X-M) \equiv S_I \equiv \Delta INW \tag{2.1}$$

One qualification must be made clear at this juncture: a nation's current
S_I (vis-à-vis non-residents) is only a first measure of the change in its
INW since it is possible that outstanding assets or liabilities may change
in value (in their currency of denomination) quite independently of
both the balance on current transactions and changes in the set of
exchange rates. For example, if interest rates were to decline in the
United Kingdom, the induced increase in the price of bonds denominated in sterling would enhance the wealth of US residents who owned
such bonds and the US INW would, *ceteris paribus*, increase.[6] The rôle of
the exchange rate is very important: since international accounts must
report assets and liabilities in a single currency, an appreciation or depreciation of the home currency will prove to be an important factor in the
determination of the change in INW (pp. 106–7). The capital account is

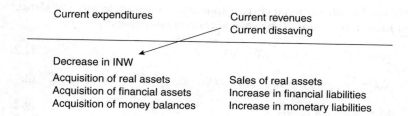

| Current expenditures | Current revenues |
| | Current dissaving |

Decrease in INW

Acquisition of real assets	Sales of real assets
Acquisition of financial assets	Increase in financial liabilities
Acquisition of money balances	Increase in monetary liabilities

Figure 2.2 The relationship between the current balance and INW

Notes: The entries above the line are current flows of incomes and expenditures and below the line are acquistions of foreign assets and liabilities by residents. The above the line flows are equal and the surplus of expenditures over revenues is the current deficit or international dissaving. This imbalance is transferred to the asset position and represents the decrease in the INW. The six categories show how the change in INW was distributed among the different genera of assets and liabilities. The apparatus is formally known as "flow-of-funds analysis" and identifies expenditures (on current purchases or asset acquisitions) as "uses" and revenues (from the sale of current goods and services or of assets) as "sources" of funds.

This apparatus does *not* allow for changes in the values of pre-existing assets and liabilities in the currency of record.

important[7] but *the focus of policy is likely to be the current balance since it is on the current-account balance that the available policy tools can have their most direct effect.*

III   The world as a closed economic system

The fact that the world economy is a closed system imposes some constraints on global activities and it becomes possible for the totality of nations to want (for domestic reasons such as political agency or for reasons of mistaken ideology) to thwart those constraints. Such efforts impose stress on the system and can be suppressed by passive financial markets. The interdependence of the global economy can be seen with a simple set of Keynesian relationships. Using the net value of exports over imports $(X-M)$ to represent the net balance on current transactions, a satisfactory level of global capacity utilization is independent of the volume of international trade. Let there be a hegemon (h) and the rest of the world (rw). Each is viewed as a single nation with a single currency. Output (Y) in the two countries depends on the rates of consumption (C), investment (I), government spending on goods and services (G) and net exports $(X-M)$. In a two-country global economy, one country's exports are definitionally equal to the other's imports and vice versa: therefore global income (Y_g) is independent of both the volume of international current transactions as well as any imbalances of such transactions at the level of individual nations.[8]

$$Y_h = \sum C_h + I_h + G_h + (X - M)_h \tag{2.2}$$

$$Y_{rw} = \sum C_{rw} + I_{rw} + G_{rw} + (X - M)_{rw} \tag{2.3}$$

$$(X - M)_h + (X - M)_{rw} \equiv 0 \tag{2.4}$$

$$Y_g = \sum (C + I + G)_h + \sum (C + I + G)_{rw} \tag{2.5}$$

$$(X - M)_h = S_{Ih} = -\sum (X - M)_{rw} = -S_{Irw} \tag{2.6}$$

$$A_h^* = \sum (C + I + G)_h - S_I \tag{2.7}$$

This does not mean that individual current balances are unimportant. They serve to distribute global aggregate demand among the countries differently from that which would occur in their absence (Equation 2.6). A current surplus adds to national aggregate demand but this presents no problem as long as there exists a counterpart nation willing to run a current deficit.[9] But, there is no guarantee that the short-run *target values* of $(X-M)$ for the rest of the world of $(n-1)$ countries will be zero (or negative). For a passive hegemon, this is approximately what (with sign reversed) its own $(X-M)$ will tend towards as a result of the interaction between the net flows of capital and the rate of exchange. If the hegemon's current account is negative as may be expected if rest-of-the-world countries wish to increase their net international reserves or to acquire real or financial assets in the hegemon net,[10] the hegemon's international net worth is fated to decrease. While this is not important provided that the hegemon's liabilities are, in some sense, "locked in" and if the magnitude of the negative INW does not cumulate far below zero because of "alternating" years of positive and negative S_I, it is a potential source of danger when the hegemon's liabilities can be easily transferred out of the key-currency. This is the essence of a potential system-wide international financial instability as distinct from national or regional crises.

The use of resources and output by a country is known as its absorption (A^*) (Equation 2.7). This is an important concept since it determines the rate at which a country is using up output (from home and abroad), and contributing to global aggregate demand. A^* will be compared, in Chapter 3, with the rate of production of goods and services. In this way, the current account becomes the difference between the values of output absorbed and output produced.

The focus of this monograph is positive not normative but one normative point is worth raising here. There are grounds for opposing the idea that the hegemon or any other nation be allowed to run cumulating current deficits of a magnitude that exceed the desires of other nations to accumulate international reserves. The hegemon as, ostensibly, the richest large country in the world, should not, in a world committed to helping the development of the poorer countries, suck in (absorb) more than the share of global saving, which it produces and many would advocate that "rich" nations (a group which will include the hegemon) should transfer resources to the developing world net. Such a computation would not be a simple one since it would involve both foreign direct investments in developing countries as well as unilateral payments to them – either directly in the form of foreign aid or indirectly through private parties or supranational organizations.

The global constraint (Equation 2.6) also applies to the international net worth of the individual nations (to stocks as well as to flows). Global international net worth, as defined, must equal zero. Under a system of double-entry bookkeeping, a nation with a positive net INW has, somewhere, a counterpart (or counterparts) with a negative INW. This relationship is crucial because it implies that a hegemon cannot increase its INW without another country reducing its INW in exactly the same way that a nation cannot run a surplus on current account without the rest of the world running a deficit (whether the deficit be desired or not).

There tends to be a bias for nations to want to run current account surpluses. A surplus is needed to increase the level of international reserves which is desirable when economic involvement is itself increasing or when the domestic economy is growing. A surplus also has the advantage of adding to domestic aggregate demand and employment. This reason underlies the concept of "beggar my neighbour" commercial policy examined by Robinson (1947) and was very important in the period of economic breakdown in the adequacy of global aggregate demand between the two world wars.

Built-in interdependence among national economies is the basis for the importance of foreign aggregate demand being high when a country is seeking to extricate itself from the after-effects of financial instability. High foreign aggregate demand in an open global economy provides an outlet for exports, which contribute to international saving and which can ease the fragility of its financial system. Contrast this set of conditions with those that prevailed between the two world wars, in which all countries in the world had lost confidence so that there was no buoyancy in the export market to aid a country's economic recovery. Thus, a single country in recession in a buoyant global economy is much more happily positioned than one in which even prosperous foreign countries have no strong desire for its exports. This point becomes crucial when the absorption theory of balance-of-payments adjustment is applied to the hegemon (in Chapter 3).

IV   The costs of adjustment after a major financial shock

The need to avoid financial instability derives in large measures from the damage which such an event will inflict on the real economy.[11] The adjustment costs are, of course, not independent of the type of shock or of its magnitude. A major international shock will require that resources be transferred, in individual countries, from sectors or industries due to decrease in proportionate (domestic) importance to those required to increase their share of total output. Thus, workers at all levels are likely to be surplus in some industries and sectors and must make themselves available to be employed in a different sector (possibly in a different city or region of the country). There will, at best, be substantial frictional unemployment. Part and parcel of the costs of reallocation will be the loss of industry-specific skills and, probably, lower incomes. Lower incomes will also be suffered at the aggregate level if the shock is adverse (i.e. for the deficit nation). It is reasonable to assume that the economic and social costs of an adjustment rise at an increasing rate with the size of the shock. The larger is the shock, the greater the proportion of total resources which have to be transferred among industries and, the less easily will the transfer be made as difference in skill levels and in specific skills are needed for transfers among starkly different industries.

V   Asset positions and functional currencies

Differences in the investment behavior of residents of different countries derive in large measure from the difference in their *functional currencies*: Private economic units in the United States, firms, families and individuals, regard the dollar as their *functional currency* because, respectively, they report to their shareholders their records of achievements in dollars and compute their wealth and incomes in that same currency. Non-resident individuals and families normally use the currency of the country of residence and corporations use the currency of the nation where headquarter offices are located, as their functional currencies. When the dollar is the currency of denomination of their foreign (portfolio) assets non-residents will give weight to the effect of a possible weakening of the dollar when considering the composition of their portfolio. US residents will take into account the possible effect of a change in the value of the dollar on their foreign assets in much the same way. Both sets of people will try to avoid having assets denominated in a currency that is expected to lose value in the foreign-exchange markets. Thus a German who owns stock in an American firm may consider unloading that investment if s/he believes that the dollar will weaken against the euro (by more than transaction costs). There is, clearly, a potential self-reinforcing mechanism here (see Chapter 4). One can draw the inference that residents of countries outside the United States may react more sensitively (i.e. more quickly and on a smaller expected percentage depreciation of the dollar) than will US residents – if only because many US residents will not as easily recognize the vulnerability of the dollar. US residents are perfectly capable of buying foreign equities and bonds and are likely to speculate against their own functional currency if it is expected to weaken. Quick action is likely to be dominated by people already involved in the international financial sector on a daily basis.

The analysis regards both foreign-owned physical assets (mainly the assets of foreign-based multinational corporations) as being denominated in the host country's currency (i.e. in the currency of the affiliate's location) and all financial assets as being denominated in the currency of the country of issue and location. While this is an adequate working assumption, it is not entirely precise: for example, many loans to developing countries, inter-governmental and private-sector, are specified in the currency of the lending nation. Another complicating factor is the possibility that a single multinational enterprise (MNE) may affect the *composition* of assets and liabilities: for example, a foreign MNE's assets may include physical assets in the United States financed in part with dollar-denominated bond issues or loans from US banks or by loans raised in a third country.

Official reserves and assets are also usually denominated in the key currency, that is, in dollars, but the governments of major industrialized nations will (or should) be concerned with the stability of the international financial system rather than with short-term maximization of wealth.

VI   The burdens of hegemony[12]

The rôle of financial hegemon, as briefly noted above, imposes several "duties" so that the hegemon may usefully contribute to the efficient functioning of the global financial/economic system. Four tasks can be identified: (i) free acceptance of the international saving of both official and private non-resident entities; (ii) acting as the "Keynesian locomotive" to ensure the adequacy of aggregate demand in the global economy; (iii) providing leadership in negotiating reductions to the impediments to international trade and, necessarily, increasing the transparency of any such policies; (iv) playing the leadership rôle in eliminating national or regional financial crises.

(i) Free acceptance of net international saving by the $n - 1$ countries requires that the hegemon not be concerned unduly with the loss of aggregate demand that derives from running a current deficit. The inflow of saving may consist of increases in government reserves or of the acquisition of assets in the hegemon by non-resident firms or families. Given that the value of reserves needs to increase over the long run for prosperous economies and as the ratio of international transactions to gross domestic product increases, the hegemon is likely to find its own INW declining over time. Under ordinary circumstances, the annual increase in the demand for international reserves of the "rest of the world," will be quite small but these flows cumulate. Much more important than planned increases in official reserves will be increases in key-currency assets made by foreign nations, which seek to enjoy or continue to enjoy the advantages of an undervalued national currency and the accompanying current-account surplus for domestic political goals.[13]

The rôle of economic hegemon imposes costs on the hegemon's economy in terms of the reduction in the international competitiveness (global market share) of its industries deriving from the overvaluation of the currency but it also may permit a faster rate of growth as foreign saving is attracted to the economy to permit capital formation.[14] The unemployment effects of an overvalued currency are likely be a source of political discontent with the responsibilities of the position (Godley, 1999). A current deficit undermines the "price-competitiveness" of the hegemon's industries as the key currency strengthens in foreign exchange markets and begins to exert long-run effects as its firms tend to have profit margins squeezed by foreign competition. Moreover, where the ability to maintain competitiveness requires investment in research and development and knowledge capital, firms within the hegemon may lose ground against their foreign competitors (Milberg and Gray, 1992). The excess of absorption over income is more directly germane to the thrust of this monograph, because "borrowed growth" (Ozawa, 2001b) can become excessive and the aftermath will be either a slower rate of growth coupled with positive international saving or steadily waning international economic strength.[15] Economic hegemony can require that policymakers impose unpleasant economic measures on the home economy because of its duties to the global economy. If these measures are "built-in," they are likely to generate discontent, which is primarily "domestic" – for example, dissatisfaction with income distribution and unemployment rates. However, when serious changes in policy are overtly imposed as a result of hegemonic responsibility, there may be both a tendency for policymakers to *delay* needed action and an induced dissatisfaction on the part of the electorate with the primary cause of the action – the hegemony. The importance of the hegemony will be brought to the attention of the public (the electorate) by a free press which will connect cause-and-effect in the minds of its readership. This consideration suggests that the United States will encounter domestic resistance in efforts to scale back absorption in order to increase its INW.

(ii) The adequacy of global aggregate demand is crucial if the global system is to operate efficiently. High levels of capacity utilization are needed if the political climate is to be supportive of greater freedom of international economic involvement, and if regional and/or national financial or economic crises are to be uncommon. Supporting high levels of global capacity utilization is, together with the provision of an "open" financial system, the key duty of the hegemon and the one which most seriously affects the decline in its INW. For a hegemon willing to accept this responsibility, it must run a current deficit equal to the sum of the target surpluses of the $n - 1$ other countries – otherwise the international saving of the $n - 1$ countries will represent a leakage from the global spending stream. It is this required passivity that has resulted in the hegemon sometimes being referred to as the "*nth country.*"

The danger here is that the erosion of the ability effectively to play the *nth country* can be slow and gradual so that the costs of this task are neglected until the world approaches crisis.[16] A second source of danger is that important countries will amass assets in the key currency as a part of their own financial system. A part of the large amount of Japanese assets denominated in dollars can be attributed to the use of dollar assets as guarantees for loans, which have ultimately become questionable. The idea that the global economy needs a spender of last resort becomes more important as the global economy becomes more closely integrated and as international transactions increase as a percentage of (an increasing) national product.

(iii) The British were the global leaders of free trade during the hegemony of the United Kingdom in the late nineteenth and early twentieth century and the United States continued this link between hegemony and the drive towards freer trade in the second half of the twentieth century. In fact, the United States went further and, as early as the 1950s, was the champion of free convertibility of currencies and the elimination of capital controls on international capital movements with greater enthusiasm than many nations felt it to be appropriate to the ongoing conditions.[17] This task involves long drawnout negotiations and the leader must set an example. Thus, the United States tended to be drawn into a position in which concessions in free trade multilateral negotiations often opened US markets by more or faster than the concessions of trading partners.[18]

(iv) The existence of local crises is likely to destroy assets and reduce the ability and/or willingness of nations to extend credit to countries with bad credit ratings. The key-currency nation is, together with the International Monetary Fund, responsible for ensuring that there exist lines of credit for nations which have suffered adverse shocks. Such crises use up the reserves of the key-currency country.

It is in this guise that the dominance of the hegemon comes into play: the hegemon must "discipline countries" to live within their means but there is always the danger that a socio-political breakdown in a debtor nation will be more destructive to the global system than providing some financial help. Discipline will involve lecturing ("jawboning") and will not increase the popularity of the hegemon.

VII   Enlarging the burdens of hegemony

When the United States assumed the burden of financial/economic hegemon at the end of the Second World War, its world view caused it to assume two other responsibilities as well. The United States made a conscious choice to take on the economic leadership rôle. It saw a surplus on international trade in goods and services as a counter to the inherited fears of the need to allot a large economic role to the government and government spending in the domestic economy in order to avoid a 1930s-type depression or, at least, some low-level equilibrium of capacity utilization (Schwartz, 1994a, 1994b). According to Dean Acheson (1944), the post-war economic policy of the United States was to avoid a large rôle for government in the home economy by generating aggregate demand internationally through a surplus on current international transactions – to be financed in substantial part by "foreign aid" although Acheson did not use this term. Further, the Roosevelt Administration took the position that open goods markets and open financial markets were necessary for an export surplus and that, given the economic potential of Germany and Japan, a security umbrella was necessary for open markets. The provision of the security umbrella required that the United States also assume the rôle of military hegemon.

While internationalism was viewed as inherently desirable, there was a straightforward logic involved and the three-part burden of hegemony: key-currency (financial); locomotive (economic) and security (military) was a means to a desirable end. The existence of potential constraints was recognized but at the end of the Second World War, the United States was dominant in all three dimensions of hegemony. It can be argued that, at some time but before the United States lost its economic and financial dominance, the means became ends in themselves and that policymakers lost sight of the need to recognize constraints and of the original plan of action.[19] It would also be arguable that politicians would have lost support for such a program had the costs to the domestic economy been made clear.

The financial hegemony required that the United States be the recipient of foreign international saving but this was negligible in the early years of hegemony because the technological lead of the US economy prevented European nations, even ex-allies, from running surpluses on current account, try as they might. Like the financial and economic leadership rôles, the military hegemony also imposed a direct foreign-exchange cost both by transferring military equipment to allies through military aid programs and through maintaining troops abroad: there were also indirect costs in using up much of the saving of the economy (although the transfer of equipment did serve the purpose of high employment at home). The development of military technology generated some valuable spillovers for civilian industry and this helped to offset the foreign-exchange costs as did the sale of military equipment to affluent allies. However, the Vietnam war was an important drain of foreign exchange but it released Japan and other Asian economies from severe balance-of-payments constraints (Fetherston and Gray, 1998). Not only did these burdens exert macroeconomic effects but they also diverted research-and-development expenditures away from "commercial research" so that US firms producing technology-using goods were disadvantaged compared with firms in Europe and those benefitting directly or indirectly from the Vietnam War.

All of these aspects burdened the US economy but they were not responsible for the focus of this book – the likelihood that the huge volume of easily-encashable foreign-owned assets coupled with a perceived need to depreciate the US dollar by a substantial amount can induce financial instability. The major decreases in the US INW can be attributed to policies during the last twenty years when the only war in which the United States was involved was the short-lived Gulf War of 1991.[20] Indeed, in the years 1981–97, the United States seemed to be acting conscientiously as the macrofinancial hegemon but with little, if any, awareness of its steadily decreasing INW.[21]

VIII   Regulation of financial markets and allocative efficiency[22]

Eonomic analysis has traditionally focused on obtaining optimum allocative efficiency so that global output is maximized. Because this argument has always been couched in models based on long-run static equilibrium, the possibility of instability was not considered and, even more surprising, the efficiency of the allocation of flows of investment was not integrated into the analysis (Walter, 1993). The latter would have involved the introduction of the efficiency of capital markets and financial variables and the simple assumption that all national economies had similar Northian institutions (North, 1990) would have had to have been discarded.

The possibility of financial instability introduces the desirability of regulation of financial firms and market.[23] Clearly, if financial firms assume risks which could contribute to instability, they need to be regulated if only because the potential costs of financial instability can be huge. However, the regulation of financial firms and markets will, inevitably, inhibit the allocative efficiency of asset allocation. There is therefore a trade-off between the two goals of allocative-efficiency and stability-efficiency, where the latter is defined as the magnitude of an adverse shock which can be survived without sending the prices of financial assets into a downward spiral. It is difficult to find the appropriate level of regulation and its structure when the appropriate level and structure will change with the conditions of the firms and markets. Moreover, since conditions can change rapidly and the essential problem is one of unwarranted exposure to risk, different individuals will have quite different views over both the actual and the appropriate degree of risk exposure. There is no straightforward answer to this problem of what is the optimum degree of freedom of financial intermediaries and markets but many economists advocate allowing market forces to allow financial firms to fail (if only *pour encourager les autres*) (Maehara in Herring and Litan, 1994).

This study addresses, effectively, the need to recognize a latent threat of stability-inefficiency of very large proportions. It remains important to assess the way in which financial regulation will impede real economic performance when conditions are tranquil and to provide the most efficient regulation possible. This question will be important in Part III.

IX   Recent years: a retrospective

In the absence of the sudden surge of inward direct and portfolio investments in the last four years (1998–2001), the US dollar would be less overvalued (i.e. the rate of international dissaving would be much smaller) and the liability position less vulnerable.

Developments in Europe and in Asia may have contributed to the recent burdens placed on the US rôle as locomotive. The elimination of regulations on foreign investments by many European (and other) countries in the late 1970s and early 1980s opened up the possibility for European residents to acquire assets in US financial markets (Herring and Litan, 1994, ch. 2). These inflows did not reach their full force quickly but grew gradually over time as European investors became familiar with investing in US financial markets and, probably more importantly, as European mutual funds and unit trusts were formed to facilitate investment in North America for people with little specialist knowledge. The opportunity existed for European investors to diversify their portfolios internationally. The inflow of portfolio capital to the United States began to surge in the early 1990s and should, in theory have subsided. The bubble of "irrational exuberance" on the New York Stock Exchange in the second half of the decade of the 1990s undoubtedly led to large inflows from European (and other) countries and strengthened the dollar.

A second European development, which may have contributed to the burden of the locomotive duty of the United States, can be traced to the formation of the euro after the Treaty of Maastricht. The Treaty of Maastricht imposed on EU member countries, which wanted to be absorbed into the euro bloc, well defined limits on the federal deficits which their governments could run (Rehman, 1997). The purpose of this requirement was to reduce any stress on economic relationships among the members of the bloc. A side-effect of these requirements was that countries within the euro bloc were limited in their ability to indulge in contra-cyclical tax policy. The millennial recession in Europe was, therefore, longer-lasting and perhaps deeper than it need have been had the negotiators at Maastricht confronted the question of this sacrifice of a tool for the ease of introduction of the euro. It would have been possible, given the high degree of integration of the member economies to allow for variable degrees of the ratio of federal deficits to gross domestic product to be instituted when the bloc was in a sustained recession and the members' economies were not responding to low interest rates. The recession in "Euroland" has also kept the major European stock markets in the doldrums and, in this way, affected the flow of portfolio capital to the United States.

The possibility of conflict between the duties of the authorities in the hegemon towards their domestic economy and towards the global economy[24] will be important when, for example, the two duties of providing a global money to act as a medium of international exchange and acting as the supplier of aggregate demand to the global economy (the Keynesian locomotive) are in conflict because the supply of aggregate demand to the rest of the world involves incurring debts with other (non-hegemonic) nations and will, over a protracted period, drain the INW of the hegemon.[25] In addition, the measures, which put into force policies which augment global aggregate demand will tend to have unfavorable domestic repercussions for some industries made visible by the strengthening of the dollar. The effect of current deficits on the demand for labor in the hegemon make any policy that requires a deficit a potential source of political opposition.[26] Policy in the United States in 2003 seems to seek to defuse the domestic aspects of this issue by attributing the current deficits and the unfavorable "balance of employment" to slow growth in foreign countries and to "unfair" commercial policies imposed there.

The potential clash between the needs of the domestic economy and the needs of the global economy has existed in principle since the United States assumed the role of hegemon after the Second World War. The recent substantial increase in the liberalization of international transactions in both economic and financial markets and the deeper international integration that results from the communications revolution, in short "*globalization*," have increased the burdens of hegemony. The relative importance of international transactions has increased substantially and national (non-hegemonic) governments are likely to want to increase their international reserves. To this end, they must "save" vis-à-vis the United States and lodge the savings in their international reserves in the global key currency. At the same time, the liberalization of international capital transactions has allowed residents outside the United States to acquire dollar-denominated assets as a means of diversifying their portfolios (Table 5.2). This inflow of foreign saving will have a transitory component as the reallocation of portfolios is a stock-adjustment process. This new international mobility of financial assets creates a danger that a country will be able to invest in physical assets (domestic capital formation), which have a much longer life than the term on which the easily encashable international liabilities (the corresponding liabilities) have been funded. This problem played its part in the July 1997 crisis of the Thai baht (Gray and Dilyard, 2002). This problem can also affect the hegemon. The data in Chapter 5 (Tables 5.3 and 5.10) show that the United States has increased its capital stock (of both physical and, it must be assumed, knowledge capital) by accepting from abroad easily encashable liabilities traded in secondary financial markets ($I_D > S_D + IFDI$). This ability to finance long-term investments with easily encashable liabilities has been made possible by non-residents' great faith in the reliability of the dollar. Such behavior contravenes the *maturity matching* approach to financing assets whereby a firm will attempt to match the maturity of its liabilities to the length of operating life of the counterpart asset (Brigham and Gapenski, 1985, pp. 597–8). At the firm level, the concern is that the liabilities will have to be refinanced at higher costs than those used in the investment decision. The analogy is not exact because obligations to refund foreign exchange when foreigners encash their dollar-denominated assets resembles more closely the problem of a bank, which must pay its liabilities "on demand." However, the comparison does indicate the macroeconomic danger of financing domestic capital formation with easily encashable foreign saving.[27]

3

A Theory of Balance-of-Payments Adjustment for the Hegemon

I Introduction

The absorption theory (Alexander, 1952) (Johnson, 1958) is the basic theoretical analysis of the elimination of a balance-of-payments deficit. However, this theory is not, in its original form, directly applicable to the subject matter of this book. In its original form, the theory applied to a world of ostensibly fixed rates of exchange in which, with the exception of the key-currency country, which had, at that time, a very large positive INW, international capital movements were both screened by the authorities in the exporting country and were small relative to the volume of current transactions. Second, the theory applied to a relatively small nation so that it is in need of a major restatement when it is to be applied to a large country (the key-currency nation).

Section II of this chapter briefly summarizes the standard version of the now-dated absorption theory of balance-of-payments adjustment and adapts it to modern conditions in which international capital movements are fully capable of outweighing current international transactions in value and in which exchange-rates react to the net flows of funds. Section III emends the theory to make it applicable to the problems facing the hegemon. These elaborations will give the reader a logical/theoretical basis for understanding the problems facing a hegemon which is nearing exhaustion of its capabilities. Section IV addresses the determinants of a nation's "income on international assets" and US data for this minor component of a country's current account balance. Section V summarizes the implications of the model for the United States and the exhaustion of the dollar.

II Updating the absorption theory

Since the absorption theory was created in the 1950s, the institutional setting in which international transactions take place, has changed substantially. The immediate post-war international financial system relied upon widespread governmental controls on international transactions on both current and capital accounts (except in the United States which had tied itself to gold and to open markets), and a system of ostensibly fixed exchange rates. That system has evolved to one in which both current and capital transactions are largely unregulated in the major countries from a balance-of-payments point of view and in which rates of exchange are free to flex with autonomous flows of funds. The existing system comes close to what has been the goal of US international economic policy since the Second World War (Acheson, 1944). In attaining this very liberal system, the United States received a helping hand from the Thatcher governments of the United Kingdom. Both President Reagan and Prime Minister Thatcher and their advisers were unquestioning believers in the virtues of a system of free markets.[1]

A second major feature of the evolution was the growth in the absolute value of *private* international capital movements (and the accompanying increase in the ratio of the value of capital transactions to current transactions). Machlup (1958) and (1965) distinguished between accommodating and autonomous transactions in international payments: capital movements, which were designed to finance some short-term indebtedness, were "accommodating" (they owed their existence to a "minor malfunction" in the existing system). Project-specific loans to developing countries were autonomous but they were carefully designed and accommodated the need for capital formation in a developing nation. In practice such loans, usually long-term, were largely devoted to financing imports of capital goods and therefore self-financing in a balance-of-payments sense for the lending country. Activities, which were undertaken for their own sake were "autonomous" or "spontaneous" and private sector transactions of this kind are profit-seeking and/or are intended to be wealth-increasing. The growth of international capital movements in the last quarter of the twentieth century was dominated by the increase in private autonomous (profit-seeking) transactions. If all of the assets held abroad were either illiquid (as in the fixed capital of multinational corporations) or owned by governments concerned more with the efficient functioning of the global financial system than with avoiding short-run pecuniary loss, the problem of adjusting to the exhaustion of the dollar would be much less difficult.

McKinnon (2001) gives a careful explanation of how such a well-behaved system might work to effect the necessary adjustment without financial crisis.

In addition to the reduction in controls, the growth in private capital flows can be attributed to three major changes in international economic and financial affairs. First is the growth of foreign direct investment by multinational corporations. This phenomenon started to gather momentum in the 1960s and has grown quickly since then.[2] The flows of direct investment began largely as greenfield ventures, which added production capacity to the host economy and which concurrently induced certain imports of capital goods (usually from the parent country of the new affiliate).[3] Cross-border mergers with and acquisitions of operating firms (M&As) result in the acquisition of more than a 10 percent share of the equity and they have, in recent years, grown in relative importance. In developed economies, M&As have increased from about $80 billion per annum in the early 1990s to roughly $700 billion in 1999: other FDI (greenfield) has grown from about $100 billion per annum in industrialized countries to approximately $150 billion (UNCTAD, 2000, Figure IV.8a). Mergers and acquisitions among industrialized countries are usually undertaken by the purchase (or swap) of the equity of active corporations at negotiated prices so that the effect of such a transaction on the balance of payments closely resembles, at least in the short-term, a financial transaction. In developing countries, greenfield ventures still dominate.

The second category of transactions to grow rapidly is portfolio investments: these *financial* assets are traded in secondary markets and are effectively denominated (or traded) in the currency of the host nation (as distinct from the functional currency of the non-resident asset holder[4]). For simplicity, data on portfolio investments are assumed here to include changes in money balances of non-residents. Portfolio investments have grown in response to the liberalization of capital markets and the effective elimination of controls over the international movement of private funds. The liberalization resulted from the belief in the greater allocative efficiency of free financial markets uncluttered by restraints imposed on investors' behavior.[5] Modern international flows of portfolio capital seek international diversification for their owners and have been facilitated by the technological developments of high-speed communications (as has the management of their affiliates by multinational corporations). The development of new types of services is particularly important in the growth of portfolio investments where the newly developed international mutual funds and unit trusts are now the major means by which private individuals acquire foreign financial assets. In periods of stress, these institutions are capable of instigating major movements of assets very quickly (much more so than individuals).[6]

The third category of fast-growing international investment is credit extended by financial institutions (commercial banks) to firms abroad.[7] For the claims and liabilities of banks, the currency of denomination is not as clearly defined as for portfolio assets and, in times of stress, banks may not, in their own self-interest, be able to forego renewing some outstanding loans.[8]

It is important to recognize that the various categories of private transactions (greenfield, M&As, portfolio investments and bank loans and liabilities) can have quite different effects on the time profile of a country's balance of payments. Nearly all direct investments will impact upon the balances on goods and services of both the home and host countries in future years. Greenfield investments increase both the volume and the sophistication of the productive capacity of the host country (Fry, 1996) (Dunning *et al.*, 2001). Both greenfield and M&As investments will affect the foreign demand for exports and the demand of the host economy for imports as the multinational parents link new affiliates into the parent corporation's global productive and sales networks. These investment flows will, then, affect the rate of exchange between the host- and the home-country currencies compatible with balanced trade in goods and services (given the absence of capital flows, levels of aggregate demand in all countries and the existing price levels in domestic currencies). Call this rate "*the balancing rate of exchange*": this rate is a reference rate and it is the financial equivalent of the net barter terms of trade in formal models of balanced international trade. The balancing rate of exchange is *not* observable. Portfolio investments and bank activities are, like direct investments, expected to yield a return on invested capital so that "net income on international assets" (a component of the current account) will respond to changes in both the net position and the mix of assets and liabilities as well as to changes in the spectrum of returns.[9]

Given the importance of capital flows, it is useful, under modern conditions, to identify *two* effects of capital flows on rates of exchange. The first is a *direct* effect, which may lead to induced imports by the capital-importing country and which will, through capacity creation and other linkages, affect the balancing rate of exchange. The direct effect of an individual investment will be delayed: Each investment will have its own unique effect so that the balancing rate will vary through time and the direction of movement cannot be precisely foreseen.[10]

There is also an *indirect* effect, which works on current transactions through the effect of ongoing net capital flows on the *market-clearing rate of exchange or the observed financial rate* (at which the total flow of funds is equal in both directions). The indirect effect of an individual investment takes place immediately but, being part of a flow, its effect has a short duration. The distinction is important because net inflows of capital of any kind will strengthen the currency of the capital importer and reduce the international price-competitiveness of its value-added. Under current conditions, capital flows are less exchange-rate-sensitive than current transactions and, therefore, the net volume of capital flows tends to be the prime determinant of the market-clearing rate of exchange.[11] In the absence of capital flows, the balancing and the market-clearing rates would be identical and, if the mix of capital flows is unchanged, it is legitimate to assume that, as the volume of net investment decreases, the gap between the two rates (and the degree of overvaluation of the deficit nation's currency) will get smaller. Both the flows and the accumulated stocks of the three kinds of capital flows must be distinguished if only because the composition of the stock and of the concurrent flows will affect both rates of exchange (as well as the net income on international assets).

The absorption theory of balance-of-payments adjustment can be summarized in its original form in terms of a set of Keynesian (flow) equations. For an individual country, the net value of exports over imports $(X-M)$ represents the net balance on current transactions (neither the balance on unilateral transfers nor net income on international assets is allowed for in this summary). Output (Y) depends on the rates of consumption (C), investment (I), government spending on goods and services (G) and exports of goods and services (X). Absorption (A^*) is equal to income-less exports plus imports. Clearly if A^* exceeds Y, the country is absorbing goods and services in excess of the value of its own production (it is "living beyond its income") and must finance the difference either by running down its international assets or by "borrowing" from its trading partners.

$$Y = \sum(C + I + G + X) \tag{3.1}$$

$$A^* = \sum(C + I + G + M) \tag{3.2}$$

$$Y - A^* = X - M = S_I = \Delta \, \mathrm{INW} \tag{3.3}$$

If the balance on current account is negative, the country is dissaving vis-à-vis non-residents and, if its INW is already negative, the total net "indebtedness" is increasing. International dissaving $(M > X)$ implies an overvalued currency (defined here as being stronger than the balancing rate). The imports of goods and services will exceed the rate compatible with the balancing rate of exchange: the more sensitive the demand for imported goods and the supply of exports to the market-clearing rate, the smaller the degree of overvaluation for a given imbalance on current transactions.

The original version of the absorption theory of international payments adjustment recognizes that, if dislocations are to be minimal, the elimination (or reduction) of a current account deficit requires the adoption of three interrelated policies. The first policy measure is, an *expenditure-switch*. This is usually thought of in terms of a depreciation of the national currency (although impediments to imports and subsidies on exports would have much the same effect if global agreements were to permit such actions). The advantage of a currency depreciation is that it is neutral across sectors so that it does not contain any biases likely to affect the mix of goods traded and produced. The purpose of the expenditure-switch is to change relative costs of domestic value-added in order to increase the foreign demand for the exports of the deficit country and to reduce its home demand for competitive imported goods.[12]

Second, *an expenditure-reducing measure* is needed. A current deficit indicates that the economy is absorbing at a rate in excess of the value of its output ("living beyond its income") and the expenditure-reduction is required to scale down aggregate absorption. Monetary or fiscal policy would be the usual means of achieving the expenditure-reduction. This policy measure was obviously important when an overly exuberant domestic economy verging on or subject to demand-pull inflation was the principal cause of a current deficit.[13] As a first approximation, the proportionate expenditure-reduction must equal the deficit on current account $(S_I < 0)$ as a percentage of total absorption. The expenditure-reduction, which is implicit in the earlier model, is generated entirely by the change in the terms of trade (the balancing rate of exchange) and would, even under very optimistic assumptions, take significantly longer to eliminate a given deficit.

The third measure is the *arrangement of financing* to cover the negative cash flow during the time taken for the policies to eliminate the deficit. Inevitably, the absorption theory requires emendation and/or elaboration if it is to adapt to a particular set of conditions. The expenditure-switch will, to the extent that it is successful, add to aggregate demand for the output of the deficit country so that the decrease in capacity utilization will be less than the proportionate expenditure-reduction, but there is, almost inevitably, an appreciable lag between the institution of the expenditure-switch and the induced increase in net exports: the expenditure-reduction can be expected to work the more quickly of the two.

This chapter identifies those aspects of the standard version of the theory, which must be changed, if the theory is to be applicable to the elimination of a series of apparently chronic current deficits incurred by the global financial hegemon in a world in which autonomous capital transactions dominate current transactions in volume.

In essence, the standard version of the theory states, straightforwardly, that a nation running a deficit on current account is in danger of not being able to finance such a deficit (i.e. to have non-residents provide it with liabilities) and must, if serious dislocation is to be avoided (at home and in its creditor countries), eliminate the deficit by reducing the level of domestic prosperity by *both* constraining domestic aggregate demand and shifting the terms of trade (the balancing rate) against itself. Clearly, there was room for case-by-case differences in the size and speed of availability of the potential line of credit, which a nation might hope or expect to enjoy and, therefore, in the immediacy of the need for deficit-reducing measures. This was likely to depend, in part at least, on the component of its INW, which could be quickly realized by non-residents.

In the early institutional setting, the theory was valuable because it emphasized, albeit implicitly, the passive role of arranged (accommodating) capital flows and the need to recognize the limits of such flows as a means of avoiding or postponing socially costly and politically unpopular remedial policies. The major indicator was a negative balance on current account ($S_I < 0$). Recognition that chronic deficits led to the possibility of crisis was understood and identification of the two dimensions of deficit-eliminating policies was an important advance because it emphasized the need for a proactive policy reducing aggregate demand in addition to the expenditure-switch.

When private capital movements became quantitatively dominant in the later years of the twentieth century, the major change in the analysis was that the balance on current account (S_I) became the (relatively) *passive* element, levels of income assumed constant, because the rate of exchange was allowed to flex in response to the flows of funds, and a deficit country could no longer change the international value of its currency by some announcement. The only way for a country to change its market-clearing rate of exchange without interfering with current transactions (trade in goods and services or its rate of domestic capacity utilization) is to work through the capital account: to acquire foreign assets or to exclude some potential inward investments. If the country was seeking to weaken its currency because foreign capital was flowing in at a rate deemed excessive and chose to weaken its currency, the country had to "*counter-invest*" (to reduce the net credit on capital flows). This raises some delicate questions as to whether a (creditor) nation would allow a foreign government to intervene in its capital markets on an important scale: the activity would tend to resemble non-neutral open-market operations. If counter-investing were to be carried out on a scale large enough to affect values in financial markets, its practice would be likely to require some *a priori* globally-negotiated agreement. It is possible that governments would agree to inter-governmental loans so that counter-investment would not require activity in secondary markets. In effect such an agreement would lead to a new rôle for governments in the international financial system.

Second, a country, which was a popular place in which to invest capital, could find itself with a high rate of inflow and with what could be an excess stock of foreign capital (direct or financial): this state of affairs would necessarily be accompanied by an unacceptably strong exchange-rate and a rapidly deteriorating INW.[14] This condition removes the short-term pressure to finance the current deficit since the autonomous inflow of capital finances and, indeed, helps to generate the current deficit. For most countries, this would be likely to be a short-lived phenomenon because the resulting strength of its currency could reduce the country's attractiveness as a base for inward FDI and the larger deficit position on assets, and the implicit threat of depreciation of the host currency, would discourage the inflow of portfolio investment. However, a large country with a strong currency, could generate a large deficit on INW before the inflows ceased spontaneously and the economy would then be in danger of a herd-instinct motivated by, large-scale withdrawal of portfolio capital.

What would matter would be the potential volatility of the stock of non-resident-owned assets denominated in the country's currency (i.e. assets which could be traded in local secondary financial markets and the proceeds quickly liquidated in foreign-exchange markets).[15] Here it is necessary to note that inward *direct* investments are not "easily-encashable" and therefore carry with them no threat of sudden withdrawal.[16] This attribute of inward FDI must be qualified by recognition of the fact that multinational corporations are quite capable of using their working capital to their own advantage when sudden and important changes in values in foreign-exchange markets are either foreseen or occur. Moreover, because these corporations seek to minimize the cost of working capital on a routine basis, they are well equipped to be alert to and to take advantage of any actual or anticipated shift in spot or future foreign-exchange rates.

In the past, when private capital movements were not dominant, the indicator of balance-of-payments stress was the (negative) current balance and any string of recent current balances. In a world of fixed rates of exchange, such current deficits were likely to have arisen because of different inflation rates at home and abroad or through faster rates of economic growth in the deficit country. In the more liberal, current international financial system, there is no single indicator. At present, *current and historical data on the net international investment position and its rate and direction of change (S_I) are the measures by which international financial performance must be judged.*[17] There are no exact criteria of the need for immediate institution of corrective policies and the judgments of the policymakers are important. It is self-evident that the need to impose an expenditure-reduction on the deficit country will be politically unpalatable in a democracy in which the electorate is prone to punish elected incumbents for inflicting painful measures on them. There is, therefore, a tendency in almost every country to postpone instigating those policies, which, however necessary, are likely to promote a backlash and economic policies, particularly international financial policies, tend to be instituted less quickly than is desirable. The use of the complex indicator is more important in a world committed to the unimpeded functioning of free markets for goods and services and for all of the different forms of capital as well. Capital controls (direct controls over investment flows) are inefficient because they are both ponderous and porous, so that the balance on current account (S_I) remains an important indicator because it is the first measure of the ongoing change in INW.

The global financial system now provides for freedom of capital movements and flexible rates of exchange in almost all countries whose residents are involved in international investment. Capital flows affect the (market-clearing) rate of exchange: a net inflow of capital strengthens the recipient country's currency and that country will tend to run a current deficit as its stronger currency makes foreign-made goods and services more attractive to the domestic population and its own exports more highly priced in foreign currency. In this way, the balance on capital tends to finance the deficit on current account *ex ante*. In a short-term, cash-flow context, this is the crucial change: *effectively, capital flows provide the financing for the current deficit, which they induce.* Modern conditions expose the global macrofinancial system to the stability/instability characteristics of asset (financial) markets rather than of goods markets.

The advocacy of complete freedom of international capital movements finds its intellectual antecedents in the same theoretical construct that underlies the basic argument for trade liberalization. Both arguments rely on the principle that unhindered international movement of goods and services and capital will result in an optimum international and inter-industry allocation of global resources. This condition is prerequisite to the maximization of global income. Both arguments neglect, *inter alia*, the potential costs of (major) instability in financial or goods markets and do not consider a trade-off between allocative efficiency and stability-efficiency (Gray and Gray, 1981, 55–61). In principle, the argument in favor of complete freedom of capital movement has built-in dynamic aspects because international capital movements become part of the mechanism by which the global flow of international saving is allocated among competing end-uses (although there are no transfers of international saving entertained in the argument for free trade). The argument for freedom of capital movements neglects the difference in the speed of reaction of flows to changes in conditions. The sensitivity of the current account to the rate of exchange is slow to achieve its full effect[18] while capital flows, particularly portfolio investments, can react to a change in conditions, particularly in investor confidence, and reverse the direction of net flow very quickly and in large volume. It is this difference in capacity for adjustment that introduces the costs of resource-reallocation when exchange rates change appreciably. Volatility is likely to be much greater for portfolio than for direct investments.[19]

III Emending the theory for a large country

The original version of the absorption theory applies only to small countries. Analysis of the balance-of-payments adjustment process for a large country and, particularly, for the hegemon, requires that the theory be expanded. There are four major qualifications to the standard theory which apply to a hegemon. They are: (1) the effect of hegemonic attempts to eliminate a current account deficit on the level of global aggregate demand; (2) the likelihood that the hegemon cannot expect to depreciate its currency against all others (i.e. without a retaliatory offset); (3) the effect on the sensitivity of the hegemon's current balance of having world prices of important primary products denominated in its own, key currency; and (4) the sensitivity of the adjustment process to the magnitude of the adjustment (i.e. to the magnitude of the deficit and the time during which a deficit has existed).

Global aggregate demand

The (original) absorption theory gave explicit attention to the level of aggregate demand in the deficit country by requiring that that country's level of resource utilization be included in the analysis. Aggregate demand in the deficit country had to be reduced if that country were at full employment, in order to make resources available to those industries destined to expand after the expenditure-switch policy had taken effect. If the country was operating at less than full employment of resources before the policy package was instituted and had sufficient spare capacity to increase production of exports by the required amount, there was no need, except for what might be called "psychological reasons," for an expenditure-reduction. If the country was not operating with excess capacity, the necessary capacity had to be created by restricting domestic aggregate demand. Thus, expenditure-reduction was usually but not inevitably required.[20]

There was, in the original version, no equivalent concern with the expansion of aggregate demand by the surplus nations on the presumption that the foreign demand for the goods of the deficit nation would increase solely as a result of the depreciation of its currency (in real terms). Thus, global aggregate demand would be smaller when the expenditure-switch policies of the deficit nation took hold but this reduction in global aggregate demand was presumably deemed small enough to allow market forces slowly to return the system to full capacity utilization without pro-active demand-expanding measures by surplus nations. It follows from this presumption that the deficit nation was a very small component of the global system. The logic underlying the omission was that a small nation would have smaller lines of credit and would be forced to act to counter a cumulative string of current deficits very quickly, so that the problem of the level of global aggregate demand could be neglected.[21]

When the deficit nation is the hegemon and, perforce, the Keynesian locomotive for the global economy, neglect of global aggregate demand is not permissible. The current deficit of the hegemon can be a substantial element in global aggregate demand. If, as suggested above, the United States would have to reduce its aggregate demand by the ratio of the current deficit to total absorption, this decrease in global aggregate demand – roughly $480 billion in 2002 – would, if successfully achieved, have to be divided among the other countries of the world and their collective levels of capacity utilization would fall. Clearly, a hegemon near exhaustion should be careful lest by continuing to act as the Keynesian locomotive by running further current deficits, it would enhance the risk of a loss of confidence in its currency. The task of adding to global aggregate demand must fall on the surplus nations but, if recent experience provides evidence, this will not occur spontaneously from an understanding of what is needed for the re-establishment of global prosperity.[22]

Expenditure-switching measures

The original version of the absorption theory assumes that a deficit nation will be able, and indeed should, instigate expenditure-switching measures, which are identical for all nations (subject to the effects of membership in a customs union or a common market). This is unlikely to be possible under current conditions and even less likely if the deficit nation is the hegemon. First, an expenditure-switch policy incorporating a weakening of the currency of the deficit nation is difficult to effect. To instigate a depreciation of the currency in a world in which exchange rates depend on the flows of funds would require that a government intervene in foreign capital markets to acquire net assets denominated in foreign currencies (counter-investment). This presumes that the economic authorities have the required funds. The funds needed for counter-investment could be acquired by imposing an expenditure-reduction (through a tax increase) to increase the surplus in the government sector and then to use these funds to buy foreign securities. *In this way, the two major measures of the absorption theory come together.* Even with the best will in the world, it would not be possible for the hegemon to effect an equal depreciation of the deficit nation's currency against all others simply because the distribution of the effects of the depreciation on flows of funds among the rest of the world is not knowable. There is also a very real possibility that trading partner nations would, themselves, indulge in counter-investment in an attempt to try to offset the acts of the hegemon.

The effectiveness of a given expenditure-switch to the deficit country's current account will depend upon the size of the elasticities of demand and supply for tradable goods and services at home and in foreign countries. The greater the sensitivities, the greater will be the change in the current deficit of a given depreciation, incomes held equal.[23] Given the virtual inevitability of the inequality of depreciations across countries, the question of the sensitivity of the current account balance to different mixes of full and partial depreciation warrants investigation. What follows is purely illustrative since there is no practical way of knowing what the actual mix of currency depreciation would be.

Table 3.1 shows the effect on the US current deficit of a 10 percent depreciation when supply elasticities are infinite and demand elasticities are unitary. The computations do not allow for induced changes in levels of capacity utilization in countries. Taking the actual totals of exports and imports of goods and services of the United States in 2001 and assuming incomes remain unchanged, the specified elasticities produce an overall reduction of the balance on goods and services of 39 percent of the deficit.[24] If countries in the western hemisphere offset the depreciation of the US dollar, the reduction of the deficit is reduced to 25.6 percent. If Japan joined the western hemisphere nations in offsetting the formal depreciation of the dollar, the reduction of the deficit is reduced to 21.1 percent and, self-evidently, the reduced breadth of the depreciation implies the need for a larger depreciation of the currency if the deficit is to be eliminated.[25] While these numbers only provide an

Table 3.1   The effectiveness of a 10 percent depreciation of the dollar

Extent of depreciation	Sum of exports and imports ($ billions)	Change in balance on goods and services (percentage)[a]
Total	2,507.5 (1,069.5 + 1,438.0)	39.0 (From −368.5 to −224.7)
Excludes western hemisphere (Western hemisphere data)	1,582.5 (201.4 + 227.7)+ (248.6 + 247.3)[b]	25.6 (From −368.5 to −274.2)
Excludes western hemisphere and Japan (Japanese data)	1,318.2 (98.9 + 165.4)[b]	21.1 (From −368.5 to −290.8)

Notes
[a] Computed, for simplicity, on the basis of unitary elasticity of demand for exports and imports and perfectly elastic supply of exports and imports (i.e. constant prices of US goods in dollars).
[b] The data give the exports to Canada and to Latin America in that order: the equivalent imports are given in the second parentheses. Japanese data are given below in the same way.
Source: *Survey of Current Business* (April 2001), pp. 50 and 64–5. Based on preliminary US data for 2000.

illustration, they suggest that it is imperative that any depreciation by the dollar be as general against all currencies as possible.

The required magnitudes of the expenditure-switch and the expenditure-reduction are positively correlated, respectively, with the ratio of the flow of dissaving to total current-account credits and with GDP. The interaction between the expenditure-reduction and the expenditure-switch is very difficult to assess if only because the effect of the expenditure-reduction on the rate (and distribution) of global capacity utilization is unknowable. Economists have little knowledge of the sensitivities of international trade patterns to changes in price-competitiveness because the new conditions of a globalized world have not been in force for a long time and such disequilibria as exist among industrialized nations have been suppressed by allowing the hegemon to appreciate its currency and to dissave internationally. Such evidence as exists does not point to large increases in exports in response to a weakening of the dollar (Galbraith, 2002, 10). The needed expansion of capacity in import-substitute industries could take a great deal of time because the import-replacement industries will have been operating at low capacity rates with low, if any, profits in recent years and will, therefore, need to update their equipment and to expand their capacity.

Ultimate recognition that the dollar cannot continue to support its current outflows and that the system must undergo a major adjustment seems likely to involve the national authorities in giving serious consideration to renouncing many features of the existing liberal framework. The system faces a possible return to a world of negotiated exchange rates and controls of varying severity over the freedom of international movements of portfolio capital. The longer, the existing state of affairs is left to continue, the more likely is some sort of new short-term arrangement to be needed. This suggestion of a return to a world of controls should not be seen as a response to the third proposition of Chapter 1, which posits that the world will need to develop a new international financial architecture. What is mooted here is likely to be a short-term régime designed solely to effect the adjustment of the existing imbalances. However, given the enthusiasm of the financial sector for free markets, such a temporary system may be impossible to achieve if and until the seriousness of events generates acceptance of some temporary framework of controls.

Basic commodities

Many basic commodities are traded in global markets and, almost without exception, the global price is determined in the key currency. This fact has implications for the sensitivity of the hegemon's import demand for such commodities.[26] Provided always that the prices of these commodities continue to be denominated in the key currency, there is no direct link between an expenditure-reduction and the price of the basic commodity in the hegemon's currency. This suggests that there will be no great sensitivity in the current balance that derives directly from imports of the basic commodities (in terms of elasticities, the change in the market price will be zero and therefore the elasticity of demand is irrelevant). Basic commodities include petroleum and in many such basic commodities, the United States is not self-sufficient. At the margin, therefore, these products are "non-competitive goods" in the sense that marginal demand relies wholly on imports (Gray, 1976, 46–9). What has been painted is a worst case scenario because there is an indirect link between the cost of the basic commodity to users in the United States and the size of the expenditure-switch. The basic commodity with a constant price in dollars, will now be cheaper in foreign countries and demand there will increase. These increases will add to global demand and the global price should increase in dollars. Nonetheless, there is a potentially important segment of absorbed goods, which will only have their price in the United States indirectly affected. This fact does not encourage belief that import demand for these commodities will be significantly curtailed as a result of the expenditure-switch measures and this factor will put greater reliance on expenditure reductions.

This characteristic suggests that a hegemon will have a current account which is less sensitive to an expenditure-switch. Deficit elimination will either require a larger expenditure-switch or, possibly, a larger expenditure-reduction. One possible alternative strategy would be to apply an import duty or a sales tax on basic goods with the rate of tax being set equal to the degree of depreciation of the dollar.

The magnitude of the adjustment

Perhaps the most serious qualification to the original version of the absorption theory when it is transposed to the hegemon, is the potential size of the current deficit, both relatively to GDP and in absolute terms. The larger the ratio of current deficit to GDP, the greater is the need to change the mix of production away from non-traded goods and services to export goods and import-substitutes. In the present context, these industries are likely to be in a depressed state because of the prolonged overvaluation of the dollar and the intensity of foreign competition since 1983 and the more serious overvaluation of the dollar in the years from 1999 to the end of 2002 (Table 5.1). A great deal of time may be needed to re-establish the global price-competitiveness of these industries because of the necessary increase in capacity and the updating of the existing capital stock. In terms of the assumptions of the subsection on expenditure-switching measures, it is less reasonable to assume perfectly elastic supply elasticities the larger are the duration and the size of the deficit. The more capacity has to be created in some industries and the more firms have to update their plant and equipment,[27] the smaller will the supply elasticity be and, therefore, *the less sensitive the adjustment process* to a weakening of the currency in the short run. But this question of the magnitude of the adjustment affects both aspects of the adjustment process and the assumption for Table 3.1 of constant unitary elasticity of demand that acquires ever greater heroism, as the magnitude of adjustment increases.

IV   Balance on income on international assets

While it is simpler to view the balance on current account as defined in terms of the balance on goods and services, this simplification neglects the existence of unilateral transfer payments and net income on international assets.

Unilateral transfer payments are substantial net debits for the United States and average $47 billion per annum over the five years 1997–2001. These payments (particularly official development assistance) are mainly devoted by recipients to imports from the donor country: private unilateral transfers are dominated by expenditures by charitable organizations and are often made directly in goods and services rather than in money. It is, then, practical to view the balance on goods and services and unilateral transfers as a combined set of payments in which unilateral transfers generate their own value in terms of additional demand for national exports by the recipient countries. The balance on goods and serviceless unilateral transfers can be defined as the balance on trade and transfers (BTT). Together with net income on international assets, BTT determines the balance on current account.

The balance on income from international assets is disregarded in the traditional version of the absorption theory but is potentially important in the present context if only because of the substantial changes in American INW. Mann's (1999) estimates suggest that, according to her assumptions, the balance of income on international assets (BIA) could reach large negative numbers in 2005 and 2010.[28]

The balance on income on international assets must be defined as:

$$\text{BIA}_i = \sum A_i \cdot r_i - \sum L_i \cdot r_i^* \tag{3.4}$$

where A_i identifies assets of residents of country i in other countries and r_i for the average after-tax rate of return earned on those assets and where L_i and r_i^* are the equivalent values of liabilities owned by non-residents and the after-tax return on those liabilities. The expression $(\Sigma A_i - \Sigma L_i)$ is simply the INW of country i. The two aggregate rates of return, r_i and r_i^*, are sensitive not only to the level of rates of return in the host countries but also to the distribution of the assets and liabilities among public funds, private direct investments, private portfolio assets (investments in capital markets and private investments in money markets) and bank loans to foreign borrowers. Investments in portfolio assets may be expected to be reallocated internationally as conditions change in different countries so that it would be virtually impossible to develop an operational model of such reallocations because of the number of countries involved, the variation in controls affecting international movements of assets and in after-tax rates of return on foreign assets.

The balance on income flows from international assets (BIA) is a function of the stocks of assets and liabilities and these quantities change every year in consequence of an imbalance on current account and the induced changes in the value of stocks of international assets and in their rates of return. There is no reason to assume that r_i is necessarily equal to r_i^* since the composition of assets among direct investments, private portfolio assets and government-owned balances can vary substantially as can the average rates of return on groups of assets. Table 3.2 gives the balance on BIA for the United States for the years 1983–2002. The balance is reported (*before the revision made in 2002*) to have decreased by $40 billion in the five years ending in December 2001. The balance in 2002 was lower by $36.5 billion than the revised value for 2001. A comparison of Tables 5.1 and 3.2 will show that the United States had amassed a deficit INW of about one trillion dollars before BIA turned negative (according to the original data). This is thought to be due, in large part, to the greater age and consequently higher profitability of US foreign direct investment but could also be due to the tendency of inward FDI in the United States to seek a base for improved access to ongoing research in the United States so that normally defined profits understate the benefit of the investment. The return on US assets abroad was 8.77 percent and on foreign direct investments in the United States was 2.6 percent.[29]

While there exist many factors, which can affect a country's BIA in a given year, it is probable that the change in BIA will be positively related to the ongoing current deficit ($S_I < 0$). There is one factor which has a direct and major importance on BIA and which deserves recognition. Like balance-of-payments accounts, a nation's balance sheet (INW) is computed in a single currency so that when an exchange rate changes, the value of assets held abroad increases in response to a depreciation and *vice versa*. In addition to the "balance sheet" values, currency depreciation also tends to enhance the flows of repatriated interest, dividends and profits (provided always that the returns on assets owned in foreign countries are approximately constant).[30]

The two major components of the balance on current account, the balance on goods and services adjusted for unilateral transfers (BTT) and BIA work in "opposite directions" after a depreciation of the currency. The balance on goods and services will deteriorate immediately as the price of imports in domestic currency will increase very quickly until home-country users can obtain alternative, cheaper sources of supply. The balance on goods and services will ultimately increase, probably with a pronounced lag as the depreciation and the expenditure-reduction reduce expenditures on imports. At the same time, the depreciating nation's INW will increase (when measured in its home currency) and the balance of income on international assets will increase immediately if the rate of return on foreign assets remains roughly constant. However, BIA is likely to deteriorate after the immediate adjustment to depreciation as the nation's current deficit will not be immediately eliminated and the country's INW will continue to decrease. The balance on goods and services and transfers is, of course, much larger than BIA.[31]

Table 3.2 includes the original and the revised data on the balance of income on assets for the United States for the years, 1995–2001. The original data showed a trend in the value of the US net income on international assets, which conforms with the expected diminution of the US net balance through the 1990s on the basis that the substantial reductions in the INW of the United States would outweigh the effects of any changes in rates of return on asset categories and could reinforce such changes. The revisions for the years 1995–2001, published in 2002, introduce some substantial increases in both the INW and in the net balance on income on international assets.[32] The negative balances on income on international assets are eliminated.[33] The revised series on the balance on income on international assets runs counter to what is to be logically expected from the direction and magnitude of the changes

Table 3.2   The US balance on income from international assets (1983–2002) (billions of dollars)

	Original data	Revised balance	Increase
1983	+36.4		
1984	+35.1		
1985	+25.7		
1986	+15.5		
1987	+14.3		
1988	+18.7		
1989	+19.8		
1990	+28.6		
1991	+24.1		
1992	+23.0		
1993	+23.9		
1994	+16.7		
1995	+20.5	+24.6	+4.1
1996	+21.0	+24.1	+3.1
1997	+8.8	+20.2	+11.4
1998	−6.2	+7.6	+13.8
1999	−13.5	+18.1	+31.6
2000	−14.8	+21.8	+36.6
2001	−19.1	+20.5	+39.6
2002ᴾ	−12.0		

Notes: ᴾ Preliminary estimate.
Sources: For the original data, *Survey of Current Business*, July 2001, p. 47. For the revised data, see *Survey of Current Business*, July 2002, p. 51. (For revised 2001 and preliminary 2002 data, see *Survey of Current Business*, April 2003, p. 42.)

in INW during the 1990s and from the even more impressive rates of international dissaving, which began in 1999. The trend increase in the strength of the dollar from 1995 to 2001 (see Figure 2.1) would also have weakened US receipts from the assets of its residents located abroad (as, indeed, it reduces US INW). The revised data serve to remind the reader that the aggregate numbers used in this volume must be interpreted with caution. However, preliminary data for 2002 show that the US balance on income is a substantial negative number of an order of magnitude similar to the "original data."

The BIA is not negligible but it is a very small component of the current account.

V Summary

For all its glory and responsibility, the rôle of key-currency nation does not absolve the country from the basic need of living within its income in the very long run.[34] It follows, then, that having the national currency serve the global economy does not, when the currency is under pressure, release it from the need to impose on itself both expenditure-reductions and expenditure-switches. This need holds whether the excess spending has been carried out in accordance with the responsibilities of the key-currency nation or is simply the result of overspending. Debt is a great leveler.

The domain of the key currency is the global economy. It is, therefore, understandable that the difficulties of finding the appropriate policy strategy for a key currency country that is under balance-of-payments pressure, are likely to be many times greater than the difficulties of defining policy for a single nation in a similar condition. This chapter has addressed the greater complexity of balance-of-payments adjustment theory for the key-currency nation: it has found that the increase in complexity applies to every dimension of the adjustment problem for a single nation and that there exist dimensions which are unique to a hegemon.

It is a useful summary technique, in context, to provide a list of the sources of the relatively greater difficulty facing resolution of the problems of the global financial *system* when it is the hegemon that is under pressure, than when there is a national economy facing balance-of-payments problems. This distinction is vital because the failure of the hegemon can force the *system* into disarray – an outcome that is improbable even when the national economy under pressure is a large one. At the same time, it behoves the reader to recall that the effects of the several sources of greater difficulty for efficient systemic policy formulation are multiplicative. These complexities are:

1. The danger of serious global recession if global aggregate demand is not maintained and the responsibility of the traditional Keynesian locomotive is not recognized and reallocated.
2. The absolutely larger potential current deficit that must be eliminated and with it the probable larger negative INW, which must be reduced to tolerable proportions.
3. The longer the period of time over which adjustment must be ongoing, with the greater probability of spontaneous exogenous shocks during the adjustment (this is a consequence of point 2).

4. The greater the difficulties in estimating an order of magnitude of the necessary expenditure-reduction and of the requisite expenditure-switch.
5. The virtual inevitability of having to confront sequential adjustments of both the expenditure-switching and expenditure-reduction in force.
6. The expected relatively low sensitivity of the hegemon's current balance to an expenditure-switch and the greater initial reliance likely to be placed on an expenditure-reduction.
7. The need for financing a large and long-term adjustment process.
8. The danger of a widespread crisis in foreign exchange markets and, through contagion, in the capital markets of both the hegemon and the major trading nations.
9. The probably steadily increasing political discontent that follows from protracted spells of, at best, more or less constant levels of real income below that to which the hegemon's electorate has grown accustomed.

The net result of this list of greater sources of complexity is that the degree of "dislocation" (the hegemon's negative current balance and its negative INW) can and, in context, is likely to be so large that the problem of restoring a viable system may exceed the capacity of a system of free markets (Gray, 1990). Almost certainly, the liberal system so carefully created during the US hegemony will have to be temporarily renounced. The global economy may fall into a condition in which the power of a system of markets to return the economy to a position near the economy's long-run growth path is exceeded – even when key markets receive some oversight and support.

4

A Model of Instability in Asset Markets

1 Introduction

Economic analysis relies predominantly on general equilibrium solutions of *flows* of production and consumption. Few economists have addressed the problems of financial instability in *terms of stocks of assets*. Hicks (1946, 62–7), in the original *tour de force* of modern general equilibrium analysis, did address the possibility of instability in markets for goods which were concurrently produced and consumed, that is, for a flow market. This is his famous "snake diagram," which forms the basis of Figure 4.1. In this figure, excess supply increases (excess demand decreases) as the price of the good falls over a range of values but the instability is bounded by a stable equilibrium at both higher and lower prices. Because instability in markets for financial assets is crucial to an informed understanding of the dangers of dollar exhaustion for the likelihood of a "hard landing" for the US (and the global) economies, it is necessary to have a comparable model for instability in asset (*stock*) markets. This chapter provides such a model.

Serious systemic instability necessarily involves spasms of instability in a broad swath of markets, which deal in different financial (and other capital) assets. There is, inevitably, interaction among those markets, Widespread instability can also be triggered by a major fall in asset prices in a single market. The transformation of instability from a single-market problem to a systemic problem can be described as "inter-market contagion."[1] Inter-market contagion can take place in an autarkic economy, which, by definition, has no dealings with foreign countries. Instability can also be introduced from (or transmitted) abroad directly by means of a shock, which affects real variables in the domestic economy or it may derive from contagion with unstable foreign financial

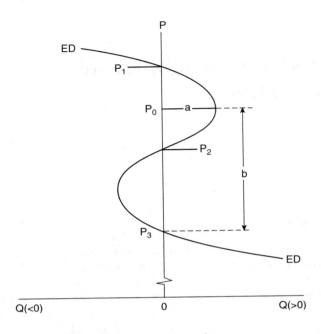

Figure 4.1 Downward instability in an asset market

markets.[2] In both scenarios, the home-country markets are, by defini-tion, "fragile" since they cannot withstand the foreign shock and insta-bility is created from a foreign source.[3] Similarly, if domestic instability is transmitted abroad and creates instability in foreign markets, the feed-back can reinforce the extant domestic instability. If international con-tagion is not broad-based, it will be most likely to occur between two national markets for the same or a very similar genus of financial assets. Once transmitted in this way, contagion can spread domestically (inter-nally) through inter-market contagion.

There exist no hard-and-fast limits to the effects of international con-tagion. The phenomenon is not limited to two countries: a shock in one country can spread simultaneously to a number of countries. In the same way, a shock may affect a range of financial markets (multiple impact markets) which differ by nation and by type of asset traded. How quickly the international contagion spreads domestically depends upon the fragility of the impact market and then on the fragility of related financial markets. The more vulnerable the system of markets is to insta-bility, either inherently or through contagion, the greater will be the effect of a given shock on the buoyancy of the system and the greater the likelihood of systemic instability.[4]

Section II of this chapter addresses instability in a single asset market. Section III extends the approach to a financial system of interdependent markets in a closed economy and Section IV uses the model to describe the potential for instability in a global financial system. The analysis will show that one crucial factor in contagion is the efficiency of the "conduit" between pairs of markets, where the efficiency of a conduit derives from the accuracy, speed, and cost of effecting financial transactions in one country's financial markets from abroad (and, indirectly, from the institutional similarity of the markets). An efficient conduit contributes to inter-market sensitivity by allowing the full effects of a disturbance in one market to be quickly, reliably and cheaply transmitted to a second market or country. This factor explains the greater efficiency of a conduit between markets for the same or a similar asset and/or within the same cultural or institutional setting: International conduits are likely to be less efficient than domestic conduits but recent information technological gains have eroded the difference and increased the efficiency of international conduits.[5]

II Instability in a single market

Figure 4.1 is an elaboration of Hicks's classic diagram and can be used for analyses of both stock and flow disequilibria. It is useful to investigate in some little detail how a flow market could be unstable. Excess demand for the good is measured to the right of the vertical axis, which signifies zero excess demand. The difference between stocks and flows is that Hicks is able to conceive of an unstable equilibrium at price P_2 on the vertical axis. For assets (stocks) such an equilibrium would not be viable: the system would not settle there. The crucial distinction is that the supply of a good being used up and produced on a regular basis will adjust to market demand very quickly so that the market may not quickly discover that it is in a potential disequilibrium. The range of prices over which the demand for the good is unstable depends largely upon the speed with which output will respond to excess supply or demand, upon the size of inventories considered normal in the industry, and on the degree to which customers are used to waiting for delivery of orders for custom-made products. The obvious and perhaps extreme example of a disequilibrium system is the cobweb theorem of agricultural production when the crop can only be planted seasonally and harvesting has long lead times so that supply cannot adjust quickly to offset shifts in demand.

An *asset* market will differ from a *flow* market for five possible reasons.

1. All of the existing stock of assets must find satisfied holders if a market equilibrium is to be re-established. Bankruptcies affect both sides of the market: potential asset holders can lapse into bankruptcies as can the issuers of the securities. But, major bankruptcies apart, changes in the quantity of assets available are so small relative to the existing stock, that they may be neglected.
2. Changes in asset values affect net wealth positions of market participants; the "degree of confidence" of borrowers (Kregel, 1976), and the willingness of "scarred" executives of financial institutions to lend money to fund the purchase of financial assets. Scar tissue, like the loss of confidence by entrepreneurs and lenders, can slow down the adjustment to new conditions.
3. Markets for financial assets are likely to have a range of stability before encountering instability. This is the reason that assets are shown in Figure 4.1 as being in equilibrium at P_1 and as having a range of stability around that price (over which the excess demand curve slopes downward and to the right).
4. In a functioning market, the idea of instability is likely to be unusual in that expectations based on recent (tranquil) experience will dominate the thinking of market participants (Tversky and Kahneman, 1982), so that the idea of significant market movements in either direction will not be widely held.
5. Once the stable range has been left, the instability feeds on itself as price declines lead asset holders both to expect and to contribute, through net sales, to further price declines. The range of instability can be substantial.

These features for a stock equilibrium are summarized in Figure 4.1. P_1 is the going short-run equilibrium price. If the excess demand schedule is shifted to the left by a change in asset-holder psychology or because of some adverse shock, which impinges on the demand and supply for securities of the particular genus of assets traded in the market, prices fall. If the leftward shift is small and causes the price to fall only slightly, the market remains stable with a lower clearing price. If, instead, the excess demand curve shifts leftward by a distance greater than a, the price falls beyond P_0, the market becomes unstable and the price of the representative financial asset will fall to P_3.

The performance of the market can be described using the two measures a and b. The distance a is a conceptual measure of the resilience or stability efficiency of the market for the identified asset group. Of course, an adverse shock, which shifted the excess demand curve to the left by an amount sufficient to induce instability, could quite possibly also change the shape of the excess demand schedule, so that the new stable price (where the changed excess demand curve cuts the vertical axis) can be above or below P_3 as shown. In practice, the ultimate value of P_3, depending as it does on the revised perceptions of actual and potential asset holders, is unknowable *ex ante*. Obviously, the greater the difference between P_0 and P_3 (the distance b), the greater is the amount of adjustment, which the real sector must undergo. This adjustment parallels the analysis of adjustment to balance-of-payments deficits (in Chapter 3). It can be seen as the reallocation of factors of production and the reduction of income levels to suit the new conditions or it could be seen as some new lower level of capacity utilization, which would exist in the absence of expansionary macroeconomic policy. The distance b, then, conceptually identifies the range of instability or the seriousness of the financial crisis.[6]

The process is not reversible. There is no reason to suppose that after a market has dropped from P_0 to P_3, a favorable event will reveal latent upside instability and that the price will revert to P_0. Even if the shock were of the same order of magnitude, bankruptcies of some asset holders and changes in the degree of confidence in the surviving actors in the market will reduce any potential for upward instability. (For an originally favorable shock creating a bubble of optimism, the likelihood of reversion to the neighborhood of the original level is greater than zero.)

The resilience of an asset market, the size of a, depends upon the expectations of the actors in the market and the degree to which they can finance their positions in the event of an adverse shock. It will be influenced by several factors. Following Tversky and Kahneman (1982), recent experience will be important in determining the (latent) degree of confidence that actors have in the ability of the market to revert to some price level in harmony with fundamentals. Thus, any market that has recently experienced adverse shocks will tend to have a smaller a. Equally, confidence in the potentially successful intervention of a lender of last resort will increase a as will the existence of hedging devices such as forward and futures markets and options – provided always that these instruments are mainly used as safeguards rather than as speculative vehicles (Keynes, 1936, 158–9).[7] The degree to which asset holders can maintain their positions in the face of adverse shocks is directly dependent upon the financial leverage in their positions as well as upon the ability of holders of hedging contracts to meet their contracts without bankruptcy, that is, hedging contracts must continue to be available during any period of substantial change in prices. Thus, the market will be more susceptible to a significant downward movement (P_3 will be lower): (i) when the adverse shock is greater; (ii) when it is expected to endure for a longer period of time; (iii) when asset holders are more highly leveraged; (iv) when the vulnerability of hedging contracts is perceived to be greater; and (v) when the degree of confidence placed in the lender of last resort, is weaker.[8]

The essence of self-reinforcing instability is that when net sales are induced by events and the price of the representative asset falls, the new, lower prices at which the sales are made and the direction of price change become additional information for and influence the expectations of other actors in the market. Thus, asset holders are more likely to sell in a falling market and push prices still lower.[9] The financial strength of asset holders also affects the degree to which the price declines may bring on self-reinforcing conduct: the greater their financial leverage and the greater the perceived likelihood that creditors will call their loans as prices fall, the more rapid the potential rate of price decline and the greater the psychological impact of such events on the ultimate value of P_3. If speculators come into the market and take short positions, this too will reinforce the downward pressure on prices.

In this picture of instability in a single financial market, the adverse external shocks must be deemed to have their sources in the real sector of the economy as opposed to other financial markets (at home or abroad).

III   Systemic instability (in an autarkic sector)[10]

The same analytic device can be used to diagnose systemic fragility and instability. Here we postulate an adverse shock impinging on one market (the impact market) and examine the mechanics and the implications of contagion from the impact market to other markets within the same national system. An external adverse shock (in the real sector) or a domestically sourced revision of expectations could affect several financial markets simultaneously so that any contagion would be merely a reaction to unequal impact damage in individual markets. The effect of a specific (single-market) shock and a general shock affecting several markets will be similar only if the contagion from the single-market shock is both rapid and substantial. The single-market shock case requires a study of the contagion linkages and is, therefore, analytically more revealing. Recognition that contagion linkages can be broken indicates that not all financial markets are equally fragile at a particular time. A general shock could be seen as seeking out the weakest market and striking the system most tellingly through that market: in contrast, the total effect of a single-market shock would depend on the fragility of the particular market hit by the shock.

It is necessary to recognize that the character of shocks may vary. For example, Eichengreen and Portes (1987, 29) report that British banks were not, in 1933, seriously threatened by a large-scale withdrawal of foreign credits from sterling:

> Since the run took the form mainly of sales of foreign-owned Treasury bills and withdrawals of credits previously granted to the discount market, it posed little threat to the banking system.[11]

The resilience of the system will be greater than that of the impact market if the shock induces an inflow of funds to the impact market from other markets. In this way, the shock will be dissipated among a series of markets and instability (crisis) will be avoided. *Per contra* the system can be as or more fragile than the impact market so that, if the impact market becomes unstable (the shock exceeds the value of the market's *a*), the repercussions will trigger defaults and bankruptcies in other fragile markets. A full-scale systemic crisis emerges if all of the financial markets are precipitated into their *b* domains. The crucial elements in such a scenario are the magnitude of the shock, the resilience of the impact market, and the efficiency of the network of conduits to other financial markets together with the inherent lack of resilience of these markets.

Financial markets are interdependent because asset holders can be expected to have diversified their risk by holding assets traded in different markets. Thus, an adverse shock in the impact market will automatically affect the solvency of asset holders in other markets. If the asset holders have enough reserves to support their position in the impact market, then funds will flow into the impact market and crisis will be avoided, albeit at the cost of a weakening of the resilience of the other markets where asset holders will have experienced an induced increase in leverage.

If the asset holders in the impact market are leveraged as highly as the availability of credit permits, an adverse shock in the impact market will result in their assets being sold out from under them and the impact market will enter its *b* domain. Once the impact market becomes unstable, a revision of expectations will probably take place in other financial markets, and fully leveraged asset holders in these markets will have their assets sold out from under them. The rôle of linkage is clearly vital. If the impact market is mainly linked to a robust market in which asset holders have strong reserves of liquid assets and retain positive net worth (i.e. they are not leveraged), the shock will not generate a crisis. The weaker the related markets and the less resilient the financial intermediaries, the greater is the likelihood of a full scale systemic crisis. To the degree that the buoyancy of perceptions is like to be much the same system-wide, the buoyancy of all markets will vary together though there may not exist the same absolute level of resilience in each market.

The more fragile is the system, the greater is the need for prompt and strong action by the lender of last resort. The more highly leveraged the asset holders and the financial institutions, the smaller is their capital adequacy and the greater is the probability of a crisis and the deeper that crisis is likely to be.[12] The greater the system's value of b is, the greater is the reduction of community net wealth and the less likely is the economy to avoid depression. Once the national economy has lost its normal tendency to revert to its long-run growth path, that is, it is depressed, the first priority of holders of financial assets and of financial institutions will be to rebuild their liquid assets and their net worth. This process and the critical experience will lead to pronounced risk aversion toward investment projects by both entrepreneurs and lenders.

It is necessary to distinguish between perceived robustness and actual robustness (even though the latter is not objectively measurable and is sensitive to the nature of the disturbance). It is quite possible for actors in a market to overestimate the robustness of a market or of the system. The size of a depends on actual robustness, while the size of b is determined in part by the perception of robustness. The implications of any excess in perceptions over actuality can best be seen in terms of actors assuming that their positions are warranted when they are, in reality and given the probability of either a shock or of an inadequate response by the lender of last resort, excessively aggressive.[13] If actors believe that there exists a support system for the market in the face of some perturbation, they will dare to incur greater leverages than they would in the absence of such a belief. In other words, an excess of perceived over actual robustness, enhances the size of b so that, following a destabilizing shock, the fall in prices will be greater (and the adjustment more painful). The change in excessively positive perceptions can either come gradually, in which event the financial markets will be able to adjust in an orderly fashion, or a sudden awareness of the general overly leveraged position of market actors can communicate itself through the market and the system. Such an event will induce what Kindleberger (1978) and Minsky (1977) refer to as a "pell-mell rush to liquidity" and the market will be forced into its *b* domain.

The crux of market instability is the reserves of liquidity of the asset holders and of the lender of last resort. The less euphoric the perceptions of asset holders, the less likely is the market to be unduly fragile. However, the possibility of an adverse shock of sufficient magnitude to thrust a market into its *b* domain cannot be overlooked. This is clearly a matter where Thatcher's law should be kept in mind at all times.[14]

IV Fragility in an internationally integrated system

The increased volume of international investment in financial (portfolio) assets will have increased the fragility of the global system and its component markets in five ways. These are:

1. The increased rôle of foreign-exchange markets;
2. The increased volume of foreign portfolio investment by households;
3. The increased efficiency of conduits;
4. The greater institutional distances among markets;
5. Cultural (or institutional) distance.

Increased rôle of foreign-exchange markets

Fragility has been increased by the increased importance of foreign exchange markets in the global system of markets for financial assets and by the volume of international easily encashable portfolio investments. Foreign exchange markets are more prone to violent fluctuations than autarkic markets presumably because they are the nerve centres of international interaction. The greater volume of international assets, both proportionately and absolutely, owned by individuals and economic units whose functional currency differs from the currency of denomination of their assets, can contribute to potential instability. A stampede of flows under the control of mutual fund managers can take place very quickly and can be intensified by speculative positions. Individuals who manage their own portfolios are likely to react to perceived volatility in a foreign exchange market defensively by liquidating holdings denominated in a currency expected to depreciate. These transactions can be handled but the investors are less likely to have the expertize to augment the volatility by taking an exposed, speculative position. Capital markets are inherently subject to substantial volatility, partly because so many assets are controlled by people who receive the same data and interpret those data with similar approaches and models and partly because of the herd instinct of investors (Recall Paul Volcker's axiom that the "trend is your friend"). Add to this, large-scale exposure to the reactions of foreign residents and the result is the existence of concerted responses by foreign-based asset holders.

Foreign exchange markets are, in effect, the interface between the economies of two ostensibly independent (but actually interdependent) nations and they are likely to reflect every disturbance occurring in either country or any disturbance affecting either country as a result of some event in a third country. Such disturbances are not limited to economic or financial phenomena and will most certainly include political phenomena, which have repercussions on foreign economies.

Markets, which are freely open to foreign investments and disinvestments are more susceptible to substantial shocks than are autarkic markets or those in which domestic asset holders predominate (Gray, 2002). The probability of a currency crisis, in a developing country particularly, will be susceptible to the share of total assets owned by foreigners.[15]

Increased volume of foreign portfolio investment by households

Liberalization of regulations governing international portfolio investments has allowed individuals to hold assets denominated in currencies, which are not their functional currency so that a whole new dimension of risk has been created for families. This risk ties in with the inherent greater volatility of foreign exchange markets and, possibly, with the greater political risk and lesser economic sophistication of the institutional economic environment in developing countries.[16]

Increased efficiency of conduits

The increased efficiency in the conduits of international investments is the third factor. It combines with the first two, the natural volatility of foreign-exchange markets and the much greater volume of profit-seeking, possibly speculative investments from abroad, to provide the major contribution to international contagion. The efficiency of a conduit (the accuracy, speed and cost of effecting transactions in a country's financial markets from abroad) has increased substantially since the wave of relaxation of controls over international portfolio investments. This increase in efficiency derives from the developments in information and communications technology, from the establishment of mutual funds and unit trusts specializing in foreign portfolio investment, which largely channel and safeguard the assets of small investors and the attendant increase in financial news in the media. Thus, reaction to an event can come much more quickly and, because the stock of portfolio assets is greater, on a much larger scale than would have been possible a quarter of a century ago.

In principle, the establishment of affiliates of large banks in developing countries should also add to the efficiency of conduits in that locally established affiliates should serve as sources of reliable, local information. However, in 1997 when the Thai baht collapsed, reliable information on conditions in financial markets was not generally available in Bangkok (Rahman, 1998, 51). Undoubtedly, lenders are, in the post-Bangkok era, much more careful about the creditworthiness of borrowers but this sophistication of the Thai financial system has been improved at tremendous cost to the local economy.

Greater institutional distances among markets

Many emerging markets are neither as efficiently overseen and regulated as investors from industrialized countries might expect, nor are their major participants as sophisticated about global financial practice (Gray and Dilyard, 2002). Using the Thai experience as an example again, the introduction of a fixed rate of exchange between the dollar and the baht was a formula for collapse (Shelburne, 2002) if only because the measure seems to have neglected the possibility that the dollar would appreciate so steadily (see Figure 2.1).

Cultural and institutional distance

No individual international investor can be as familiar with foreign countries as with his/her home country and this lack of familiarity increases the risk of errors in portfolio management. The lesser familiarity with local conditions in foreign markets and the danger that information from such markets will be transmitted to the home country of the asset holder with a delay or in language that could be misinterpreted (Rahman, 1998). Either possibility could contribute to instability.

The sources of fragility, autarkic or international, are more likely to take hold the lower are the transaction costs of moving assets from one currency denomination or from one form of asset to another or from one country to another. James Tobin (1978), recognizing the potential instability of speculative international portfolio investments has suggested that economic and financial authorities impose a tax (now known as "the Tobin tax") on transactions according to the length of time they are invested in the market. In this way, the return on a speculative short-term investment based on two transactions in the foreign-exchange market would incur the costs of two transactions and two taxes. The total transaction costs would increase. Tobin's proposal has met with, at best, a mixed reception. Most critics are concerned that the levy will reduce the allocative efficiency of financial markets. Any increase in transaction costs will do this if the financial markets are stable and efficient. However, when weighed against the potential costs of a currency (or some other financial) crisis, the Tobin tax would obviously be the lesser of two "evils." [17]

V Conclusion

The essence of crisis is that a downward movement in the price of assets be large enough to precipitate a self-reinforcing momentum whereby asset holders become fearful of the magnitude of b or, having overextended themselves, they are forced by their sources of credit to sell. Further selling will reinforce the downward momentum of the market. This phenomenon will spread through inter-market (domestic) and international contagion until the pessimism and the excess leverage have become exhausted. Almost inevitably, a collapse will follow from a bubble of irrational optimism that has pushed prices into a state of suppressed disequilibrium. Both the bubble and the crash will be driven by the herd instinct, which the availability of leverage can create in financial markets.

A combination of the balance-of-payments adjustment model in Chapter 3 and the model of financial instability presented here present a dismal basis for assessing the existing condition of the US economy and its currency. For the United States to reduce even the rate at which it is reducing its international net worth, requires cuts in absorption with either a renunciation of its free trade stance or a weakening of the dollar in foreign-exchange markets. Since such a process will take time, the acquisition of financing for its continuing international dissaving is necessary and such saving will not be easily generated if the claims are to be denominated in a currency seen as susceptible to depreciation in foreign-exchange markets. Part I has focused predominantly on the loss of ability of the key currency to continue to inspire the confidence needed to continue to finance the country's international dissaving and its negative asset position.

The second potential source of instability derives from the possibility that the continued sacrifice of the short-term interests of its domestic economy (and its domestic employment rate with a current deficit equal to 4.8 percent of GDP) is equally important. This source of instability has been alluded to in Part I but is developed in greater detail in chapter 5.

The potential interaction between the two potential causes of instability is very important. Chapter 5, pp. 108–10, shows how the two sources of instability, the financial or international trigger, and the willingness or domestic trigger (with its real-sector, unemployment emphasis) are closely interrelated so that a crisis in both sectors can be triggered by events in either the real or the financial sector.

Part III

Exhaustion: Soft, Hard or Very Hard Landing

5
The Data

I Introduction

The essential problem faced by this monograph is that buoyant financial markets have the inherent capacity to feed a potentially unstable disequilibrium condition until markets collapse under the ever-growing weight. Financial markets can lock themselves into a position in which an accumulated overhang can threaten their stability and can end in financial crisis. The stock-market bubble in the United States in the late 1990s and the baht crisis in Thailand in 1997 are clear examples.[1] Such problems can be solved by confrontation by alert policymakers, but confrontation by policymakers can require the implementation of policies, which damage their personal reputations. Countermeasures can be suppressed for political reasons in the hope that the overhang will dissolve itself or that the crisis will not come until the policymaker is immune from the probable reaction of the electorate (political agency). Failure to identify and to eliminate the potentially disequilibrium financial condition will create distortions in the "real" economy so that the real economy must undergo substantial change in the output mix. When the financial disequilibrium collapses into crisis and financial flows quickly clear the market for assets, the real economy can be thrown into deep recession or worse "as goods and labor respond to price signals from the [international] financial sector much more sluggishly than do financial assets" (Tobin, 1978, p. 154). For most financial markets, this possibility affects a national economy, at worst a region, but a suppressed disequilibrium of the value of the key currency in foreign exchange markets, can affect the world.

Part II begins by presenting (Chapter 5) and assessing (Chapter 6) the data, which warrant consideration of the first two propositions.

The data are divided into two sets. The first set bears on the possibility of the exhaustion of the dollar being triggered by international events (the state of *suppressed* financial disequilibrium collapses). The immediate international cause of the exhaustion of the dollar would be the loss of foreign confidence in the ability of the dollar to perform as a key currency (to act as a store of value through time in the asset-owners' functional currencies). This trigger leads to an exodus of foreign-owned funds from the key currency. This is the *"capital-account" or "international" trigger* and the data are presented in Section II of this chapter. The second set of data addresses the possibility that the end of the capability of the United States to continue to perform the responsibilities of the key-currency nation, will have a "domestic" origin. Politically appointed and elected American policymakers and office-holders can only hope to continue in those rôles, if the US economy is operating at or near capacity and with satisfactory levels of employment. An election during or immediately following a severe recession will oust many incumbents and will probably involve a change in the majority party. Allowing the United States to act as the global locomotive, by supplying net demand for goods to the global economy, when imported goods and services are seen as generating higher than acceptable unemployment rates and slower than acceptable economic growth, is a sure prescription for change in both policies and the party elected to carry them out. If sub-par economic performance is maintained for so long a time that it eliminates any hope of a quick resurgence to a satisfactory level of capacity utilization, it must call the domestic social and economic costs of being the global locomotive into serious question. This is the *"current-account" or "domestic" trigger* whose implications are described in Section III.[2] (Section V will show that the two triggers are closely interdependent. Nonetheless, the text will identify the two phenomena separately because they involve, in the early stages, different actors and involve different sectors of the economy.)

Section IV examines and offers data on the rôle of the income-on-international-assets account. While the negative balance on this category is currently a quite small component of the current account, it has the potential to grow. This balance reacts to currency depreciation in the opposite way from the balance on goods and services.

Section V is devoted to analysis rather than data. It shows the virtual inevitability of contagion between the financial and real sectors of a heavily indebted economy. Which trigger precipitates the end of the passive acceptance of the string of current deficits, becomes a secondary issue, though it may well have an effect on the path-dependent process of establishing a new international financial architecture (see Chapter 9). Whether the actual trigger be "international" or "domestic," the advent of either will set in motion forces that will lead to the activation of the second trigger as contagion brings about interaction between the financial and real sectors of the US economy.[3] This phenomenon of mutual interaction (contagion) is crucial. The stability of the financial system is in inherent danger from both the easy-encashability of so many foreign-owned dollar-denominated assets *and* from stress born of inadequate levels of global aggregate demand. *Any analysis of the unsustainability of the US international financial position based exclusively on only one of the two sectors, is inadequate.* The probability that exhaustion will take hold is, then, the *sum* of the two probabilities that an individual trigger will be activated. Neglect of this contagion was the primary weakness of the *Report* of the US Trade Deficit Review Commission (2000), which focused exclusively on the problem of attracting capital inflows to cover the chronic current deficits while completely neglecting both the question of retention of foreign saving which had been co-opted earlier and the possibility of the deficit on goods and services inducing a major recession. While the ongoing deficits in the first half of the 1990s were not negligible (Table 5.3a), particularly when they accumulated, the rapid increase in the magnitude of the current deficits did not arise until after the charge to the Commission was written with the result that the Commission was not charged to and did not confront the global financial implications of the continued erosion of the US INW. As events developed, this was a grievous omission.

II The international trigger

The relevant data are presented in ten tables. They are:

Table 5.1   The Changing Mix of Foreign-owned Liabilities of the United States (1983–2002)

Table 5.2   The Mix of Private Foreign-owned Financial Liabilities of the United States (1983–2002)

Table 5.3   The US Net International Investment Position, 1983–2002

Table 5.4   The *Relative* Size of International Dissaving and the International Net Worth (1983–2002)

Table 5.5   Rates of Exchange of the Dollar 1992–2002

Table 5.6   Cumulative Current Balances for 24 Countries (1983–2001)

Table 5.7   Ratios of Private Foreign-owned Financial Assets to US Official Reserves (1981–2002)

Table 5.8   US Bankruptcy Filings, 1980–2002

Table 5.9   A Pro-forma Estimate of the US INW at the end of 2010
Table 5.10   US Ratios of Current Credits to Current Debits (1990–2002)

The international trigger of the "exhaustion proposition" derives essentially from the loss of confidence in the dollar as a denomination for profit-seeking and wealth-preserving financial assets. The trigger will sharply reduce the further acquisition of dollar-denominated assets by non-residents and will, for the same reasons, set off withdrawals of foreign savings from dollar-denominated assets acquired before the loss of confidence.

One of the most important changes in the global financial system over the past twenty years has been the growth in the absolute and relative volumes of private, wealth-enhancing *easily encashable* assets denominated in currencies other than those of the functional currency of the asset holder. Tobin (1978) was one of the first people to draw this point to the attention of the economics profession but chose to emphasize a "sand-in-the-machinery-of-speculation" approach – the so-called "Tobin tax." The focus of this monograph is a fundamental flaw in the international financial architecture in which the key currency can be weakened by the conscientious performance of its "locomotive duty" over a period of years and in which concern with maintaining the quality of the key currency can impair the locomotive function. The problem of having foreign investments in easily-encashable assets that increase the fragility of a national currency, is not restricted to the United States. This problem has affected emerging stock markets as well as the financial sectors of industrial countries (Gray and Dilyard, 2002).

Table 5.1 provides the data on the growth of three broad categories of US liabilities over time: foreign official assets; direct investments and privately-owned assets which can be easily-encashed in secondary markets (financial assets). The composition of privately owned assets is given in Table 5.2. The data provide the total or gross value of assets owned by non-residents not net assets. *One presumption of this monograph is that non-resident owners of dollar-denominated assets are likely to be more sensitive to exchange-rate risk than residents and will, therefore, withdraw their securities more quickly or in response to a smaller perceived loss of strength of the dollar than residents will take an exposed, speculative position in foreign currencies.* Non-residents with functional currencies other than the dollar, will see their wealth (in their functional currencies) at risk of being reduced and will activate the international trigger. Residents of the United States may contemplate taking a position in a foreign currency but depreciation of the dollar threatens a smaller proportionate

Table 5.1 The changing mix of foreign-owned liabilities of the United States (1983–2002) (billions of US dollars)

Year	Official assets	Direct investment[a]	Private financial assets	Total	Column 4 as a percentage of column 5	Column 4 as a percentage of columns 2 and 4
(1)	(2)	(3)	(4)	(5)	(6)	(7)
1983	194.5	193.7	524.4	912.6	57.5	72.9
1985	202.5	247.2	783.4	1,233.1	63.5	79.5
1987	283.1	334.6	1,128.9	1,746.6	64.6	80.0
1989	341.7	467.9	1,520.7	2,330.3	65.3	81.7
1991	398.5	533.4	1,663.8	2,595.7	64.1	80.7
1993	509.4	593.3	1,957.9	3,060.6	64.0	79.4
1995	682.9	680.1	2,585.0	3,948.0	65.5	79.1
1997	873.7	824.1	3,703.2	5,401.0	68.6	80.9
1999	945.6	1,100.8	4,696.7	6,743.1	69.7	83.2
2001	1,027.2	1,514.4	5,625.7	8,167.3	68.9	84.6
2002[p]	1,132.5	1,504.4	5,939.5	8,576.4	69.3	84.0

Notes

[a] Direct investment values are measured at current cost.

[p] Preliminary.

Source: US Department of Commerce, *Survey of Current Business* (July 2002), pp. 18–19, and (2003).

Table 5.2 The mix of private foreign-owned financial liabilities of the United States (1983–2002) (billions of US dollars)

End of year	US treasuries	Corporate stocks and bonds	Currency	Liabilities reported		Total
				by banks	by nonbanks	
1983	33.8	113.8	36.8	278.3	61.7	524.4
1985	88.0	207.9	46.0	354.5	87.0	783.4
1987	82.6	341.7	55.6	518.8	110.2	1,128.9
1989	166.5	482.9	67.1	637.1	167.1	1,520.7
1991	170.3	546.0	101.3	637.2	208.9	1,663.8
1993	221.5	696.4	133.7	677.1	229.0	1,957.9
1995	330.2	969.8	169.5	815.0	300.4	2,585.0
1997	550.6	1,512.7	211.6	968.8	459.4	3,703.2
1999	462.8	2,351.3	250.7	1,067.2	564.9	4,696.7
2001	389.0	2,855.7	275.6	1,306.4	564.9	5,625.8
2002[p]	503.6	2,861.1	297.1	1,407.4	870.3	5,939.5

Note: [p] Preliminary.

Source: *Survey of Current Business* (July 2002), pp. 18–19 and (July 2003), p. 19.

loss of wealth for residents because of the large reliance on domestic goods and resources. *There currently exists no mechanism whereby the US government can require resident holders of assets denominated in foreign currencies to sell such assets and to repatriate the proceeds or to forbid them from speculating against the dollar.*[4] Thus, the sale of dollar-denominated assets by non-residents will not be countered by a large-scale repatriation of foreign assets to the United States, and the sale of dollar-denominated assets by non-residents may be reinforced by the sale of such assets by residents of the United States, probably largely for speculation. In this way, a loss of confidence in the dollar as a store of value over time will affect all holders of dollar-denominated assets.[5]

Table 5.1 provides background data showing the division of US liabilities among "official" or government-owned assets; foreign direct investments and financial assets for purposes of comparison. The absolute growth of private financial assets has been spectacular (five trillion dollars in eighteen years). There is a presumption that "official assets" will not be used to aggravate symptoms of general instability and to reinforce large private capital flows in foreign exchange markets,[6] but, given the degree of diplomatic stress that exists between the United States and many important countries (Joffe, 2001), foreign central banks and treasuries may lose sight of the costs of instability to their own economies.

Table 5.2 shows the composition of the steady increase in the outstanding volume of assets denominated in dollars owned by profit-seeking non-residents (as distinct from official holdings of international reserves). Most of the privately owned assets are easily encashable though they are not "liquid" by the usual definition. The increase in portfolio assets and the inflows of foreign direct investment contribute to the strength of the dollar and constitute an important direct cause of the chronic current-account deficits since 1983 (see Figure 2.1 and Table 5.3).

In many ways, Table 5.3 is the single most important data set for the assessment of Proposition One. The dominant contribution to "exhaustion" derives from the continuing and cumulating international dissaving and the consequent steady decline in the INW of the United States.[7] This statement implies that the capital-account trigger has a higher probability of being activated.

The way in which official data have been knitted together must be described. Table 5.3 traces the generation of the large current negative INW of the United States from 1983 on.[8] The data are taken from two series reported annually in the US Department of Commerce's monthly publication on economic data, *Survey of Current Business*. The series are

"U.S. International Transactions" which reports data on flows of trade and transfers, and the "International Investment Position of the United States," which reports the year-end stock of international assets denominated in foreign currencies and owned by American residents as well as the possessions of dollar-denominated assets of non-residents. For analytic and accounting purposes, foreign direct investments are deemed to be denominated in the currency of the country in which they are located. Direct investment assets are *not* easily encashable because their sale would involve heavy transaction costs (although working capital can be quickly shifted in response to suspicions of instability).

Table 5.3 is based on the flow-of-funds identity described in Chapter 2 (pp. 37–9). This identity states that the net stock of assets of an economic unit at the end of the year will be the arithmetic sum of its net stock of assets at the beginning of the year plus the unit's balance on current revenues and current expenditures, *provided that the values of the pre-existing assets and liabilities have not changed in the currency of their denomination and that the rate of exchange has not changed in the interim*. Table 5.3 takes, as givens, four numbers for each year from the data sets: the net stock of assets at the end of the preceding year and at the end of the year in question; the current-account balance; and the "statistical discrepancy" from the data on current transactions. No compilation of aggregate data, can avoid some discrepancy in the data. The reported current balance is used to measure the nation's flow of international saving or dissaving vis-à-vis non-residents.[9] The "statistical discrepancy" is an explicit qualification of the estimate of international saving or dissaving because it represents "unexplained net debits or credits" in the international transactions data.[10] There is, of course, also a "balancing item" in the computation of the international investment position. While in the flow or current data, this discrepancy is identified separately, in the data on the investment position, the balancing item is a composite. It comprises: price changes of pre-existing assets in the currency of denomination, the effect of changes in exchange rates; and a residual category which allows for changes in coverage, statistical discrepancies and miscellaneous adjustments.

It is not possible to combine two sets of aggregate, independently generated data, one dealing with stocks and the other with flows, and to obtain an exact "fit." There is a need in this data set, then, for a "balancing item" which allows the four independently determined data (taken from the official data) to be consistent: this item is called "total adjustments." By explicitly identifying the statistical discrepancy for current transactions as a qualification to the current balance, the Table

Table 5.3 US INW (1983–2002) (with direct investments at current cost)[a] ($ billions at end of year)

	INW (end of prior year)	Current account balance	Total adjustmetns	Statistical discrepancy	INW at end of year	*Memorandum* With direct investments at market value
1983	+329.0	−38.7	−8.1	+16.1	+298.3	+257.4
1984	+298.3	−94.3	+26.6	+16.7	+160.7	+134.1
1985	+160.7	−118.2	+28.3	+16.5	+54.3	+46.9
1986	+54.3	−147.2	+28.1	+28.6	−36.2	+100.8
1987	−36.2	−160.7	+125.9	−9.0	−80.0	+50.5
1988	−80.0	−121.2	+42.0	−19.3	−178.5	+10.5
1989	−178.5	−99.5	−31.1	+47.1	−259.5	−47.0
1990	−259.5	−79.0	+58.0	+23.2	−245.3	−164.5
1991	−245.3	+3.7	+22.1	−48.6	−309.3	−260.8
1992	−309.3	−48.0	−25.9	−48.0	−431.2	−452.3
1993	−431.2	−82.0	+204.2	+1.8	−307.0	−178.0
1994	−307.0	−117.7	+123.3	−10.5	−311.9	−123.7
1995	−311.9	−105.2	−98.9	+20.0	−496.0	−343.3
1996	−496.0	−117.2	+1.3	−19.3	−595.2	−386.5

1997	−521.6	−127.7	−93.4	−90.5	−833.2	−835.2
1998	−833.2	−204.7	+10.5	+129.7	−918.7	−1,094.1
1999	−918.7	−290.8	+352.8	+59.1	−797.6	−1,068.8
2000	−797.6	−411.5	−134.5	−44.1	−1,387.7	−1,588.2
2001	−1,387.7	−393.7	−177.7	−20.8	−1,979.9	−2,314.3
2002	−1,979.9	−480.9	+119.5	−45.9	−2,387.2	−2,605.2
Cumulative sum						
1983–93	—	−985.1	+504.0	33.3	—	
1994–2002	—	−2,249.4	+102.9	+22.3	—	
1983–2002	—	−3,234.5	+606.9	+55.6	—	

Note: The current account surplus in 1991 was an anomaly. It can be largely attributed to payments by non-participating allies in the Gulf War. In 1991, net unilateral transfers increased from $−26.7 bn. in 1990 to $+10.8 bn. in 1991 only to sink back to $−33.0 bn. in 1992 and to remain at or above that level for the ensuing ten years.

Data notes

[a] Gold is valued at year end market price. INW at market valuations is given in the memorandum. For detail, see sources.

"Total Adjustments" includes value changes of both real and financial foreign assets in US dollars. This number is clearly sensitive to changes in exchange rates. "Statistical Discrepancy," when positive, shows "unexplained credits" in the international accounts (and vice versa).

[p] Preliminary.

Source: Survey of Current Business, July 2003, pp. 58−9 and 20−1 and Landefeld and Lawson (1991).

Table 5.4 The *relative* size of international dissaving and the INW (1983–2002)

Year	Dissaving/GDP (%)	Dissaving/ current credits[a] (%)	INW/current credits[a] (%)
1983	1.4	10.9	Positive
1985	2.9	30.5	Positive
1987	3.6	35.2	−17.5
1989	1.8	15.3	−40.0
1991	0	0	−42.5
1993	1.3	10.6	−39.5
1995	1.5	10.9	−51.2
1996	1.7	11.2	−55.2
1997	1.8	11.7	−81.4
1998	2.6	18.2	−93.9
1999	3.6	26.1	−86.8
2000	4.0	35.8	−154.3
2001	3.9	30.7	−154.1
2002	4.6	39.5	−194.1

Note: [a] "Current credits" are gross earnings from non-residents including income on assets.

Source: *Survey of Current Business* (various issues).

must attribute any remaining discrepancy to the factors, which contribute to the "balancing item" of the data on the international investment position. "Total adjustments" can be seen as providing an estimate for the net changes in value of the pre-existing assets and liabilities during the year. To give some measure of the magnitudes of the two balancing items, the cumulative balances on current account, statistical discrepancy and "total adjustments" are given as a note to the Table.

Table 5.4 gives a time series of three ratios that give measures that may be preferable to the absolute dollar amounts shown in Table 5.1. The first two ratios show the flow of international dissaving (the current deficit) to gross domestic product (GDP) and then to total current credits. The reason for providing both denominators is that the ratio of the deficit to GDP provides a first indication of the relative size of the expenditure-reduction required to eliminate the current deficit (in the absence of any expenditure-switch).[11] The second ratio, of the deficit to total current credits, shows the size of the deficit in terms of the country's gross current revenues from foreigners and it provides an indication of by how

Table 5.5 Index numbers of the dollar's annual effective rate of exchange (1992–2002)

| Year | Nominal | | "Real" International Monetary Fund Series[c] (1990 = 100) |
	Federal Reserve Series[a]	International Monetary Fund Series[b]	
1992	86.61	105.2	—
1993	93.18	108.4	—
1994	91.32	106.4	93.7
1995	84.25	100.0	86.4
1996	97.43	105.2	89.5
1997	104.44	113.8	94.5
1998	116.48	119.3	100.7
1999	116.87	116.3	99.2
2000	119.68	121.0	106.7
2001	126.08	129.1	116.7
2002	127.19	127.7	116.1

Notes

[a] The Federal Reserve Series was completely revised in 1998 but was backdated to1996 (Leahy, 1998). Prior to 1996, the series is trade-weighted against the rates of exchange of ten industrial countries. After 1996, the numbers refer to the so-called "broad series," which includes 35 national currencies.

[b] The weights applied to the different currencies are the value of trade in manufactured goods with industrial countries averaged over the three years, 1989–91.

[c] The weights are the same as in note b. The adjustment of internal costs was accomplished by allowing for "normalized unit labor costs in the manufacturing sector" to the weighted average of those of its industrial trading partners.

Sources: Federal Reserve Bulletin (various issues) and International Monetary Fund, World Economic Outlook (various issues).

much net current revenues from foreigners need to be increased. *A fortiori*, the second ratio could also indicate how much of a currency depreciation is required provided that some degree of the sensitivity of the current balance to depreciation can be postulated. The third ratio, the negative INW to total current credits also provides an insight into the magnitude of the long-run cumulative reduction in absorption needed to get the INW to a sustainable level. These ratios provide some approximate indication of the magnitudes of the economic adjustments.

Table 5.5 provides two versions of the average annual effective nominal rate of exchange from 1992 on. The table also supplies a series of

Table 5.6   Cumulative current balances, 1983–2001 for 24 countries

Country	Cumulative current balance (billions of US dollars)
Argentina	−101.4
Australia	−253.1
Austria	−40.2
Belgium	+177.2
Brazil	−170.0
Canada	−136.0
Chile	−24.6
China (mainland)	+141.6
Denmark	+13.6
Finland	+19.6
France	+154.4
Germany	+120.4
Italy	+48.7
Japan	+1,667.7
Mexico	−172.4
Netherlands	+195.5
Norway	+103.8
Portugal	−42.0
Spain	−127.5
Singapore	+150.0
Sweden	+13.6
Switzerland	+235.6
Taiwan, Province of China	+180.6
United Kingdom	−272.0
United States	−2,756.7*

Note: * See Table 5.3.

Source: International Monetary Fund, *International Financial Statistics* (various issues), Washington DC. Source of data for Taiwan, Republic of China, *Statistical Yearbook*, 2002, Taipei, 2003.

inflation-adjusted rates for the dollar. All three series are given in the form of index numbers. Index numbers identify the change from some base year. Unless the current balance was equal to zero in the base year, the "real rate" must be adjusted if it is to be used to infer its effect on a later current balance. Note the trend in the strengthening of the dollar over the eighteen years.[12]

Table 5.6 shows the cumulative current surplus or deficit of 24 countries from 1983 to 2001. A cumulative surplus shows a reliance of domestic macroeconomic/employment policy on the international sector. If a country can obtain the same expansionary effects for its home economy

Table 5.7 Ratios of private foreign-owned financial assets to US official reserves (1981–2002)

| Year | Numerator[a] | | US[b] official reserves ($ billions) |
	Tradable securities	Total financial liabilities	
1981	0.87	2.44	124.6
1983	1.50	4.26	123.1
1985	2.90	6.64	117.9
1987	2.96	6.83	162.4
1989	4.25	9.01	168.7
1991	5.14	10.45	159.2
1993	6.38	11.87	164.9
1995	8.34	14.68	176.1
1997	16.88	27.47	134.8
1999	22.47	34.43	136.4
2000	25.52	40.18	128.4
2001	24.96	43.27	130.0
2002	21.22	37.45	158.6

Notes

[a] "Tradable securities" comprise foreign holdings of Treasury securities, private equities and bonds traded on secondary markets and currency. "Total financial liabilities" include, in addition, liabilities to unaffiliated foreigners by non-banking concerns and liabilities to foreigners by banks not included elsewhere.

[b] Official reserve assets are the sum of the gold stock valued at market price, special drawing rights, the reserve position in the International Monetary Fund and holdings of foreign currencies. In the last four years the gold stock comprised over fifty percent of reserve assets and there must be some doubt as to whether it could be sold at the given market price in a period of substantial financial upheaval.

Source: *Survey of Current Business* (July 2002), pp. 18–19.

by having non-residents owe residents money as from having the home government owe money to the residents/taxpayers, the choice is fairly simple. Of course, the simplicity of the decision does presume a docile electorate willing to accept a weaker currency, smaller per-unit gains from trade and a lower real income. The data in Table 5.6 will also be needed in Part III since chronically surplus nations necessarily impose a greater strain on the hegemon by requiring that other countries run correspondingly larger deficits on current account (see equation 2.4, p. 40).

Table 5.7 shows the ratios of privately owned dollar liabilities to US official international reserves.

III   The domestic trigger[13]

Chapter 2 (p. 42), indicated that acceptance of the rôle of hegemon imposed two major (and two minor) duties on the United States: (1) to supply a key-currency, which was a reliable store of deferred value in both domestic and foreign currencies; and (2) to provide positive net aggregate demand to the global economy as needed.[14] The two areas of responsibility generate different triggers. While residents of the United States have no alternative to the dollar without incurring transaction costs and exchange-rate risks, non-resident owners of dollar-denominated assets are unavoidably concerned with the possibility that the key currency weaken in foreign-exchange markets because of domestic inflation in the United States, because of adverse shifts in the U.S. terms of trade or because of net withdrawals of funds from financial markets in the United States. The "domestic trigger," in contrast, will derive from stresses generated in the real sector rather than financial causes. The burden of the provision of aggregate demand to the "rest of the world" will, sooner or later, impair the ability of the key-currency economy successfully to maintain adequate aggregate domestic demand. The latter will be the cause of the domestic trigger launching the destruction of stability in the international financial system.[15]

Godley (1999), drawing on Godley and Milberg (1994), developed a model that could be used to anticipate the behavior of an economy by examining the sources of expansion as deriving from *ex ante* increases in demand from three sectors. These are the *private* sector, comprising business and personal (or household) sub-sectors; the *government* sector including sub-national units of government and the *foreign* sector (the external current balance). The three sectors determine whether there is sufficient aggregate demand for domestic output to generate a satisfactory level of employment. They are interdependent in that, *ex post*, the three balances (of expenditures in excess of available financing) have to sum to zero (total injections are equal to total leakages). If an increase in aggregate demand is necessary for expansion of the economy, the behavior of each of the sectors can be examined to see whether the three of them as a unit are capable of generating the necessary increase in financing either internally or from one of the other sectors. This approach, albeit Keynesian, had the great virtue of examining possible constraints on sectoral expansion, which resulted from the net asset position of the individual sector or sub-sectors. For example, the sudden growth in concern of the US electorate with government deficits in the Reagan and post-Reagan years restricted the degree to which the government sector could be expected to add to aggregate demand to generate expansion or to limit recession.[16] In the 1990s, consumption expenditures increased and were ultimately restrained from further growth by the debt burden of many households and the unavailability of further debt to many potential spenders.[17] Consumer debt burden (interest and scheduled repayments) of the personal (household) sub-sector reached new heights and was estimated by the Federal Reserve System to reach 14.3 percent of household disposable income in the first quarter of 2001 Once households had reached maximum consumption, the personal sector's contribution to the corporate sub-sector's demand for investment funds became negligible. The household sub-sector was, together with large-scale investment in cost-reducing new technology by the business sub-sector, the locomotive for the expansion during the Clinton presidency. The personal sector financed much of its expansionary input by using profits generated by the bubble caused by irrational exuberance on the New York Stock Exchange, consumer credit from financial intermediaries and from credit card accounts, that is, by raising spectacularly its ratio of debt to disposable income.[18] Since the credit available to households wishing to enhance expenditures raised the ratio of debt to disposable income and since that has a very clear limit, this source of expansion of aggregate demand was finite and ran the risk of generating large numbers of personal bankruptcies. The increase in personal/household bankruptcies matched a logical interpretation of the data. The number increased by almost five hundred percent in 22 years (see Table 5.8).

The international sector is seen as passive and, reminiscent of Mann's (1999) approach, its contribution depends largely on the levels of domestic and foreign income and rates of exchange. For the external balance to be conceived as being passively determined is consonant with fulfilment by the United States, of the locomotive rôle of the key-currency nation.

The strength of this approach is that, by focusing on the sources of credit needed by each sector to maintain its existing contribution to total aggregate demand, it can assess the ability of individual sectors to contribute to (or detract from) economic expansion. This amounts to identifying constraints on the stock of debt, which each sector both has and can support. *In brief, the Godley approach introduces balance-sheet (stock) items into a Keynesian (flow) framework of the rate of capacity utilization, employment and economic growth of a national economy.* The approach also allows for severe dangers to be anticipated (Godley, 1999) (Godley, 2003). In the existing, early 2003, context of the US economy, the long

Table 5.8   US bankruptcy filings (1980–2002)

Year	Business	Non-business (households)
1980	43,649	287,570
1981	48,125	315,818
1982	69,300	310,951
1983	62,436	286,444
1984	64,004	284,517
1985	71,277	341,233
1986	81,235	449,203
1987	82,446	495,553
1988	63,853	549,612
1989	63,235	616,226
1990	64,853	718,107
1991	71,549	872,438
1992	70,463	900,874
1993	62,304	812,898
1994	52,374	780,455
1995	51,959	874,642
1996	53,549	1,125,006
1997	54,027	1,350,118
1998	44,367	1,398,182
1999	37,884	1,281,581
2000	35,472	1,217,972
2001	40,099	1,452,030
2002	38,540	1,539,111
2003	35,037	1,625,208

Source: American Bankruptcy Institute data (www.abiworld.org).

expansion of household demand has so increased the debt of the household sector, that it would be excessively optimistic to look to that sub-sector as a source of expansion in demand, and a decrease in demand was almost inevitable.[19] The corporate sub-sector is suffering from less than robust profits and inadequate pressures on its capacity utilization. The external sector is in substantial deficit and the effect of decreasing demand from the personal sector is having little effect in 2002. The sector lacks any obvious source of substantial improvement.

The analyses emanating from the Levy Economics Institute show that the US economy is headed for a serious recession with higher-than-acceptable levels of unemployment. Papadimitriou *et al.* (2002), working before the elevation of military expenditures in the Middle East, uses

Table 5.9   A pro-forma estimate of the US INW at the end of 2010

| Data at the end of 2002 | International Net Worth: | $ −2,387.2 billions (Table 5.3) |
| | Easily encashable liabilities: | $ 5,939.5 billions (Table 5.2) |

Year	Hypothesized deficit on trade and transfers[a] ($ billion)	Increase in non-resident private financial claims ($ billion)	Income on assets[b] ($ billion)
2002	500	300	0
2003	400	240	−15.0
2004	300	180	−27.0
2005	200	120	−36.0
2006	180	108	−42.0
2007	162	97	−47.4
2008	146	87	−52.26
2009	131	79	−56.64
2010	118	70	−59.26
Total (8 yrs.)	1,637	981	−335.36

Totals at end of 2010[c].

INW = −$4.360 trillion (smaller than INW at the end of 2002 – i.e. a larger negative – by $1,637 + 335.56 bns).

Easily encashable assets $7.12 trillion (greater by $981 bn. plus 60 percent of $335 bn.).

Notes

[a] This column does not, below the line, include the effect of the assumed reinvestment of net income on assets on the outstanding balance of easily encashable instruments: it is, therefore, the BTTs.

[b] This column computes the balances of income on assets starting from balance in 2002. The computed balance is equal is equal to 3 percent of the sum of the current deficits beginning in 2002. The computation assumes that interest on the decrease in INW is credited on December 31 of the following year. The balance of income on assets in 2005 is 3 percent of $(500 + 400 + 300) billion.

[c] The data for INW of 2002 are preliminary: this fact qualifies the computations.

the Godley approach. Relying largely on models of the future level of US economic activity developed by the Congressional Budget Office, the baseline scenario estimates that US unemployment levels will approach 8 percent by 2006 (Papadimitriou *et al.*, 2002, p. 9).[20] Following Godley and Izurieta (2002), the authors offer a so-called "dream scenario," which relies for the economy's expansion on an improvement in net export demand stimulated by a substantial (25 percent) depreciation of the dollar in early 2003. This stimulus is estimated to halve the current deficit down to two and a half percent of GDP. While such a reduction in the rate of current dissaving would ease the accumulation of the

Table 5.10 US ratios of current credits to current debits (1990–2003) ˙

Year	Current credits ($ billion) (2)	Current debits ($ billion) (3)	Ratio of debits to credits (4)
1990	707.0	754.3	1.074
1991	727.6	734.6	1.010
1992	748.9	763.7	1.020
1993	776.9	821.8	1.058
1994	868.5	948.6	1.092
1995	1,005.6	1,075.7	1.070
1996	1,077.1	1,155.5	1.073
1997	1,195.0	1,281.3	1.072
1998	1,191.2	1,347.5	1.131
1999	1,255.7	1,499.8	1.194
2000	1,416.9	1,772.7	1.251
2001	1,284.9	1,632.1	1.270
2002	1,229.6	1,651.7	1.343
2003	1,294.2	1,836.1	1.419

Source: *Survey of Current Business* (July 2002), p. 59.

Note: The space has been inserted into the columns to draw attention to the obvious increase in the annual trend rate of increase in the ratio (Column 4).

"dollar overhang," this flow is by no means negligible. Papadimitriou *et al.* (2002, pp. 11–12) recognizes the need for an increase in absorption by the rest of the world to offset the decline in the US current external deficit.[21] Failing this partial handing over of the locomotive responsibility by the United States to the rest of the (industrialized) world, the expectation of the study is for a steep rise in unemployment in the United States and, as a result of the decrease in global aggregate demand, in the rest of the world.[22]

Table 5.10 identifies the ratio of current debits to current credits. Together with the elasticities of the demand for imports and exports, it is this ratio that determines the requisite ["real"] depreciation of the dollar. The rate at which this ratio has increased since 1997, is sobering.

IV Income on assets

The simple analytics of this component of the current account were considered in Chapter 3, Section IV. The purpose of this section is to examine the probable magnitudes, which future deficits on income on assets might add to the balance on goods and services and transfers.

Two authors Mann (1999) and Blecker (1999b) have recognized this potential drag on US international saving in estimating future current deficits. The balance on income on assets involves the debits, which accumulate at some rate of compound interest on the outstanding assets and liabilities. It is, of course, necessary to allow for the fact that the United States has managed to achieve a zero balance on income on assets while having a substantially negative INW. Given the revision of the income on assets data for 2001 to a positive flow (Table 3.2) and the fact that the account returned to deficit in 2002, it is practical to take the end of 2001 as having an approximately zero balance.

Table 5.9 reports the implications of the sub-component of net income on assets based on some hypothetical numbers about the international dissaving for the eight years from 2003 through 2010. The same apparatus is used to estimate the future (negative) values of US INW in 2010 as well as the estimated value of gross liabilities in easy-encashable foreign-owned assets in the absence of either confrontation or collaborative efforts to resolve the ongoing weakness of the key currency. The estimates are, deliberately, quite conservative to the point that the estimated (negative) INW in 2010 is less than half of the negative number that derives from Mann's 1999 computations. One reason for this discrepancy is that the current deficit on trade and transfer decreases over the eight years because some gradual easing of the dollar is built in (on the basis of experience in 2002) and the effects of different relative growth rates on import values are not incorporated.[23] But this monograph serves a different purpose than Mann (1999) and there is little fear that using these data for illustration will unnecessarily enhance the probability of activation of either trigger. The increase in easily encashable non-resident-owned dollar-denominated assets is estimated by assuming that these foreign-owned assets will comprise 60 percent of the estimated deficit on trade and transfers. The technique and income on assets used to estimate the balance on net income on assets in 2010 is straightforward. The decrease in INW since the end of 2002 consists of the sum of the deficits on trade and transfers (column 2) plus the total debits on income on assets (the sum of column 4).[24]

According to these computations, the negative INW of the key-currency country decreases from $2.387 trillion at the end of 2002 by $1.637 trillion in 2010 plus $335.56 billion which is the cost of financing the marginal decrease in INW. The probability of activation of both triggers has increased with the negative magnitude of INW and with the volume of foreign-owned easily encashable assets, which has increased by more than a trillion dollars.

V   The contagion of the two sectors

Both the absorption theory presented in Chapter 3 and the data presented above recognize that exhaustion can be triggered in one of two ways. The first derives from transactions in the capital account when private non-resident holders of dollar-denominated assets liquidate a substantial amount of their easily encashable dollar holdings (at the end of 2002, these holdings amounted to in excess of \$5.9 trillion). This trigger has its major and more probable source outside the United States. The second trigger will be activated by domestic political pressures and shows itself in the current account as the key-currency nation attempts to reduce the rate at which its INW is being reduced (its current deficit). Analytically, these two possible phenomena have been considered separately. That approach, however useful for expositional purposes, exaggerates the difference between the two triggers. The first point to be made is that the two sectors are mutually interactive and reinforcing so that the source of the disruption that promotes exhaustion, be it the international or the domestic trigger, is of secondary importance. The potential contagion also requires that any steps taken to reduce the magnitude of the problem address both the international financial and the capacity-utilization aspects of the potential crisis at the same time. Instability in one sector will transmit itself to other sectors, that is, from the capital to the current account and *vice versa*, through contagion. Essentially, the conduits for contagion revolve around the familiar Keynesian distinction between the financial sector and the real economy comprising Godley's three sources of injections and leakages into and from the expenditure stream.[25] Instability in the financial sector (the international trigger) derives, at bottom, from the work of Minsky on instability in financial markets and its repercussions on the resilience of the system of financial intermediaries.[26] Instability caused by inadequate aggregate demand will generate the familiar multiplier effect in an international analytic framework. The approach in this section will be to hypothesize the activation of, first, the international (financial-sector) trigger and to examine the way in which this will transmit the shock to the real sector in the United States and, through current transactions, to foreign countries. The section then examines the reverse scenario. There is, in principle, no limit to the potential number of "waves" of interaction,[27] but the reliability of any analysis will diminish as it hypothesizes about the later "waves" of interaction.

Activation of the *international trigger*, a large net exodus of privately foreign-owned assets brought about by expectations of a future depreciation of the dollar,[28] will constitute a deflationary shock for the US financial sector, which cannot help but be passed through to the real sector. If the US financial sector were backed by strong international reserves (in hard foreign currencies), these reserves might be used to reduce the net impact of the exodus of funds but the existing level of official reserves is minimal in relation to gross liabilities of easily encashable instruments owned by private non-residents (Table 5.7). The weakening of the dollar, brought about by the exodus of funds from dollar-denominated assets, will raise the cost of loanable funds directly and indirectly as the central bank tries to stem the hemorrhage. Given the sophistication of commercial banks in the United States, it is to be expected that the rate of bank failures caused by the shock will be small and that the Federal Deposit Insurance Corporation will prevent any major repercussions on the household sector.[29] The withdrawal of assets from stock exchanges, will increase the cost of equity capital in the United States and create a substantial negative wealth effect on the resources of the household sector. In addition, the reactions will sap both the animal spirits of corporate America and the consumer confidence of households. Add any induced effects from the sale of financial assets by US residents (including foreign-owned as well as domestically owned multinational enterprises) and the effects could be doubled.

There will be straightforward contagion between the financial sector and the real sector in the United States. The crucial question is the magnitude of the changes in the real sector induced by the disruption in the financial sector. Nothing, even in the most pessimistic scenario, suggests that all of the private foreign deposits will be withdrawn, but Tables 5.1 and 5.2 indicate that between 1997 and 2002, more than $2.2 trillion foreign-owned private financial investments have been attracted to dollar-denominated assets tradable in secondary markets (totaling over $3.9 trillion at the end of 2002). The potential shock and its impact on the dollar price of US financial assets are, then, of major proportions.. The spectrum of interest rates must rise and the market values of both financial and real assets will decline. Together these forces will put great stress on private parties (households and corporations) with high ratios of debt to net income and net worth: the greater the leverage, the larger the magnification of the original action by its induced effects. Provided that the shock is not great enough to push the economy into a depression mode (Gray, 1990), the effect on the real sector in the key-currency country could be mitigated by the inevitable weakening of the dollar in two ways: some parties will repatriate assets held abroad; and depreciation of the dollar will add aggregate demand to the US economy.

Activation of the domestic trigger will invoke both of the same variables. To reduce the current deficit, the authorities must weaken the currency and restrict domestic aggregate demand. These two variables will affect the financial sector by encouraging an outflow of assets (possibly at less favorable terms than under the international trigger) and by imposing restrictions on aggregate demand.

The original effects will be very similar regardless of which is the activating trigger.[30] It may be inferred that the domestic trigger will have smaller initial effects and some preplanning, arranging financing for spreading out the process of adjustment, may have been carried out.

VI   Concluding remarks

Two points need to be emphasized. Somewhat contradictorily for a chapter ostensibly devoted to the provision of data, the chapter has also developed an extremely important analytic point. Given the increased efficiency of the conduits for the international flow of funds, for financial information among national financial sectors and between financial and real sectors in national economies,[31] the question of which trigger is activated is a matter of minor importance. The contagion and the mutual-reinforcement that can be expected after the dollar has been subjected to stress by non-resident asset holders or by (domestic) macroeconomic policymakers, require recognition of the need for analysis of both the real and the financial sectors. To concentrate exclusively on one sector would be misleadingly simple in any study of exhaustion.

An international financial system in which the hegemon finances decreases in its INW by increasing its rate of dissaving (as non-residents acquire more and more dollar assets) is a case study in Ponzi finance (Minsky, 1986, 335–41). While Ponzi finance, when committed by private parties, is "evocative of fraud," there is no such attribution here (see Chapter 11). The existing predicament is better seen as arising because neither the US authorities nor their counterparts in other countries confronted the problems facing the hegemon and neither, therefore, foresaw the need for the United States to finance its locomotive responsibilities by international dissaving at the annual rate of 4 percent of GDP (the average rate for the four years, 1999–2002) or understood the limits of the country's ability to do so. There was a general enthusiasm for a market system and there was no awareness of the possibility of the steady, secular erosion of international stability efficiency.

6
Assessing Propositions One and Two

I Introduction

This chapter assesses the evidence that, in the absence of major (and improbable) spontaneous policy initiatives, the *"exhaustion proposition"* is a high-probability event that would impose serious costs on the global macrofinancial system.[1] The chapter is, then, an exercise in applied political economy. It uses the broad-ranging approach suggested by Robbins (1981).[2] In quantitative terms, the chapter draws directly on the numerical evidence given in Chapter 5 as well as on the conservative (read "optimistic"), pro-forma estimates of the US INW and the volume of easily encashable financial assets owned by private non-residents through 2010 (Table 5.9).[3] In addition, Section II draws on the estimates of those economists who have identified the linkage between the deficit on current account and the domestic performance of the US economy. The reader must, however, recognize that past behavior is not necessarily a reliable guide to future behavior,[4] if only because the background conditions (national and global Northian institutions) evolve through time. Moreover, in the current international political climate, political responses are likely to change. The inferences drawn in this chapter assume the absence of substantial real exogenous shocks. The focus is on the degree to which continued international dissaving by the United States at the historical and postulated future rates is likely to (or not to) generate malfunction in the global economy. Because there exists very little empirical knowledge about the ability of economies to adjust to new international financial conditions without disruption and severe adjustment costs and because this lack applies even more importantly to problems when the hegemon is the direct source of the financial instability, this inquiry penetrates unknown territory. The details of its conclusions must be seen as being subject to some considerable uncertainty.

Section II will provide a first consideration, based on available data, of the proposition that the dollar is fated to lose its key-currency status. Section III examines the susceptibility of the conclusions drawn in Section II to changes in the three major assumptions: the possibility that international dissaving by the United States will not decrease as quickly as Table 5.9 indicates; the sensitivity of the current account balance to changes in the real rate of exchange is exaggerated; and the possibility that erstwhile surplus nations do not expand their aggregate demand. Section IV summarizes the arguments and the inferences drawn with respect to Proposition One. Section V applies the available arguments and evidence to Proposition Two.

It would be pleasing and efficient if the discipline of economics were capable of supplying policymakers (and analysts) with an approximate statement of what must be done to reduce the probability that exhaustion will take hold and/or a measure of the degree of dislocation that exhaustion will entail in countries in the global system. Unfortunately, as will become painfully clear in this and the following chapters, there are simply too many unknowns, in terms of the economic performance of individual countries (or blocs), of current quantitative economic relationships and of political responses to events by the major industrialized nations, for such a tidy analysis. The change that will have taken place in the world is such that earlier studies would have almost negligible relevance to responses under the specific conditions of financial stress in a globalized world. The "unknowability" of the effects of exhaustion derive from the huge scope of the problem and the high [underestimated] degree of interdependence of national economies that exists. Other than the abdication of sterling's tie to gold in 1931 under very different conditions, exhaustion of the key currency is unprecedented.

II   A soft or a hard landing? A first assessment

As noted in Chapter 5 (pp. 120–2), the probability that "exhaustion" will take hold and disrupt the functioning of the global macrofinancial system is the *sum of the probabilities* that one of two triggers be activated. The probability that the international trigger will be activated will increase as the negative INW of the United States increases absolutely. In terms of Figure 4.1, increases in the negative value of US INW will steadily diminish *a* by moving the excess demand schedule to the left. No exogenous shock is required, in principle, for the ultimate activation of the international trigger. The implications of self-reinforcing disruption from activation of the international trigger, dimension *b* in Figure 4.1, can be expected to increase with the volume of outstanding easily encashable assets owned by non-residents. Continuing current deficits by the United States will generate a smaller *a* and a larger *b* and the larger the deficits, the more quickly will *a* decrease and *b* increase. Both the likelihood and the scope of global macrofinancial disruption will increase. There is no requirement that *a* reach a value of zero (in terms of Figure 4.1) for the symptoms of exhaustion to set in. Exhaustion will be tied to the loss of investor confidence so that, given the vagaries of herd behavior, neither the position of the excess demand schedule nor that of the inflection point is set in stone, as might be inferred from the figure.

The evidence points strongly toward exhaustion taking place. Table 5.3 shows substantial ongoing international dissaving by the United States in 2002 reaching a rate of 4.8 percent of GDP and over 4 percent of GDP on average over the years 1999 through 2002.[5] If exhaustion is not to materialize in the future, there has to be some sign of a declining rate of international dissaving and, given the rate existing in 2002, the rate of decline must be substantial. In contrast, Godley (2003, p. 5), in an extension of his earlier work suggests that this ratio will grow in 2008 to between 8 and 9 percent of GDP. While Godley's estimate of the future deficit relies on his assumptions, the scenario that he paints, is one of steady worsening of international dissaving – indeed Godley estimates that the negative INW of the United States in 2008 will approach $8 trillion (or 60 percent of GDP). His estimates are closer to those of Mann (1999) than to the conservative, even optimistic assumptions of Table 5.9.[6] That table provides estimates consistent with a steady reduction in annual current deficits through 2010. Even with these assumptions, the INW of the United States will decrease to an estimated negative value of $4.36 trillion by 2010.

The changes needed to eliminate current deficits, be they policy-induced or the natural workings of the financial system, must weaken the dollar in foreign-exchange markets (although different kinds of expenditure-switch instruments can be used). The estimates in Table 5.9 must, then, imply a steady depreciation of the dollar and the more pessimistic estimates of Mann (1999) and Godley (2003) imply the need for even greater rates of depreciation. This weakness may be seen as inevitably destroying the image of the dollar's invulnerability that has existed since 1945. Once the faith in the dollar's invulnerability is lost, it cannot be quickly restored.

Godley and Izurieta (2002) have confirmed the need for a weakening of the dollar and have suggested that a reduction of the value of the dollar of 25 percent would be good policy. Papadimitriou *et al* (2002) have incorporated this number into their "ideal scenario." This recommendation assumes that these reductions are reductions in inflation-adjusted (real) rates of exchange.[7] It is also optimistically assumed that all countries allow the dollar to depreciate against their own currencies by the full amount;[8] and that foreign nations enhance their aggregate demand so that total global aggregate demand is constant.

A 25 percent depreciation may be insufficient. The ratio of the US deficit on current transactions to earning of foreign currencies in 2001 was 30.7 percent (Tables 5.3 and 5.6). In 2002, the equivalent ratio was 39.0 percent. If the sensitivity of the US current deficit to depreciation is based on unitary elasticity of demand for both exports and imports, a 10 percent depreciation will, if export and import supply schedules are perfectly elastic, reduce the current deficit by approximately 10 percent of the average of foreign-exchange revenues and expenditures. As a quick rule of thumb, a 30 percent deficit ratio would require a depreciation of 30 percent, combined with a reduction in US aggregate demand of 4.8 percent and a matching increase in foreign aggregate demand. Non-resident owners of dollar-denominated assets would face a loss in value, in their own functional currencies, of about 30 percent plus any effect, which the expenditure-reduction of 4.8 percent of US GDP would inflict on the dollar value of the assets. The total loss in, say, euros, of leaving assets in dollar-denominated assets would certainly exceed 30 percent.[9] The prospect of losses of value of this magnitude would be very likely to bring about a sizeable exodus of foreign-owned funds and would make a hard landing inevitable – easily sufficient to offset an inherent growth rate of 3 or even 4 percent *per annum*. Such a growth rate is highly improbable during a period of adjustment, that is, of retrenchment of aggregate demand and of large-scale reallocation of inputs among sectors with all of the havoc that this would wreak on the labor market.

The mutual reinforcement of the two sectors and their triggers will come into play. The probability that the domestic trigger would be activated depends importantly on the awareness of the executive branch of the vulnerability of the dollar and on the political courage of office-holders: the [US] *Economic Report of the President*, 2003 (pp. 59–62) does not convey any such awareness. This position is fully compatible with an essential faith in the benefits of a strong dollar. The prospect of a (passive) policy of simply allowing the dollar to weaken is greater since the exchange rate is profoundly influenced by the net flow of capital: policymakers can continue the passivity towards net capital movements that has marked recent years. The dollar weakened perceptibly (by almost 20 percent against the euro) between January and December, 2002, but by far less against the inflation-adjusted index of the "broad" rate of exchange (Table 5.5). There was no clear induced reduction in the current deficit. The latter could be attributed to the inevitable lag in the reaction of current transactions to the rate of exchange (Dornbusch and Krugman, 1976). Contrary to theoretical expectations, the relatively low level of US economic activity in 2002 did not seem to have any observable influence on the current deficit. It is quite possible that this relationship is also subject to a (shorter) lagged reaction and that it interacts with the effect of the weakening of the dollar. A continuation of market-determined weakening of the dollar and its lagged effects underlie the steady but moderate declines in current deficits postulated in Table 5.9.

Unless the current account deficits of the United States can decrease gradually without activating the international trigger, the outlook must almost inevitably point to a *hard landing* for the US economy.[10] But, the danger in a gradual rate of depreciation of the dollar is the greater length of time before the current account approaches zero and the greater is the string of successive deficits. Similarly, non-resident asset-holders must disregard the effect of the weakening of the dollar on their wealth positions, and domestic policymakers must tolerate the drag of current deficits on domestic unemployment rates for longer periods of time.

Still heavier economic costs are likely to ensue in the United States as domestic confidence falls after the dollar has weakened and domestic output fallen. What cannot be known is the degree to which a widespread loss of confidence would affect the buoyancy of aggregate demand over a longer term. If the loss of asset values were substantial, the repercussions would exceed recent experience and there is no guide to the depths of the recession that could ensue. It could extend the effects to the third degree of disruption – a crash landing.

If the current rate of international dissaving is to grow smaller, the dollar must weaken in foreign-exchange markets. Neither trigger has yet been activated but no-one can know *ex ante* which straw will break the camel's back. The international trigger in particular has a large component of mob psychology since investors, regardless of nationality, tend to obey herd instincts. Once a break occurs, all indicators and reasoning suggest that the depreciation will, in the absence of energetic and combined actions by the major nations, be a substantial one.

III   Easing the assumptions

In addition to the assumption of the absence of exogenous shocks, three major assumptions underlie the inferences of Section II.

1. A decreasing trend in current international dissaving by the United States based on the spontaneous easing of the foreign desire to acquire dollar-denominated assets and an induced steady easing of the strength of the dollar (Table 5.9);
2. A sensitivity of the current balance to change in the rate of exchange based on the assumption of perfectly elastic supply schedules of both exports and imports;
3. The deliberate, non-discriminatory maintenance of the rate of global aggregate demand by surplus nations.

The effects of these assumptions are considered in sequence. Each of the assumptions reduces the perceived probability of the activation of one of the triggers so that their release makes exhaustion more likely and disruption more severe (i.e. reinforces the expectation of a "hard landing" and its severity).

Decreasing trend in current international dissaving by the United States

The assumption of smaller future rates of international dissaving by the hegemon than may prove accurate, must almost inevitably have reduced both the assessed probability of exhaustion and the degree of disruption of the international financial system.

The estimates in Table 5.9 are "optimistic" in the sense that the table foresees substantial monotonic rates of decrease of the current deficits of the United States beginning with reduction of $100 billion *per annum* in the first three years (2003 through 2005). Consider instead the effect of reducing the rate of decrease of international dissaving to $50 billion *per annum* for the first three years and maintaining the same rate of reduction (10 percent *per annum*) thereafter. The value of the sum of the deficits of the eight years will increase from $1.6 trillion to $2.5 trillion so that the INW of the United States in 2010 will have decreased to a negative $5.25 trillion (instead of –$4.1 trillion).[11] The increase in the value of easily encashable dollar-denominated assets owned by non-residents will grow from $981 billion to $1.5 trillion to a total of $7.4 trillion in 2010. The danger of the activation of the international trigger is enhanced. The larger current deficits postulated in the variant of Table 5.9, are also more likely to activate the domestic trigger because the unemployment effect will increase as the deficit is eroded by a smaller amount. It is doubtful that the alternative scenario proposed here will have much of an effect on policymakers. The current deficit will still be smaller than it will have been and this could constitute an excuse for continued passivity.

This original scenario (Table 5.9) with its steadily decreasing chronic deficits scenario can be seen as the optimistic scenario believed in by people who foresee the chronic deficit easing gradually down to zero without overt pro-active policy measures being introduced. The following statement from the "preface" to the report of the US Trade Deficit Review Commission (2000, pp. ix–x) illustrates this view:[12]

> Some witnesses believe that the most likely scenario is that reasonable adjustments in the exchange value of the dollar, together with economic recovery abroad will produce a "soft landing". In this case, the trade deficit comes down substantially in a normal adjustment process that would not generate significant adverse effects on the United States. Both American and foreign investors thus benefit. Indeed, this has been our experience in recent decades. This is a view that we share.

Such a scenario implies a steady weakening of the dollar as a result of market forces, the assumed absence of instability in the foreign exchange markets, and a corresponding reduction in domestic absorption without inducing a substantial recession. Given the size of the current deficit in 2002 as a percent of GDP, the scenario must be seen as extremely "optimistic."

Change in rate of exchange based on elasticities of export and import supplies

The assumption of perfectly elastic supply schedules simplifies the algebra of computing the sensitivity of the current balance to currency depreciation (Robinson, 1947, p. 91) but the perfect elasticity of schedules assumption is heroic – especially when the context is a (roughly) 30 percent depreciation of a currency. A depreciation of this magnitude implies broad-ranging changes in the mixes of both output and absorption in the depreciating nation and in its major trading partners. Presumably, the larger the change in the volume of production of a good, the more heroic does the assumption of a perfectly elastic supply schedule become. Perfect elasticity requires that the individual producers in the country with the depreciating currency have about enough excess capacity on hand – given the expenditure-reductions – to allow the required increase in output to be effected (within the time frame of the inevitable lags in reaction). When a firm (or industry) approaches the limits of its physical capacity, unit costs of production are fated to increase even with constant costs of inputs so that the effective depreciation (price competitiveness) will be eroded.[13]

The heroism contained in the assumption of perfectly elastic supply schedules depends directly upon the combination of the degree and duration of currency overvaluation. This relationship can be illustrated with reference to the steel industry in the United States, which became the focus of attention when the Bush Administration chose, in 2001, to put a tariff on imports of steel. The ostensible reason for the tariff was that domestic producers had been badly damaged by price-competition from foreign suppliers (including much suspected dumping). Inevitably, there was an uproar from foreign exporters of steel and these resulted in several formal complaints to the World Trade Organization (WTO). There was also much weeping, wailing and gnashing of teeth from diehard proponents of free trade reported in the US media including, not surprisingly, users of steel who competed in foreign markets.[14] There were accounts of the inflationary impetus of the tariff on the prices of products that used imported steel and of the damage that would be done to US export industries when other countries retaliated in accord with WTO provisions. The WTO ruled against the United States in the last week of March 2003, and, in this way, allowed other nations to retaliate by protecting their other home-produced goods against imports from the United States.

The "need" for a protective tariff for the US steel industry can be attributed wholly to the overvaluation of the dollar (Blecker, 2002). The exchange rate determined in financial markets resulted in a substantially stronger dollar than was compatible with balanced current account in the absence of net capital movements). An overvalued dollar has the effect of imposing a subsidy on foreign goods and services (i.e. a negative tariff) and a tax on US export goods and services (Yeager, 1970). Thus, steel imports were effectively being subsidized by the US failure to counter the steady strengthening of the dollar during the decade of the 1990s. The ability of an industry to maintain its competitiveness in both price and quality requires that it have funds available to upgrade the technology of both its design and its product line. An industry whose member firms were being squeezed by competition from abroad will not make robust profits (or generate free cash flow) in the amounts, which allow the needed investments in cost reductions and quality improvements to be carried out (Milberg and Gray, 1992). The greater the degree of currency overvaluation and the longer its duration, the greater is the cash-flow squeeze imposed on any industry competing with foreign goods. This is where the hegemon, with its very large "line of credit" and its responsibility for adding to global aggregate demand, is severely endangered and has some claim to constituting a "special case." The series of chronic deficits that can be financed is long because of the assumed invulnerability of the key currency[15] and home industries that may well be viable under conditions of balanced free trade, lose their price-competitiveness and their markets.

> By early 2002, more than thirty steel firms have been pushed over the edge into bankruptcy including major integrated producers such as Bethlehem and LTV as well as many smaller companies – firms that together accounted for about one third of industry employment. (Blecker, 2002)

However, the issue is more complex than simply allowing the US steel industry to be protected. There exists a mix of internationally traded goods and services, which would be produced with a given rate of exchange and the corresponding deficit on goods and services (the deficit mix) and a second mix, which would be produced under conditions of a cheaper dollar and balanced goods and services (the balance mix). If the national economy is to eliminate its deficit on goods and services, it must have available, or be able to move towards having, the mix of productive capacities corresponding to the balance mix. The greater the ongoing deficit, the larger is the amount of adjustment needed in the mix of output and, therefore, the larger is the potential discrepancy between the two mixes of capacity by industry or service. Under a free-market system, the need for internally generated cash flow is crucial in creating confidence sufficient to decide on the investments needed for the expansion of capacity and for the financing of that expansion. This is the "capacity-mix" problem facing a hegemon that has run cumulative deficits on goods and services for 20 years.[16]

The traditional choice of a currency depreciation over a mixture of import duties and export subsidies is that the currency depreciation is neutral with respect to the individual components. In contrast an administered mixture could attempt to wring a competitive advantage for the nation's industries. The Bush Administration's tariff on steel was as much politically – as economically motivated. Steel is a complex industry covering a wide range of products of which only some would be viable under balanced free trade.

Non-discriminatory maintenance of global aggregate demand

If the United States is to reduce its negative INW and to repay the liabilities, which have financed its years of dissaving (see Table 5.3), it is important that it takes the steps, which are necessary for repayment to be made. But it is also important that the rest of the world be willing to accept (import) goods so that the United States can earn the money with which to reduce its obligations. This scenario recalls the problems which faced Germany in its attempt to pay the reparations imposed on it by the Treaty of Versailles when the countries scheduled to be recipients of reparations did not want to accept goods which would put ever greater pressure on their futile attempts to increase domestic employment. Galbraith (2002, p. 10) is aware of the similarity and suggests that there is serious doubt that "the world would quickly rally to purchase increasing quantities of made-in-America exports: ... Exports to the rich regions may not be very price sensitive." The idea that depreciation of a currency would not reduce the US rate of international dissaving, recalls the inter-war years and involves the strong nationalist, *sauve qui peut*, economic policies of that time.[17] Such actions would leave a greater onus on a policy of expenditure-reductions with all of the concomitant scope for a worldwide recession in the absence of deliberate expansionary measures being taken by the other major industrialized countries (but see pp. 39–42). It is this increase in the understanding of how the world works that offers some hope since the knowledge will pressure the surplus nations to expand their demand. The distinction between expenditure-reductions and expenditure-switches may not be as easily identified as the absorption theory suggests but both forces will work in the same direction.

Everyone who addresses the problem of preventing serious repercussions being caused by the ever-growing negative INW of the United States, must confront the need for large-scale and wholehearted co-operation among nations and supra-national institutions. In the absence of this order of co-operation, the prospects become ever more disheartening. But, if the US policymakers persist in ignoring the steady (absolute) increase in the negative INW, there can be little hope that policymakers in other countries will take the initiative so that a hard global landing can be avoided. Passivity on the part of the United States will mean that the country will remain the hegemonic leader in global policymaking, for want of a substitute, until the dollar has reached exhaustion and the full implications of exhaustion have sunk in on both sides of the Atlantic and Pacific oceans. It is vital that the major surplus and industrial powers recognize that what is needed is a massive variant on what is generally understood by Keynesian policy. Instead of old-fashioned Keynesian policies instituted at the national level, the focus must be on global aggregate demand and there will be serious negotiations over the allocation of expansionary responsibility. Here, of course, the United States will play only a minor role as befits the largest deficit nation.

The effects of changes in national income levels on the flows of current transactions cannot be ignored. The greater affluence of some countries (whose currencies strengthen against the dollar) and the reduced affluence of the United States will affect the pattern of demand for imports of internationally traded goods and services. The change in the value of the key currency in terms of a range of foreign currencies, will exert an effect through the substitution of cheaper for more costly goods. Mann's (1999) estimation of the sustainability of the US trade deficits was based on the asymmetry between the marginal propensity to imports of trading partners and that of the United States. Mann's model relied on earlier studies that attributed a marginal propensity to import ($\partial M/\partial Y$) of 11 percent to the US economy while the weighted sum of the marginal propensities to import of trading partners, was only 5 percent.[18] These values were estimated in earlier periods and may have little relevance to the current problem – especially given the size of the changes in exchange rates that will be affecting the demand for imports of all countries. But, a substantial depreciation could be seen as enhancing foreign growth and imposing negative growth on the depreciating country.

There does exist the real danger that trading partners will not fulfil or be able to fulfil their expansionary "responsibilities." It is useful to distinguish between political stress and purely economic factors here. It is necessary, if adjustment is to take place and to bring the global macrofinancial system quickly back to a satisfactory rate of capacity utilization, that the world avoid the traps of the Treaty of Versailles after the First World War.[19] But there exist "built-in" (economic) factors, which are likely to impede major nations from expanding the level of aggregate demand in their domestic markets to the degree needed. The countries, which use the euro as their currency, have opposed the potential use of expansionary fiscal policy by the (discontinued) Stability and Growth

Pact of the Treaty of Maastricht (Rehman, 1997). The importance of this constraint will depend upon the relative force of currency appreciation and the aura of prosperity versus currency appreciation and the replacement of output by imports from the western hemisphere.[20] Asian countries may find the loss of export markets to be a serious constraint on "open policies." Table 5.6 shows that Japan and China are among the nations, which must allow their recent current surpluses to be eroded. China is in a delicate stage of development. The Japanese economy has been mired in a long-standing recession because of weaknesses in the reserve positions of the major commercial banks. Possibly even more important are the cultural impediments to escape from the ongoing economic weakness (Ozawa, 2001, 2001a) (Mundell, 2003).

IV   Assessing Proposition One

When a system has been used to having leadership in identifying necessary collective initiatives undertaken by a responsible nation, there will, almost inevitably, be a lag before the renunciation of that responsibility (by the United States) sinks in deeply enough to allow the other members of the system to make the necessary commitment to the expansion of their aggregate demand. This likelihood of delayed action on the part of nations with positive INWs suggests that, at a minimum, there will, by recent standards, be a severe global recession while nations come to grips with the change in conditions.

To this point, this chapter has utilized a wide-ranging body of evidence from Chapter 5 and has made reference to the work of several scholars who have addressed in detail some aspects of the chronic international dissaving of the United States. These studies address the problems likely to activate the domestic trigger. Several conclusions may be drawn from the data and the detailed analyses.

First, no-one has investigated in detail the problem of the chronic US international dissaving since its quantum increase in 1999 and come to the conclusion that it is *not* a potentially serious problem. However, several earlier studies have assumed the problem away by placing professional faith in the forces that operate within a set of markets to restore a viable balance without serious disruption.[21] All of the first seven tables in Chapter 5 show a tendency for the magnitudes which point towards a danger of the activation of one of the two triggers, to increase secularly. Even in Table 5.9 where an optimistic scenario was deliberately developed, the INW of the United States continued to decrease through 2010. Table 5.6 shows that many countries have long series of current accounts with the same "sign." Japan has run current surpluses for the full 20 years covered by the table and the United States, with a negligibly small transitory surplus in 1991, has run chronic deficits for eight- and eleven-year periods. In the absence of crisis there seems to be a tendency for a deficit or surplus to continue for several years – pointing to a certain monotonic quality by which a surplus or deficit tends to feed upon itself.[22] Moreover, the deficits of the hegemon have increased substantially over the last four years and, as this is being written, there exists no evidence of a reversal of that trend. The costs of the Iraqi war in early 2003 and its aftermath offer little hope for a reduction in the rate of US international dissaving.[23]

Those who have addressed the problem in detail, many associated with the Levy Institute of Economics,[24] have all concluded that the danger will not be self-eliminating and foresee, at best, a long period of stagnation in the United States. There can be little doubt that this outcome would have a depressing effect on the world's macrofinancial economy and lead to a protracted global recession.

Despite a love affair with the existence of "a strong dollar," the Bush Administration has not provided any argument or evidence to rebut the pessimism of those studies, which foresee a hard landing of some severity.[25] The assertions that "all will continue well" are protestations of faith rather than serious studies in political economy. Not since the publication of the *Report* of the US Trade Deficit Review Commission (2000) has there been any serious attempt in Washington to consider either the causes or the implications of chronic international dissaving.

There currently exists a large "overhang" of claims denominated in dollars and owned by people with different functional currencies. Blecker (1999b) aside, this issue has not attracted widespread attention by economists in government, business or academia. Yet its implications are potentially tremendous. Given the overvaluation of the dollar, which is a concomitant factor, it was to have been expected that the corporations and industry associations as well as the labor organizations would address this problem. The three groups have not launched combined major expressions of concern although individual statements have been made. It seems that leadership does not involve confronting unpleasant realities.

The major areas in which new factors are likely to arise derive from international political stress. The rifts among erstwhile close allies which resulted from the US policies towards and in Iraq in 2003[26] are likely to deepen during a global recession and, in this way, likely to diminish the hope for constructive international co-operation.

The major concern in the immediate future, that is, before exhaustion becomes a recognized fact, is likely to be the absence of a national economy to provide those international public goods that have allowed the global economy to function acceptably well over the last 50 years.

V   Proposition Two

No data in Chapter 5 rebuts Proposition Two. The Proposition states that *"attention must be given immediately to the problem of ensuring the availability of financing for the long period of adjustment to the change in conditions (the elimination of the chronic international dissaving by the key-currency country) so that the dollar does not weaken catastrophically in the process."* Given that the Proposition is essentially a corollary of Proposition One, it is hardly surprising that data which support Proposition One support its corollary.

The amount of time available for remedial measures and the magnitudes of the imbalances imply a necessary *rate* of adjustment. If the adjustment process suffers from diminishing returns to absorption reduction as the size of the imbalances increase (i.e. the social and economic costs of adjustment will increase more than proportionately with the rate and the size of the required adjustment), then Proposition Two must be valid. Put another way, Proposition Two asserts that there is some maximum rate of adjustment which can be supported by the global economy and by individual national economies without the system incurring a major crisis in the form of either a financial meltdown (activated by the international trigger) or a very deep global recession (activated by the domestic trigger).[27] Given the contagion between the financial and the "real" sectors, a crisis involving both sectors may be seen to follow merely from the passage of time or from one serious adverse event.

The likelihood of a financial crisis depends heavily on the fact that the greater the necessary degree of dollar depreciation perceived by non-resident owners of easily encashable dollar-denominated assets, the greater will be their incentive to change the currency of denomination of those assets and the greater the probability (and the magnitude) of crisis in the foreign exchange market. The activation of the domestic trigger, derives from the assumption that the greater the required rate of adjustment or the size of total adjustment, the greater is the shortfall in global aggregate demand likely to be as surplus nations do not promptly increase their total aggregate demand. The capacity to confront adjustment will increase with the degree of constructive international co-operation that can follow from identification of the depth and urgency of the problem.

Consideration of Proposition Two raises an issue which, in one respect, simply deepens the policy problem. Every delay in confronting the problem of exhaustion will raise the absolute rate of adjustment imposed because, in addition to the higher level of strain imposed, there will be less time available for creating and putting into effect an international, co-operative plan for a phase-out of the US current deficit. At the same time, the more quickly confrontation is launched, the smaller will be the required total adjustment of bringing the negative INW of the United States to a tolerable but still negative level. Identification of and agreement on the size of what constitutes a tolerable negative INW for the United States would be one of the variables to be considered internationally.[28]

Proposition Two implies that quick united action would reduce the stresses imposed by adjustment and would help to keep the dislocational costs below. As such, it must be accepted in the general sense. However, there can be no guarantee that there remains adequate time even as this is being written. The evidence presented in the data given in Chapter 5 and the analyses of the activation of the domestic trigger both offer convincing proof that the process of confrontation of potential exhaustion is a very serious undertaking and that the probability of a (very) hard landing has a sufficiently high probability that keeping the severity of the landing within tolerable bounds must be recognized as vital.[29]

Possibly what matters most is the combination of putting an end to the simple financing of the international dissaving by the hegemon and the refusal of the major nations to confront the need for *collective* international action. This statement is true as long as the rate of US international dissaving continues to increase or, in fact, does not diminish noticeably (say at the rate hypothesized in Table 5.9). There is nothing magic about the numbers postulated in Table 5.9 but numbers of roughly that magnitude could endow national leaders with an optimism that something can constructively be done at manageable political and economic cost and provide the international consultation process with an aura of optimism. It would be difficult, in context, to overestimate the importance of collective confidence.

VI Summary

No-one would suggest that the data (and the data sources) are beyond cavil but they present a strong argument in support of the hypothesis that the existing state of affairs will end with major global disruption.

It will require remarkable insights and co-operation among the leading financial powers for the international financial system to be made resilient again without incurring a crisis of major proportions.

Chapters 8 and 9 in Part IV address, respectively, possible policies for the transition and for the new system of architecture and develop the relations between what will have been inherited from the past and what might be the best strategies to control the depth of disruption.

7
The Efficiency of Adjustment

I Introduction

Despite its current magnitude, the problem of the major overhang of "indebtedness" facing the US economy and its currency is of fairly recent origin. This chapter focuses on the identification of three categories of factors, which are likely to adversely affect the efficiency of policy measures designed to eliminate the international dissaving. The factors consist of three types: "natural phenomena;" "contrary or counterproductive measures" and "internal inefficiencies." "Natural" phenomena are largely beyond the control of policymakers in either surplus or deficit countries. "Contrary" measures can be seen as deliberate, defensive measures adopted by policymakers in surplus nations. Contrary measures can also be instituted by groups in the deficit country who have the power to neutralize policies which adversely affect their private interests. "Internal inefficiencies" consist of existing arrangements that reduce the effectiveness of some policy instruments to be used in the elimination of a sizeable deficit. This does not mean that the latter measures were without social merit at the time of legislation but that the legislative process did not allow for the side-effects when reductions in the rate of international dissaving had to be imposed.

For expositional ease, national tastes and the marginal rates of substitution in production functions, are taken as given so that the sensitivity of the current deficit to the two basic policy measures; expenditure-switch and -reduction, are pre-determined. In terms of the absorption theory, the first can be seen as the sensitivity of the current balance to changes in the price competitiveness of value-added in different countries and the second as the way in which the value of exports and imports (current credits and debits) react to changes in income levels.[1] The sensitivity of the current account to price-competitiveness is simply the elasticity of substitution of internationally-traded goods and services or, in old fashioned, Marshallian terms, the "sum of the elasticities" of demand.[2] When these relationships are given, the efficiency of adjustment hinges on the degree to which the economic authorities in a deficit nation are capable of inflicting on their constituents both an expenditure-reduction and an expenditure-switch; on the degree to which constituents can offset these measures and thwart the attempted reduction in national absorption and on the degree to which surplus countries undertake expansion of their own aggregate demand in order to provide markets for foreign-made goods and services.[3]

The ability to thwart policies by both constituents in the deficit country as well as on the ability of foreign governments to carry out "contrary measures" will depend heavily on the degree of international co-operation in force when the adjustment is being undertaken. If the system remains open and market-oriented, that is, with relatively small impediments to international transactions, then the authorities in deficit and surplus countries will not have great latitude to interfere with the process of adjustment. However, if the relations among the major nations are strained, the probability is that the open system of international involvement will be discarded and the world will have barriers to trade raised in desperate efforts to reduce the domestic social costs of the adjustment. It is, therefore, very important that global co-operation be high and that there be a full understanding of the potential problems that could come from furthering economic *national* welfare at the expense of approaching the problem in terms of the *global* interest. Statesmanship of the calibre needed for global co-operation of this magnitude has always been a rare commodity and there is little evidence that this attribute will be in plentiful supply on this occasion.

II   Natural phenomena

A depreciation of the currency of the deficit nation, the expenditure-switch policy *par excellence*, is likely to be offset, in part, by natural *"slippage"* resulting from forces largely beyond the short-run control of the economic authorities in debtor and creditor nations.[4]

Define *"exchange-rate slippage"* as identifying the erosion of changes in the net barter terms of trade (price competitiveness) by factors which do not directly impinge on the financial rate of exchange.[5] The consequence is that the improvement in the price-competitiveness of the national economy is smaller than could be expected from a given depreciation. Exchange-rate slippage can be formally defined as an elasticity – the percentage change in the price competitiveness of a national economy divided by the percentage change in the financial rate of exchange: alternatively, slippage can be defined as the percentage change in the "real rate of exchange" per unit change in the financial rate of exchange. This relationship is very important in terms of the efficiency of the adjustment process. It assumes even greater importance when, as in the present situation, the deficit nation is the key-currency nation with a large overhang of easily encashable financial assets owned by non-residents. Non-residents will be motivated to redistribute portfolios of financial assets away from dollar-denominated assets largely by the *expected depreciation of the dollar in financial markets*, while the strength of an expenditure-switch derives from the change in the *economy's price competitiveness*. Thus, exchange-rate slippage increases the percentage nominal depreciation needed for a given deficit reduction or, alternatively, the degree of intensity of expenditure-reduction measures.

It is useful to define a nation's price-competitiveness, C, as:

$$C = r\ \frac{p_f}{p_d} \qquad (7.1)$$

where r is the national currency's rate of exchange measured in the number of units of domestic currency needed to purchase one unit of foreign exchange. (Thus, an increase in r weakens the currency and increases price-competitiveness.) The terms, p_f and p_d, represent the foreign and domestic price levels so that foreign inflation in excess of domestic inflation increases price competitiveness and *vice versa*. Slippage is embodied in the degree to which the two price-level components of C diminish the change in its value brought about by an increase in r.[6] The concept, C, can also indicate the way in which, under a system of fixed (nominal) exchange rates, a national currency can become overvalued if domestic inflation exceeds that which takes place in trading-partner nations.[7] As long as the consequent international dissaving can be financed, the country can run deficits in fixed rate-of-exchange system until the termination of international credits generates a crisis. Historically, most cases of overvaluation brought about by domestic inflation, have tended to end in crisis because the deficit nation and its leaders find enjoying the overvaluation and the diminution of the country's INW to be preferable in the short run to the social (and political) costs of eliminating current deficits.

As noted above (p. 100), the "real rate of exchange" is a concept and not a fact. It is an index number with a base year and its value denotes a change from that year – not necessarily from a year with balanced current account or some absolute, known imbalance. Some bodies produce estimates of real rates of exchange for individual currencies but complexities in calculation require that such numbers be used with care. The technical difficulties of compiling a series of real exchange rates and the implications of these problems for the accuracy or reliability of real exchange rates are summarized in Box 7.1.

Box 7.1   Estimating the "real" rate of exchange

A "real" rate of exchange is the nominal rate adjusted for inflation over some specified period of time (between the current year *t* and the base year). No practical system exists for generating a perfect estimate of the "real" rate so that the concept and estimates of its value must always be used with caution. This does not mean that the estimates are not useful but they are orders of magnitude rather than the precise numbers. In contrast, a bilateral nominal rate has existed at a certain point in time. However, because a country trades with many partners, it is useful to compute a "trade-weighted" index of the many nominal rates in order to trace the performance of a currency over time – whether it has strengthened or weakened against its trading partners and at what rate. This is an "effective" rate. In other words, an "effective real rate" will indicate how the price competitiveness of Country d (C_d) will have changed over a specified period. Using equation 7.1, the nominal rate at time *t* is compared to its equivalent in the base year for each trading partner. These nominal rates are adjusted for relative rates of inflation on a per-country basis and for the rate with each trading partner currency is weighted (i.e. by the importance of international trade with that particular partner). In theory, if a country has 10 trading partners, there will be trade weights with 10 partner currencies for the year *t* and the index of the individual nominal rates (in *t* as opposed to the base year) will be introduced into the real rate according to the importance of trade with a particular currency. Each ratio is adjusted for the difference in the price levels between the base year and *t*.

It is easy to see where the approximations creep in. Putting aside errors in the raw data, the compilation process is usually streamlined. First, the sample of nations is not complete and usually comprises only the major trading partners. The weights showing the importance of international trade are not revised for each year. The measure of relative inflation is usually approximated by the use of an available index – either the wholesale or the retail (or consumer) price index when what should be used is a weighted index of inflation in the prices of goods which are involved in the bilateral international trade. One important *caveat* is that some series are based only on physical goods and omit international trade in services. The omission of services is likely to derive from the individuality of many service transactions and the probable vagaries of their prices. Since trade in services has grown rapidly in recent years (both absolutely and relative to trade in goods), its omission can damage the value of a series when it is used to trace evolution of a nation's price competitiveness over time. Table 5.5 shows a large discrepancy between the change in the real effective exchange rate of the dollar between 2001 and 2002. The index number reported by the Federal Reserve System shows a strengthening of the dollar by 0.0088 percent. In contrast, the IMF series indicates a weakening of the dollar by 1.09 percent. This discrepancy is undoubtedly due to differences in the weights applied to different currencies and to the number of currencies used in the computation. However, it serves as a warning to anyone using indexes of effective rates of exchange for evidential purposes: in extreme cases, one might need to construct one's own index.

The obvious and unavoidable source of slippage derives from the degree to which internationally traded raw materials or intermediate goods are used as inputs in the output of finished goods to be sold to both foreign and domestic buyers. Once inventories of intermediate goods and raw materials have been run down,[8] imported intermediate goods increase in price in domestic currency in the depreciating country and enhance the price of potential exports in home currency. When such multi-stage processing occurs, the competitiveness of home value-added is not the sole factor in determining the price-competitiveness of either exports or of domestically made goods with imports. Producers of goods with import content will find the percentage reduction in costs in foreign currencies to be less than the percentage depreciation of the home currency depending on the ratio of the value of imported inputs to total cost. Of course, the substitution of home-produced goods for imports can take place at the level of intermediate goods so that this factor is itself subject to some (reverse) erosion as resources are reallocated in the deficit country across the spectrum of production. The problem may be greater, when the imported inputs to be used in the output of a finished good is a raw material, with which the deficit nation may not be endowed.[9] The reverse effect can hold in foreign suppliers where an industry can find its national price competitiveness to have been reduced by the depreciation of the deficit nation's currency, but it may have the option of using off-shore supply as a means of partially offsetting the effect of the depreciation on its costs. Natural slippage will not, of course, affect all costs equally so that the change in price-competitiveness will vary by individual goods and services as well as at the macroeconomic level. This phenomenon puts limits on the ability of economists to hazard a guess about the correct degree of depreciation needed in any situation and seems likely to increase the costs of adjustment by requiring greater resource reallocation. There is little that policymakers can do to prevent the erosion of gains in competitiveness brought about by natural slippage, except possibly to encourage the substitution of domestic value-added for intermediate goods used in import substitutes.

If the deficit nation is a member of a free-trade area, international trade in intermediate goods may be concentrated within the bloc and the effect of slippage between pairs of members of the bloc is likely to be case-specific. It will depend to a large degree on the volume of trade in intermediate goods and services and on the degree to which the deficit country's exports embody such imports. As noted above in Chapter 3, a depreciation of a major currency does not ensure that all countries will allow the value of their currencies to increase against the weak currency by the target percentage devaluation (contrary slippage). If such behavior takes place within a free-trade bloc, the greater dependency of some members on the viability of the deficit nation could affect the degree of contrary slippage with downstream effects on the deficit nation's price-competitiveness against outsiders.

When the deficit country is a member of a large free-trade area or a common market, the issue of slippage becomes still more complex. If a bloc contains both industrialized and developing countries, the volume of international trade in intermediate goods, some of which will be intra-firm among units of MNEs, will be greater. In the twenty-first century when blocs are larger and more numerous than in the twentieth century (Olivei, 2002), natural and contrary slippage could be a bigger handicap to efficient adjustment. What is crucial is the degree to which the rules of the bloc enforce or permit depreciation of one currency against another or the reverse, denying the ability of countries to depreciate their currency with that of another member. Within "Euroland" where the currency has been unified and intra-bloc depreciation is impossible, one dimension of uncertainty has been removed. This may improve the efficiency of the bloc when its economic system is performing well, but, at bottom, it eliminates a policy variable of major importance for adjustment and places the burden of changing price-competitiveness on the ratio of domestic price levels (p_d /p_f). Given that the philosophy underlying monetary policy within "Euroland" is strongly against inflation (and, by inference, deflation) changing national price-competitiveness without exchange-rate flexibility may be very difficult.

A second problem of erosion of depreciation (slippage), is "pass through": it is neither "natural" nor a result of national policy and therefore "contrary." It is instituted at the firm level and can be considered in this section.[10] "Pass through" slippage derives from marketing strategies in industries in which technological and qualitative differentiation are important. The question revolves around the ability of large corporations to avoid passing the effects of the change in their costs in the currency of the depreciating nation through to the ultimate consumer of the product. Here, the automobile industry is a useful example. It is an important industry in international trade among the advanced nations and even between industrializing nations and advanced nations, when the corporations based in the industrializing nations have established viable market shares in the advanced world. Producers may choose to reduce the mark-up charged over full cost so that the prices of their exports in the depreciating country do not reflect the effect of the change in exchange rates. Olivei (2002) reviews the pass through problem in the United States and concludes:

> This article reexamines the responsiveness of U.S. import prices to changes in the exchange rate in a sample of manufacturing industries over the past two decades. We document a decline in the estimated pass-through elasticity for most industries in the 1990s. For the industries in our sample, pass through was 0.50 on average in the 1980s and dropped to an average of about 0.25 in the 1990s. This finding suggests that larger changes in the exchange-rate are now needed to move the dollar price of imported goods relative to the price of domestic goods.

The degree to which pass through is likely to be adopted may depend on the degree of competition within a national industry in the supplier nation. The German automotive industry dominated the US market for performance sedans and the three major firms, Audi, BMW and Mercedes Benz, maintained their prices in dollars during the early years of the euro even though their costs in dollars were declining approximately in line with the euro. Had these firms had more severe competition from the Lexus automobile, their behavior might have been different but the Japanese yen did not weaken with the euro.[11]

Olivei's study addresses the behavior of foreign suppliers competing in the US market during a period of major adjustment when the dollar strengthened against the euro. It is possible that US corporations could use the same tactics to bolster their mark-ups in foreign markets but it does not follow automatically, that US firms will have the same freedom of manoeuvre. Of course, the larger the change in the rate of exchange, the greater the incentive for "pass through" manipulation.

Depreciation will normally have a spillover effect in the form of an expenditure-reduction – most easily seen as a consequence of the reduction in real income brought about by inflation in excess of increases in money income. The rate of saving of households should also increase as they will need to build up reserves and net worth in their domestic currency to offset the effects of the inevitable inflation brought about by the increase in the price of imports. The crucial question here is whether the desire to maintain a standard of living or the rate of consumption will outweigh the desire to maintain real balances and net worth as a percentage of income. If, as may be expected, families vary in their behavior, this effect is unlikely to be large or empirically identifiable. Reduced consumption (an increased saving rate) can be seen as a "natural" phenomenon but it can be countered by contrary policies by pressure groups – a possibility considered in the following section.

The possibility that expenditure-reductions will be less effective for a depreciating hegemon needs to be recognized. When the hegemon's currency is the currency used in pricing important raw materials, the normal inflationary effect of depreciation on the reduction of expenditure may not occur. The cost of, say, petroleum in the United States will not be affected directly by the depreciation in US markets except for any relatively indirect effects brought about by the reduction of the price of petroleum in other countries with appreciating currencies. To the extent that this effect increases global demand, there will be a direct effect on the price of petroleum in the United States. Such a scenario obviously requires that the US dollar retain its rôle in the world gasoline market. Given a percentage depreciation of the dollar of something like 25 or 30 percent, this seems unlikely.

III   Contrary measures

There exists also the possibility that a serious weakening of the key currency, even one brought on by the domestic trigger, would induce a wholesale reconsideration of exchange-rate policies. Countries, which are important trading partners could, in the interest of maintaining their own rates of capacity utilization, could try to impede unrestrained market forces or flows of funds from inflicting a major appreciation of their national currency. This possibility introduces a qualification to equation (7.1) above. The value of r, the change in the nominal rate of exchange, must now be seen as a weighted average of a series of bilateral exchange rates and its value will be sensitive to the composition of the weights and the distribution of increases in bilateral exchange rates (the number of units of the deficit country's currency per unit of the foreign currency) the same qualification affects the price levels. The target increase in C will not be achieved and further depreciations must be attempted. (Table 3.1 gives an example of the sensitivity of the decrease in the absolute value of the deficit to variations in the degree of depreciation effected.) Clearly any country which is not allowing its currency to strengthen by the full amount of the attempted or target depreciation is generating contrary slippage. There also exists the possibility that surplus countries will choose to utilize transparent or covert impediments to imports as well as a failure to increase aggregate demand in their economies and the world.

The existence of a current-account deficit requires that the cost-competitiveness of the national economy improve and if, as a result of *cost–push inflation* in the economy, the cost-competitiveness actually decreases, then the current deficit will grow until the nation either takes drastic steps or the system of markets exerts the needed discipline. Forces that generate cost–push inflation can therefore be considered to be contrary measures. This possibility is important in context because the US economy did generate such a cost–push inflation in the 1970s and early 1980s when its cost of living was increased substantially by a surge in oil prices (engineered by the Organization of Petroleum Exporting Companies) coupled with a fixed rate of exchange and reinforced by an increase in food prices.[12] Both inflationary stimuli increased the cost of living in the United States and generated a reaction which tended to increase compensating wage-rates. The fixed-rate system collapsed in early 1973 and this new system of flexible rates was not confirmed until the Jamaica Agreement was reached in 1976. Although the dollar weakened against the German mark, the Swiss franc and the

Japanese yen, the cost–push inflationary forces were such that the dollar strengthened in real terms and the price of oil in those three countries fell absolutely between 1974 and 1978 although all countries suffered increases in the domestic price of oil in 1979 when the second oil price shock struck (Gray, 1981, table 1). The large increase in the cost of living led to a serious thrust in labour negotiations to protect the living standards of union members and resulted in the widespread use of a tie between the nominal wage rate and the consumer price index in addition to any negotiated increases in nominal wages. The outcome was that some workers were protected against any inflationary forces that came from the real sector (including the effects of inflationary wage increases given to workers in other industries).[13]

The United States had suffered a severe adverse shock from a major increase in the price of oil and a decrease in the share of total oil consumption that was generated from domestic sources. Anything which worked against a reduction in the absorption of imports reduced the effectiveness of the adjustment process. The tying of the nominal wage to the c.p.i. did exactly that and, in practice, came near to nullifying both the expenditure-switch, which was reversed, and any expenditure-reduction. In 1982, when President Reagan was elected, the then Chairman of the Board of Governors of the Federal Reserve System, Paul Volcker, imposed, with Reagan's support, a very harsh monetary policy which generated a global recession. The combination of monetary tightness, and the consequent high real interest rates in the United States led to large inflows of interest-sensitive money. The financial inflows strengthened the dollar in foreign exchange markets and, this effect was reinforced by such cost–push inflation as existed. The effects are shown in Table 7.1.

What was engineered, then, was the protection against inflation of an identifiable group, at least in terms of wage-rates but not necessarily in terms of employment. The idea was created that there should, in some sense, be a guarantee against a reduction in the standard of living (the real wage rate) although the concept did not seem to apply to workers in industries not subject to industry-wide bargaining or to workers in service industries. Self-evidently, attempts to eliminate a current deficit can be frustrated if the cost competitiveness of a national economy does not increase or if the economy is not forced into recession – possibly as a means to discipline an increase in price-competitiveness and certainly to make resources available for expanding sectors. In the early 1980s, the global recession sapped the demand for oil and brought about a weakening in the price of oil which had been the original disruption.

Table 7.1 Balance-of-payments adjustment in the early 1980s in the United States

Year/quarter	Real short-term Interest rate (% per annum)	Real rate of exchange of the dollar (1980–82 = 100)	Current balance ($ billion) (Annual)
1981 (1)	4.50	94.5	+6.34
1982 (1)	6.27	105.0	−8.06
1983 (1)	3.95	110.1	−40.70
1984 (1)	5.13	113.0	−107.86
1985 (1)	4.98	128.4	—
1985 (4)	4.66	113.0	−117.64

Notes: Real short-term paper rates are the rate paid on 90-day commercial paper less the change in the c.p.i. They were taken from various issues of O.E.C.D. *Main Economic Indicators* and the *Federal Reserve Bulletin*. Real exchange rate data were taken from Morgan Guaranty, *World Financial Markets*. Data on the annual current deficit were taken from various issues of *The Survey of Current Business*. Note that these data do not correspond exactly with those in Table 5.3 which have been revised. Unemployment rates were taken from various issues of the *Economic Report of the President*.

The costs were high and the United States was launched on its twenty-plus years of international dissaving.

IV   Internal inefficiencies

Any set of Northian institutions in the deficit nation, which is sanctified by legislation or endorsed by policymakers and which weakens an expenditure-switch or an expenditure-reduction, will weaken the effectiveness of adjustment measures. Any weakening of the efficiency of adjustment measures requires larger doses of expenditure-switches and -reduction. Given the magnitude of the depreciation that will probably be required, neither the United States nor the rest of the world can afford to have internal inefficiences in the major debtor nations.[14]

One potentially important internal inefficiency exists in the form of indexation used in some social measures, the United States, like many others, employs so-called cost-of-living adjustments widely as measures designed to protect some groups against inflation. The cost of living adjustment is measured by the change in the consumer price index, which self-evidently contains for its primary purpose, the costs of imported goods as well as domestic value-added. In this way, the persons whose incomes (or benefits) are indexed are protected against the inflation caused by the depreciation and suffer no diminution in real income caused by higher prices for imports. Real incomes remain unaffected.

When internationally traded goods were a much smaller share of consumption than they currently constitute and when the price of a barrel of oil was not a political football, the inclusion of imported goods in a cost-of-living index was of lesser importance. Social-security recipients in the United States have had their benefits indexed for years and some income-tax brackets are tied to the c.p.i. The efficiency of adjustment policies would be strengthened if cost-of-living indexes were tied to an index of domestic value-added rather than to the c.p.i. Protecting some people against the inflationary effects of actions of domestic, economically powerful groups is desirable but there is no normative reason for protecting any group of residents against foreign events which affect the welfare of the nation as a whole. This remedy will also apply to indexation of wage-rates. There is no way, short of crisis, that nations can ignore shifts in the net barter terms of trade and indexation to the c.p.i. would be nothing more than an attempt to do that.

There are two difficulties with this suggestion that indexation should be linked to an index of the change in the value of domestic production. What seems to be a minor correction could impose a potentially hard burden on the very poor and some means would need to be found to overcome this side-effect. The second problem is political. In a democracy, policies have to be justified to the electorate at large if they are to command popular support. When the underlying cause is technically complex, it becomes difficult for democracy to function in the textbook manner. Pryor (2002, p. 367) posits that this is a problem of technical complexity that is going to become much less rare as the issues on which voters must decide, become increasingly complex.

Two other possible internal inefficiencies can be usefully identified. Any adjustment in national price-competitiveness of the magnitude needed to counter exhaustion of the key currency will result in substantial changes in the prosperity of different industries and sectors in both deficit and surplus countries. Export industries will enjoy increased demand in the deficit nation and the reverse in surplus nations. Industries producing goods for domestic consumption are likely to prosper in the deficit country as these products replace imports but, unless aggregate demand is expanded strongly in surplus countries, firms serving domestic needs are likely to face difficulties. These patterns suggest that, if the onset of adjustment is very quick, as is quite possible if the international trigger is activated, the profitability of individual firms and their credit-worthiness will vary substantially. For this reason, it behoves the monetary authorities in both sets of countries to ensure that banks observe capital adequacy requirements very closely lest the costs of adjustment be enhanced by bad performance and possibly a crisis in the banking sector.

V   Conclusion

The material covered in this chapter demonstrates the huge difficulties in estimating the absolute amount of improvement which is required in the price-competitiveness of the deficit nation with or without some knowledge of the expenditure-reduction which will be inflicted. Not only are major periods of adjustment relatively rare so that there is little basis for empirical studies, but each case is unique. Policymakers can then best be seen as groping their way towards a viable solution. By instituting policies which institute changes in price competitiveness and expenditure, they can begin to put the adjustment process into action. As progress is made, smaller changes can be introduced and the adjustment will continue until, the world reaches a state of imbalance which is small enough to live with.

Given the potential size of the adjustment of the transfer of expenditures from one bloc to another that will amount to about half a trillion dollars, policymakers must recognize the possibility that financial instability in foreign exchange markets may add to the disruption. It is crucial that policymakers recognize the importance of the efficiency of the process and of the policies introduced. Improvements in policies that may merely generate small savings of, say, 1 percent, will be worthwhile because of the huge amount of reallocation which is involved. In the same way, policymakers must recognize that their policies will be imposed on an economy which will be quite different from the tranquil world in which they have been used to operating.

Efficient policymaking will reduce the likelihood of any overshooting in exchange rates and global aggregate demand so that the social costs of exhaustion are minimized. This aspect of the problem of exhaustion is taken up in Chapter 8.

Part IV
Confronting the Future

8
Policy Options and Constraints

I Introduction

Part IV introduces the analysis to a new world of uncharted phenomena and uncertainty. For these reasons, conclusions and proposals are tentative. This lead-in chapter addresses possible approaches to the creation of a new international financial architecture and identifies some of the constraints on both policies and the structural elements of the system. Chapter 9 will address very briefly the problems of transition from the moribund system left over from the last century and the establishment of a transitional international financial architecture. Chapter 10 will offer a possible "broad brush" design for a new long-term architecture as a basis for discussion.

The evidence in support of Propositions One and Two allowed Chapter 6 strongly to support the need for international co-operation to create a new transitional system as quickly as possible. Its task will be to avert or restrain macrofinancial disruption. The development of the international financial system for the transition period is the more important task and has the shorter period of grace. It may be assumed that the long-term architecture will evolve from the transitional system in the light of the degree of dislocation that will have been experienced. It seems efficient, therefore, to start with the same group of conferees if only because members will have developed some expertise. The fact that the United States will, inevitably, have been given some preferential treatment in the transitional system, see Chapter 9, suggests that there will be a broad-based incentive quickly to develop and to confirm the new long-term architecture.

The delegates to the conclave will face problems whose scope and scale exceed any experience from a previous time. The magnitude of the undertaking must be explicit. If crisis is to be avoided and the high degree of interdependence between the two triggers constitutes an ominous attribute of the present reality, a patchwork solution will be of no avail.[1] The transitional architecture must be created almost from scratch and, to the extent that they are not derivative from the transitional architecture, so must the details and institutions of the long-term system.

The policy goal must be to eliminate the overhang of instability brought about by the threatened exhaustion of the dollar and to facilitate a crisis-free transition from the vulnerable present state of affairs to a more resilient, longer-lasting system. The transition system is essentially required to put US international transactions on an "even keel" so that both the country's negative INW and its rate of international dissaving would be reduced to levels at which they would no longer constitute potential sources of instability. These levels would continue to be negative but of a much smaller size so that the main task of the transition period is to ensure that the *United States is committed to and allowed to make positive international saving without allowing the dollar's rate of exchange to weaken so much that foreign owners stampede to unload dollar-denominated financial assets.* The critical sizes of the two imbalances are not knowable *ex ante*.

Section II addresses the political economy of working towards global welfare when the necessary policies can inflict short-run damage on individual national economies. Section III considers the limits of unilateral action by the exhausted hegemon and, indirectly, the absolute need for international co-operation. Section IV addresses the need for a flexible, non-dogmatic approach to the problem of creating a new long-term architecture.[2] These topics must be understood by the participants of any co-operative effort to redesign the system.

II   The current dilemma

The degree of fragility of the global macrofinancial economy derives not only from the size of the US imbalances and the complete lack of experience in dealing with an exhausted hegemon, but also from the sheer lack of awareness and concern of world leaders and the potentially damaging policies, which they currently follow. The difficulty facing elected leaders of imposing harsh economic conditions on the electorate is understandable but the alternatives are very serious.

The faith of the Bush Administration in "the strong dollar policy" is based, in part at least, on a complete lack of awareness that the country's much-prized military and scientific advantages (Kissinger, 2001) are vulnerable to a financial Achilles heel. At the same time, US economic policy disregards, at its peril, the plight of its manufacturing sector in the face of a current account deficit, in 2002, of just under half a trillion dollars.[3] The willingness of American politicians and voters to accept comfortable nostra and to disregard hard economic facts shows a lack of macrofinancial sophistication as well as a well-known preoccupation with the short run (from one election to the next).[4]

In Europe, Chancellor Schroeder of Germany sought, on July 10, 2003, to have the European Central Bank weaken the euro against the dollar saying that exporters were suffering under the strong euro and that the Bank had not intervened in the currency markets for more than two years (*Financial Times*, July 11, 2003, p. 1).[5] As Table 8.1 shows, both Germany and the rest of the member nations of the euro bloc run current surpluses and use up a part of the injection of aggregate demand supplied by the hegemon. Adoption of the Chancellor's suggestion would have reinforced the "strong dollar policy" of President Bush (see Table 8.1, note a) and increased US international dissaving (vis-à-vis the European Union). Chancellor Schroeder's proposed strategy could be seen to derive in part from the inflexible limits imposed on contracyclical fiscal policy by the Stability and Growth Pact of the members of the euro bloc.[6] China has run an average current surplus of almost $35.5 billion over the last four years but, more important, is the huge increase in the last two years from less than 9 percent of the Japanese surplus in 2000 to two-thirds of the Japanese surplus in 2002. At the same time, Japan remains locked in its own deep recession (Ozawa, 2001a). The surpluses of four nations (China, France, Germany and Japan) neutralized about one half of the aggregate demand provided by the US international dissaving in 2002 (Table 8.1).

Global aggregate demand and capacity utilization can be increased only if a country is able to generate domestic aggregate demand and to run a (larger) deficit on current account, financed from international reserves held in a form other than the dollar.[7] If the United States is constrained by its inherited imbalances from providing the deficits to balance the sought-after increased surpluses of other countries, then there is no easy way to augment global aggregate demand that does not increase the probability that one of the two triggers will be activated. It is essential that governments, including the members of the euro bloc, understand that global aggregate demand is not increased by one country enhancing its current balance at the expense of another (see equation (2.4), p. 40 above).

Equally, the important financial powers must be aware that the predicament in which the global macrofinancial economy would find

Table 8.1 Current surpluses of some major nations 1990 through 2002 (Billions of dollars)

Country	1990	1991	1992	1993	1994	1995	1996	1997	1998	1999	2000	2001	2002
China	—	—	—	—	—	+22.5	+31.7	+35.9	+6.2	+8.6	+10.7	+47.4	+75.2
Euro bloc[a]	—	—	—	—	—	+57.2	+83.9	+104.5	+70.9	+33.9	-15.1	+19.4	+72.1
(France	-9.8	-6.2	+3.8	+9.2	+8.0	+10.9	+20.5	+39.5	+40.1	+42.0	+19.4	+24.0	+29.7)
(Germany	+48.9[b]	-18.0	-19.4	-13.5	-19.7	-20.7	-7.9	-2.7	-6.2	-19.1	-20.9	+3.5	+49.6)
Japan	+35.8	+68.4	+112.3	+132.0	+130.6	+111.4	+65.7	+96.6	+119.1	+114.5	+119.6	+87.8	+112.8
(Netherlands	—	—	—	—	—	+25.8	+21.4	+25.1	+13.6	+15.7	+14.1	+10.6	+12.7)
Taiwan, Province of China	—	—	+8.6	+7.0	+6.5	+5.5	+10.9	+7.0	+3.4	+8.4	+8.9	+18.9	n.a.
U.K.[c]	-34.4	-15.1	-16.7	-16.7	-2.9	-14.2	-13.6	-2.8	-8.0	-31.9	-29.1	-23.6	-29.7

Notes

[a] IMF forecasts estimate that the euro bloc's current account will increase to $91 billion in 2003 and the German surplus to $59.5 billion. Before 2000, estimates of the current balance of the euro bloc was simply the sum of the balances of the member countries.

[b] Germany's 1990 data apply only to West Germany for the first half of the year. The balance-of-payments costs of reunification are self-evident but had been overcome by 2001. France's current balance seems to have gained from the German stress.

[c] The sum of the continuous deficits for the 13 years is $238.7 billion.

Sources: International Monetary Fund, World Economic Outlook (April, 2003) and (September, 1996, p. 207). Chinese data were taken from various issues of the IMF's International Financial Statistics. Taiwanese data were given by Statistical Yearbook of the Republic of China, 2002.

itself if the US current deficit were to be eliminated. A serious global shortfall of aggregate demand would create a serious recession (even in the absence of expenditure-switches). In the absence of any deliberate expansion by other countries to match an expenditure-reduction which will eliminate the US current deficit, the global shortfall will approach half a trillion dollars.[8] This danger, while not independent of the problems of resource reallocation, puts the problem of generating adequate aggregate demand back on centre stage – albeit at the global rather than the national level.

It is also important that all governments understand that all countries will suffer economically to greater or lesser degree from any major macrofinancial disruption. There is no easy solution to restore vitality to the international macrofinancial system. The first focus must be on the potential willingness of countries with current surpluses to add to global aggregate demand by expanding their total aggregate demand and by reducing their surpluses.[9]

The term "macrofinancial" has been used to stress the interaction between financial instability and a major reduction in aggregate demand but it is also necessary to recognize the interaction between the need to reallocate resources among sectors. A shortage of aggregate demand impedes the reallocation of resources because it weakens the expansionist power of such growing sectors as exist. The efficiency of resource-allocative mechanisms depends heavily on the level of aggregate demand so that there will be expanding sectors to absorb resources released from depressed sectors. The positive correlation between the size of the imbalances and vulnerability to crisis derives directly from the fact that the larger an imbalance, the greater must be the volume of resources in need of alternative employment. From this it follows that the necessary adjustment in standards of living and the social costs of resource reallocation will also be higher: the larger the adaptation required, the more likely are policy measures to run into decreasing effectiveness in the short run as factors of production require upgrading, relocating or transforming before they can be applied to their new uses. Further, the greater the adjustment in living standards required in deficit nations, the greater will be the effort of residents to attempt to further their own welfare at the expense of the efficiency of the adjustment process. Drawing down liquid reserves provides an effective means of countering an expenditure-reduction for some period of time.

In the United States, both dimensions of deficit reduction (expenditure-reductions and expenditure-switches) have self-reinforcing characteristics. In the financial sector, sales of dollar-denominated assets and the dollar-denominated proceeds by non-residents will encourage others to sell their assets by strengthening perceptions of both the inevitability and the magnitude of depreciation. A decrease in resilience may also show itself in the financial sector as the new conditions weaken the banking system through defaults on loans. At the same time, the multiplier effect will take hold in the real sectors of trading partners. All of the historical evidence suggests that increases in net exports of deficit nations will be slow to manifest themselves unless trading partners play a very positive role by quickly expanding absorption.

It will be essential that national policymakers recognize the global constraints and approach the problem as members of a co-operating group. Recent conduct does not indicate that this awareness has come about.[10] The degree of overvaluation of the dollar,[11] underlies both the size of the current rate of US international dissaving and the danger of a flight from dollar-denominated securities. An efficient policy mix will, therefore, necessarily include some steady albeit gradual weakening of the dollar.

III   The limits of US unilateral action

This section reviews the feasibility of unilateral measures that the United States might institute in order to ease the stress and to reduce the lack of resilience of the international macrofinancial system. There are four categories of measures: (1) reduction of absorption; (2) depreciation of the dollar; (3) controls over capital exports of both residents and non-residents (i.e. the cessation of full resident and non-resident convertibility); and (4) impediments to international trade. There are overlaps among the four genera. The latter two fly in the face of US post-Second World War international economic policy and would eliminate the major impetus to further globalization.

It is useful to introduce first, in very general terms, the political difficulties which will beset the institution of such policies. It will be necessary, as Proposition Two intimates, to introduce corrective measures promptly and with a degree of domestic political consensus. The two houses of the US Congress are unlikely to be able to fulfil either requirement since a necessary part of any package of the four categories, would involve running a federal surplus to be generated either by raising taxes or reducing support for existing military and/or social programs. The debate cannot be kept brief because the issues would touch on very firmly held beliefs and would almost inevitably be referred to sub-committees in both houses. For ideological reasons as well as electoral concerns, support from the incumbent executive branch (in 2003) cannot be expected.[12] The inevitable debate could activate the international trigger and lead to withdrawals of foreign-owned dollar-denominated assets.

Reduction of absorption

A unilateral reduction in absorption by the United States could be effected by fiscal policy, by raising taxes on households so that the fiscal deficit of the central government is sharply reduced.[13] This has the negative side-effect of political unpopularity but it will also bring about a global recession with all of the prospects for activation of the domestic trigger or, by virtue of a collapsed market for equities, of the international trigger. An alternative would be for serious monetary retrenchment similar to that instituted by Chairman Volcker in 1982/83. High short-term interest rates were then and are now an inevitable consequence. In 1982/83, the policy attracted large inflows of short-term capital and strengthened the real and financial rates of exchange.[14] By itself, this proposal has little to offer beyond compounding the existing problem. Given a stronger dollar, the US rate of international dissaving relative to GDP, might increase. A major unilateral reduction of absorption by the United States would not, by itself, provide a sound basis for global prosperity nor would the induced global recession significantly reduce the degree of vulnerability to financial crisis.

Depreciation of the dollar

Depreciation of the dollar faces both political and economic difficulties. In a world in which exchange rates are free to fluctuate according to flows of funds, the way to weaken the dollar would be for the United States Government to raise financial (dollar) resources and to use these resources to acquire assets denominated in other currencies. The needed funds could be raised either by fiscal policy or by borrowing at home, so that this approach must indirectly involve the fiscal/monetary approach.

The political difficulty is self-evident. Even if sufficient funds had been raised, they would have to be selectively invested in foreign countries' capital markets by the US economic authorities. Given the magnitude of the financial *masse*, which might, in the first year, amount to $100 billion, the policy would involve major intrusion into the capital markets of other countries *by the US Government*. The US authorities would have to allocate the purchases among host countries and would, in effect, be sitting as judges on which countries should contribute to the adjustment and by how much. Such investments would threaten to reduce the positive current-account balance of the individual recipients (already endangered by the fiscal contraction in the United States) and would probably give rise to serious political concerns by unwilling host nations. This opens up the prospect of widespread negotiations with several countries thereby raising the issue to a multilateral level.

The macrofinancial difficulty derives from ignorance about the responsiveness of exchange rates to "artificial" flows of funds possibly reinforced by contrary measures by which countries would take steps not to allow the dollar to weaken against their currency. Presumably, the United States authorities would invest piecemeal with the idea of continuing the process until they have achieved some predetermined target, which might or might not be negotiated and agreed upon. There would also be considerable difficulty in determining a set of appropriate target rates of exchange. If the potential recipients of capital inflows were to co-operate with each other, the unilateral policy might devolve passively into a multilateral conference.

Controls over capital exports

Removing resident and non-resident convertibility (presumably only for large amounts lest the international tourism industry be severely damaged[15]) will instigate a major shock for financial institutions and could endanger some highly leveraged operations (particularly hedge funds whose existence can be expected to add to the potential for serious volatility as this genus of institutions reacts to instability). It might be possible to allow a certain amount of the assets of non-resident owners to be released from the controls every year or the funds which were locked into dollars might be liquidated (into foreign currencies) upon payment of some tax (presumably increasing with the permitted speed and/or the amount of the withdrawal). Such an arrangement echoes the Tobin tax except that the Tobin tax was conceived in a world of fixed rates, which were vulnerable to large scale speculation when the required direction of change of the rate of exchange was obvious. Present conditions do not offer huge opportunities for speculation and most foreign-owned dollar-denominated assets are the results of portfolio diversification rather than speculation in foreign exchange (Table 5.1).

Impediments to international trade

Renunciation of the free-trade posture, more precisely raising tariffs and introducing other impediments on goods and services, which currently enjoy zero or low rates of import duty and negligible quantitative restrictions, would be a very complex operation. Three measures bear identification at this juncture: the imposition of excise taxes on primary products; imposing or raising tariffs on imports which compete with domestic production with the threat of counter-measures under WTO rules; and the possibility of self-defeating impediments deriving from the involvement of so many multinational corporations across national boundaries.

The imposition of an excise tax on imported primary products is likely to generate some political support in the United States. The obvious choice is petroleum and excise taxes on petroleum products could be raised to European levels especially if the excise tax were designed to discriminate against imports from outside the western hemisphere. Since the United States is no longer self-sufficient in petroleum products, the bulk of the excise taxes would, by reducing imports, serve the same rôle as import duties.[16] Excise taxes would have the secondary effect of raising revenue for (as well as the political unpopularity of) the government and would therefore act as both a simultaneous expenditure-reduction and an expenditure-switch. The implications of such an excise tax, especially at a rate of something approaching European levels, would be substantial and put great pressure on passenger transportation/commutation services, which would need support from public funds.[17]

The fate of the imposition of import duties on steel by the current US administration merely gave rise to the WTO allowing steel exporters to raise tariffs on imports of those goods which the United States exported to them. To eliminate the imbalances through major reliance on impediments to international trade would be likely to destroy the WTO and could lay the seeds for a trade war. As noted above, the existing set of WTO regulations makes no allowance for a hegemon which is deliberately running a deficit on current account and, arguably, providing an international service by permitting its currency to be overvalued.

All policy-induced changes that interfere with the relatively free operation of markets lay the ground for economic dislocation. The growth of direct investment in the last quarter of a century and the huge growth in intra-firm international trade suggest that both modern economies and modern multinational corporations are very vulnerable to such a violent change in international economic policy. Further, the volume of intra-firm international trade and the differences in the way such trade is conducted among pairs of countries and within industries are so great that there is little hope that an efficient policy along these lines could be designed without causing severe damage to many firms.

The possibility of generating an efficient policy set of *unilateral* measures seems to be very slight. The difficulties are positively related to the degree of dislocation (the size of the imbalances) and the very well-established macrofinancial and intra-industry and intra-firm micro-relationships that exist. Inevitably, the repercussions of unilateral actions on the part of the key-currency nation will inflict economic pain on other countries and such pain is more than likely to generate local support for contra-action. Only when governments on both sides of a policy set can argue in its support to local electorates and firms is there a serious likelihood that some viable steps can be taken to reduce the imbalances with bearable costs.

The argument of this section can be reduced to the simple statement that there is no way in which the United States can draw down imbalances of their current size without obtaining the co-operation of foreign governments. Reducing the imbalances will inflict economic costs on the United States, trading partners and countries with which the United States is closely financially linked . Not only is the need for international co-operation dependent on the size of the flow and stock deficits when the problem is confronted, but it is doubtful if *effective* measures could be taken unilaterally.

IV   The need for an open mind

The theme of Yergin and Stanislaw's *Commanding Heights* (1998) is that the post-Second World War world steadily recognized the economic advantages of a market system over one closely administered by governments. The successes of the economic policies of Prime Minister Thatcher and President Reagan can be seen as having installed an ever-greater commitment to *laissez-faire* as the reigning economic dogma. This philosophy gave a strong boost to the political support for the reduction of impediments to international economic involvement and, in this way, to globalization. This section considers the need to consider alternatives to a purely *laissez-faire* approach in the design of a new, post-transition international financial system if only because that philosophy is the most likely to dominate thinking in the development of a new international financial architecture.[18]

Singh (2003) offers a cogent rebuttal of the hypothesis that *laissez-faire* is optimal for developing countries. His critique is strongest in rebutting the desirability of unfettered movements of portfolio capital between the industrialized and the developing worlds and in rejecting *laissez-faire* in terms of international foreign direct investment.[19]

The dollar-reliant international financial system has approached exhaustion in part because of a fundamentalist commitment, mainly in the United Kingdom and the United States, to achieving *laissez-faire* in international transactions. The commitment was so strong that it has impeded any serious consideration of the indirect effects of liberalization on both the system's efficiency and its stability.[20] Adelman (2000) observes that "the political forces making for liberalization ... are too strong to be able to put the genie back in the bottle, even if one wanted to." Faith in the benefits of free markets and in the US ability to continue to perform the responsibilities of the hegemon was possibly reinforced, in recent years, by delusions of hegemonic grandeur in Washington. Such delusions will have derived, in part, from freedom from rivalry as a superpower from the Soviet Union and in part from a pre-eminence in many dimensions of socio-economic activity – including military activities (Kissinger, 2001). Policymakers neglected the problem of how to finance the multiple burdens of hegemony. One account, which recognizes the huge US indebtedness, considers the possibility that the United States is, like a major private bank, "too big to [to be allowed to] fail". Unfortunately, this encouraging scenario requires the equivalent for the hegemon, of a central bank, which can prevent the failure of a too-big-to-fail bank in its system by injections of capital.[21]

Short-run problems will derive from instability of financial markets in national economies in the top level of the "inverted pyramid" (Figure 2.1), that is, from local currency crises. In recent years emerging markets have shown an inability to develop the sophistication of their own financial sectors at the pace needed to benefit from the greater openness of international financial markets (Gray and Dilyard, 2002) (Fischer, 2003). It is also necessary to recognize the desire of national monetary authorities to seek any solution which will benefit their home country even at the cost of imposing strain on the global system. This could be considered a problem of "moral hazard" and may, ultimately, need to be addressed by empowering some "replacement hegemon" to impose costs on "repeat offenders" (see Chapter 10). In some countries, the problems can be attributed to the remarkable rate of technological advance in information technology and to the degree to which sophisticated operators have been willing to intrude in markets that lack adequate institutional sophistication (Helliar *et al.*, 2000).[22]

Changes in technology will continue to require that unsophisticated countries either adapt their economies to adjust to innovations in the global economy or shun full involvement in globalization. Additionally, a new form of financial firm has developed (hedge funds). Such firms operate on very thin margins with very large volume of assets and are very highly leveraged: while such firms may be profitable in a tranquil environment, they could prove to be a major source of reinforcement to any instability once it has reached a certain critical level.

Certainly, the new long-run international financial architecture must countenance the possibility of instability and must build in means by which it can be prevented. A simple reliance on *laissez-faire* would be naive. While features of a liberal system will have a contribution to make, that contribution will be less than absolute. Nor can a system be regarded as permanent: as information technologies mature, the system will need to have an ongoing capacity for evolutionary change in architecture.

In the new long-run system the ultimate hegemonic authority (the "Authority") must have resources at its disposal and it is important that this need be recognized and means to supply such resources incorporated in the design of the long-run system. If the system is allowed by its institutional design to evolve, there is a need for the revenues of the authority to be able to develop as "quickly" as its burdens and this raises both political and economic questions of how the resources of the authority will grow.

V   "Managing" global aggregate demand?

The major built-in problem, which any long-run international financial architecture must confront, is macrofinancial. There exists a global constraint on infusions of aggregate demand obtained from running current surpluses with non-residents. A current surplus by one nation must be offset somewhere in the system, by a matching deficit on the part of another country. The problem exists if there is a bias of national preferences to run surpluses on current account. Such a policy bias is understandable for industrialized countries, which have to find injections of aggregate demand to offset full-employment leakages. In a key-currency system, this problem is solved by having the hegemon act as the *nth* country in the system and dissave internationally by any global shortfall in aggregate demand.

If the bias can be seen to exist and global aggregate demand falls significantly short of global productive capacity, there is benefit in finding a means to provide disincentives for net international saving.[23] There is, then, some benefit in considering including such powers in the post-transitional system. (Such disincentives would be unlikely to be applicable to developing or poor nations.)

Such a measure was contained in the proposal submitted to the Bretton Woods conference by the British delegation. Because of Keynes's major rôle in its formulation, the proposal was commonly called "the Keynes plan" (Grubel, 1984, p. 12). In fact, it relied heavily on contributions by leading economists in the United Kingdom as well as on Keynes's own contribution. Like nearly everyone else at Bretton Woods, members of the British delegation were dominated by the idea that depression or deep recession was an inevitable feature of a decentralized, capitalist system.[24] For this reason and because the authors were convinced that burdens of adjustment were unduly borne by dissaving/ debtor nations, they proposed a system by which nations which were running current surpluses would be penalized by paying the equivalent of "interest" on their accumulated stock of international saving (i.e. on their INW).

The mechanism of how this would be accomplished relies on the basic system proposed and does not warrant detailed description here.[25] However, the concept is valuable as a potential attribute of the new international financial architecture: see Chapter 10.

VI Conclusion

The situation described in Section II is perilously similar to conditions in 1919 and the decade of the 1920s. There was no sense then of the need for adequate global aggregate demand and no understanding of how incremental aggregate demand could be generated. Countries, instead, focused on national needs and, in effect, competed to gain the greatest amount of international saving possible as a means of protecting the meagre levels of domestic prosperity: in this, the major weapons were competitive devaluations and the imposition of tariffs and quotas on imports. This behaviour was aggravated by the understandable demands for reparations but, Keynes (1919) excepted, no-one connected the scale of reparations with an understanding of their macrofinancial implications in a depressed global economy. As a consequence, global allocative efficiency came to be sacrificed on the altar of *myopic nationalism*. The world is again, more than eighty years later, in a position in which there is no acknowledged hegemon capable of supplying the international public goods necessary for the existence of a prosperous global economy and no attention is being paid to the problems that follow from the exhaustion of the hegemon.

The political dimension is crucial. Notwithstanding the recent rancour over different attitudes towards the Iraqi war, US foreign policy has not been very considerate of the sensitivities of other nations for some years. Kissinger (2001) identifies the "arrogance, smugness and insensitivity" of recent US foreign policy and attributes this problem to the broad-based pre-eminence of the US power base and economic performance. The financial Achilles heel, so easily ignored in a capital in which no alternative to the dollar could be visualized, may have created an atmosphere in which other nations will be unwilling to let go an opportunity to pay back some of the irritation which they have suffered. It will be very easy for other nations to attribute the present problem to the fundamentally unsound global economic policies of the United States.[26] Such a political setting makes the task of avoiding a financial crisis that much more difficult.

In the twenty-first century, performance must be judged in terms of both global allocative efficiency *and* rates of capacity utilization. Short-run policy options are few and the situation requires multilateral input and co-operation. It is very probable that the immediate task of setting policies to address the short-run problems of crisis-avoidance will lay some of the groundwork for the larger but less urgent problem of a new world financial architecture. In particular, two fundamental constraints have to be considered: the imposition of much greater restrictions on the freedoms of trade and capital movements, have different implications for the short-run and the long-run. The argument for reversing the trend of recent years toward greater liberality is almost imperative in the short run but need not be taken as a given assumption for the long run, provided always that the new global macrofinancial architecture can create global aggregate demand.

Whether motivation by self-interest amounts inevitably to "myopic nationalism" can be disputed, but the need for a collective approach to crisis prevention seems, given the size of the imbalances, both urgent and necessary. Only by careful co-operation can major dislocation be avoided.

9
The Transition Problem

I Introduction

This chapter identifies some points to be considered when the problem of transition from the existing situation to one in which the threat of instability no longer looms over the international financial system. Ideally, transition must be confronted collectively by a group of nations to fashion a medium-run set of policies (and "rules") that will defuse the dangers of instability that derive from having a nearly exhausted dollar-reliant system. The transition must, then, be provided with a set of policies, principles and constraints (a system), which will facilitate those policies that the situation requires.[1] The crucial aspect is that the vulnerability of the US dollar to financial crisis must be eliminated. To accomplish this, the United States must *recognize the need for and be allowed to* run current surpluses without reducing the value of the dollar to the point that it would activate the international trigger.[2]

Once transition has been accomplished, it becomes possible to introduce a new long-run international macrofinancial architecture that does not have to concern itself with an immediate threat of instability. However, it is not possible to renounce the inherited, potentially unstable existing system and to convert immediately to a new long-run architecture. The latter will be path-dependent and will require international collaboration and agreement on principles.

II Preferential treatment for the exhausted hegemon?

One aspect of the exhaustion of a hegemon is that the erstwhile hegemon will have had both the reputation and the time to accumulate sufficient net liabilities to dig itself into a very deep hole. This aspect is clearly applicable when the United States has managed to achieve a negative INW equal to about 23 percent of its GDP p. 13. If the transition system is to allow the United States to accept the reduction in its level of living and gradually to rebuild its INW (or to slow the rate of "excess absorption") without generating a flight from the dollar, it is necessary to prevent the dollar from weakening excessively in foreign exchange markets. The inevitable expenditure-switch in the United States cannot, then, be achieved by a one-shot sweeping reduction in the dollar's rate of exchange.[3] In the same way, a too rapid but steady decline in the dollar over a long period would also be likely to trigger a financial crisis. A different expenditure-switch is needed. This goal can be achieved by renunciation of the level playing field in international transactions on current account during the medium-run transition period. Two possibilities are self-evident: either the United States can be permitted to subsidize exports or to levy special tariffs on imports of both goods and services. In practice a combination of the two would probably be necessary.

Recognition that protection and subsidy may be a necessary feature of the transitional system does *not* commit the post-transition system to the inclusion of some protectionism in the final, long-run international financial architecture

In trying to eliminate a large obligation (to reduce substantially the size of its negative INW) over a period of years, the United States will be in a position comparable to Germany's position in the 1920s when Germany needed to be allowed to export in order to fund the reparations payments instituted by the Treaty of Versailles. The United States must now be allowed to export to generate a surplus on current account. Some arrangement would undoubtedly require that a portion of the surplus would be earmarked for the reduction of non-resident claims.[4]

The combination of export subsidies and import duties may be an effective strategy always provided that a large required expenditure-reduction is imposed on the US economy. However, the subsidy/tariff measure need not match the estimated degree of dollar overvaluation. Such a rate of protection would be unnecessarily and unproductively high for many goods and services. This policy sacrifices the open global market system which the United States has pursued since the Second World War. It is testimony to the political sensitivity of such a strategy that, when the George W. Bush Administration imposed tariffs on imports of steel, the World Trade Organization found such tariffs to be illegal.[5] This episode provides a *prima facie* case for recognizing that a great deal of the liberal features of the system in force in the very early years of the twenty-first century, will have to be sacrificed in any global effort to institute change in net current-account flows without undergoing a financial crisis.

There exists one strategy which warrants mention even though the probability that the world (and/or the United States) would accept it, is small. The ecological practices and policies of the United States do not enjoy great global popularity. The per-capita consumption of petroleum is very high by world standards (even allowing for the country's larger distances and extreme climate). The effect of this indulgence was reinforced in 2000 when the United States withdrew from the Kyoto climate protocol (Joffe, 2001, 48). The United States commitment to cheap gasoline and its encouragement of the production of gas-guzzling automobiles, contrast sharply with the heavy taxes levied on gasoline in Europe and Asia and the willingness of residents in these regions to use smaller cars or to be made to pay for the privilege of driving at high speed.

A reduction in the consumption of fossil fuels, particularly petroleum, could serve a triple purpose. First, since petroleum imports are substantial, a heavy excise tax would constitute a major step to reducing imports. It therefore warrants serious consideration.[6] By raising the excise taxes on gasoline to, say, European levels, the country would also generate funds which could be used to reduce the chronic cash-flow deficit in the budget of the federal government. These funds could be used to purchase foreign exchange or to buy back foreign-owned financial assets, if intervention in foreign exchange markets were deemed desirable. Third, the measure would reduce some of the grounds for antagonism towards the United States because of its perceived lack of concern with the rate of emission of greenhouse gases.

Any tax on automotive use would be unpopular with the US electorate and would, therefore, be likely to invoke political agency (unfortunately, electorates seldom perceive the fact that revenues raised in one form are substitutes for alternative sources of revenues).[7] Further, a large part of the funds raised in this way might be needed to upgrade public transportation services in areas of dense population. The effect of such a tax on imports and exports of automobiles is unknowable but it would substantially reduce sales of gas-guzzling cars in the United States. More importantly, in context, there would be an inflationary effect as the measure increases transportation costs for nearly all goods and modes of passenger travel: this would be likely to require a greater nominal depreciation of the dollar.

Impediments to transactions (by residents and non-residents) on current account could help the transition process but so too could impediments to international movements of (financial and portfolio) capital. Just as a combination of tariffs and subsidies might be needed to reduce the deficit on current transactions, capital exports of both residents and non-residents would need to be regulated if an outflow of funds from the United States was to be achieved

Interference with the effectively perfect freedom of international movements of capital would also be a retreat from the *laissez-faire* ideal pursued by the United States and the United Kingdom. The details of any such tactic are difficult to imagine if only because interfering with flows of capital has not been very effective historically. The "raw material" is simply too fungible. Given the amount of (currently) easily encashable assets denominated in dollars and owned by non-residents of the United States, some impediment to capital withdrawals must be countenanced unless a heavy mixture of subsidies and tariffs on current transactions is tolerated. A second possible means of allowing freedom of private dollar-denominated capital movements involves foreign governments taking over (through purchase) the dollar-denominated assets of their residents. Such a policy would require the foreign governments to co-operate with the United States in effecting an efficient transition by accepting long-term assets. The obligations of the United States would be denominated in foreign exchange and this step would need to be accomplished prior to any serious depreciation of the dollar. Having debts denominated in foreign currencies eliminates the possibility of reducing the real value of the obligations by a bout of domestic inflation.

Whatever mix of policies can be agreed upon, it is inevitable that the reliance of the system of international involvement on *laissez-faire* will be temporarily destroyed.[8]

To institute a series of unilateral measures without obtaining (unwilling) agreement first, would be pointless. The opportunities for counter-action by the creditor nations is simply too great. One of the[9] premises of balance-of-payments adjustment by a hegemon is that its liabilities to foreign governments, as opposed to private parties, is that the governments would be prepared to sacrifice their short-run interests in order to reduce the possible degree of dislocation. High-handed unilateral capital controls would be likely to sacrifice governmental support.

Two possibilities warrant mention as means of lengthening the time over which the United States could reduce its rate of international dissaving to some tolerable level and of reducing the rate of depreciation of the dollar. The first is that the United States agree to buy private financial dollar-denominated portfolio capital with a ten-year bond denominated in foreign exchange. This measure would substantially reduce the ease of encashability of the liabilities. Foreign markets could allow the bonds to find their own levels abroad. During the length of life of the bonds, the United States could accumulate foreign-exchange funds and, possibly, buy some bonds back if the purchase appeared attractive. The second schema would have foreign governments purchase the liabilities of their citizens at their market value and that the US government agree to convert those liabilities to bonds denominated in the currencies of the owning foreign governments.[10] An arrangement of either kind, if it could be negotiated, would allow a much longer time span for the United States to reduce its rate of international dissaving to a tolerable level and, therefore, reduce the macrofinancial disruption which the global economy would face.

The scenarios contemplated in this chapter emphasize the tentativeness of suggestions about the transitional architecture. Everything depends on the negotiations and the ability of the negotiators to prevent leaks that would, in practice, trigger a crisis in foreign-exchange markets. In such negotiations, the US delegates would have to have their hats in their hands since the only bargaining chip which they would have is the potential reduction of the degree of disruption in the global economy and that would be a difficult argument to make to electorates in both creditor and debtor nations (Galbraith, 2000).

The description of some of the possibilities facing those who would bear the responsibility for avoiding a very hard landing *for the global economy* echoes Adelman's (2000) comment that "the political forces making for globalization [and *laissez-faire*] are too strong to put the genie back in the bottle". While recognizing the inevitable difficulties finding a means by which the world can escape with only meagre damage, the actuality of crisis and a very hard landing should weaken those forces that oppose "putting the genie back in the bottle." The essential problem then becomes one foreseen on a broader canvas by Pryor (2002, p. 367):

> Many of the dangers that I foresee are based on the hidden assumption that the policy steps necessary to alleviate emerging economic problems will either not be taken or will prove ineffective, either in design or implementation. I believe this assumption to be realistic: In part, this is because the complexity of these emerging problems does not permit them to be explained in a manner simple enough to become vital political issues.

10
A Proposed Agenda for Redesign

I Introduction

This chapter offers a broad-brush proposal for the development of an architecture for the international financial system in the post-transition period. The approach broadens the range of the concerns of the system to include all of the different components of the international flows of funds and, therefore, of international economic involvement.[1] Independently of the reliance on managed global macrofinancial policies in the transitional system, the proposal given here rejects a purely *laissez-faire* structure and it also rejects a world-wide monolithic system. Ultimately, the design of such a large and complex undertaking must involve not only political feasibility or acceptance but it will also require a wide range of specialist expertise.

The purpose of the proposal is less ambitious than it may seem. Any conference charged with the creation of an efficient post-transition system will need to have some basis for the original discussions: this proposal presents one possible point of departure. In accordance with the theme of this monograph, it is important that conferees manage to approach their very intricate task free of any philosophic adherence to lore inherited from introductory lectures on neoclassical models of international economics. It is particularly important that the existence of a comfortable system with a strong inherent tendency to regain equilibrium after a shock, be rejected and that the interaction of the multiple dimensions of international involvement be confronted.[2]

The proposal to be put forward addresses identified sources of stability inefficiency while recognizing the advantages of measures which promote allocative efficiency. It rests on seven basic premises. These must be laid out before the proposed structure of the replacement international financial system can be described.

The premises are:

(1) The greater are the volume and the rate of growth of inter-currency (international) macrofinancial activity to be supported, the greater is the created stress on the hegemonic system likely to be;

(2) It seems probable that agreement on intricate points can be realized more easily in smaller groups, that is, regions;

(3) Greater freedom of international movements of goods and services and capital is inherently desirable but not absolutely so;

(4) Left to the countries' own devices, the sum of the current account targets of the n independent countries (or currency regions)[3] in the world will tend to be positive ($\Sigma(X - M)^*_n > 0$);

(5) Following from the previous premise, the system must be able to create international liquidity so that nations can increase their international reserves without reducing global aggregate demand;

(6) An effective international financial architecture must have the authority to preclude chronic "borrowed absorption (or borrowed consumption)" by either industrialized or emerging countries so that the system must be capable of imposing some discipline on the international macrofinancial conduct of ostensibly independent nations;

(7) The system shall recognize the need to assist emerging economies. Developing countries face different problems from industrialized countries, a fact recognized when the Generalized System of Preferences was introduced in the early 1970s (Murray, 1973) and should therefore be distinguished in any reformulation of the "rules" of international economic involvement. The emphasis on aiding emerging economies is a matter of ethical principle. It is also important that such national economies avoid financial crises brought on by excessively deep involvement in the global financial system. Developing countries offer a convenient outlet for expanding [global] aggregate demand through unilateral transfers (Acheson, 1944).[4] The latter attribute may prove useful to the system in creating international liquidity.

Section II of this chapter will consist mainly of a description of the proposed institutional architecture and of the way in which the system is expected to work.[5] It is important to stress the need for the system to be capable of evolving as technological and political factors change the environment in which international payments take place. Some means of ensuring recognition of the need to review the organizational structure of the system periodically can be included in the proposal but the officers of the superhegemon must not allow such clauses to lapse into disuse. Section III fills in some structural detail of the proposal and identifies those facets which will require detailed consideration by people with operational experience in particular activities. Section IV puts the proposal into perspective.

II A multi-regional system of global finance

The proposal is developed in terms of three geographically large regions, each with its own "subhegemon."[6] The activities of these regional subhegemons will be co-ordinated by a superhegemon (the "Authority"). Provided that the procedures and regulations of the regional subhegemons do not clash with or otherwise impede the operations of the Authority, the members of a region will be free to determine their own intra-regional procedures. The two layers of the hegemonic system interact closely. In addition, the presidents of the individual subhegemons will be *ex-officio* members of the executive committee of the Authority.

The emphasis on internal consistency between the multiple genera of international macrofinancial activities requires that the Authority and the subhegemons must oversee some responsibilities currently assigned to the key-currency nation, to the WTO, and the IMF. This breadth of coverage follows from the great emphasis to be placed on the stability of international macrofinancial involvement: conditions governing international trade; direct investments and regulation of the international financial sector:[7] the resilience of financial firms; questions of control of portfolio capital movements by private entities and the stability of the international financial system. Clearly, the operational aspects of some of these responsibilities can be spun off to fairly, but less-than-completely autonomous affiliates. For example, the WTO would be quasi-independent, being virtually independent as far as phenomena affecting international trade are concerned except and unless such phenomena also affect the resilience of the international financial system. The WTO will, however, constitute an affiliate of the Authority so that trade matters do not escape the domain of the institution responsible for ensuring that the global system of international economic involvement works effectively.[8] The president of the WTO would be a non-voting member of the executive committee of the Authority. Similar arrangements can be made with other specialist bodies (except for the IMF whose responsibilities and assets and liabilities will be transferred to the Authority).[9]

It is useful to begin by describing the functioning of the proposed system and to describe its organizational structure. Countries will be members of regional areas under a regional authority, whose responsibilities will closely resemble, at the regional level, those of the [global] Authority. The Authority and each regional "subhegemon" will provide a unit of account, which will be the numeraire of its assets and liabilities. The rate of exchange of the currencies of member nations (or currency blocs) of a region will be defined in the relevant subhegemon's unit of account. International reserves will also be held with the subhegemon so that they are defined in the regional unit of account.[10] In turn, the subhegemon will have assets and liabilities lodged in the Authority and defined in terms of the Authority's unit of account. The regional sub-hegemon will extend short-term balance-of-payments accommodations to its members: these assets (liabilities of member countries) will also be defined in the unit of account of the subhegemon. The activities of the regional hegemon are financed by the earnings of its assets which derive from the basic subscription levied on members on entry and any current income derived from balance-of-payments loans and any revenue raised by taxes imposed on surplus nations (see Chapter 8). The Authority will also need its own assets to serve as a source of income. The Authority will, therefore, be provided with 50 percent of the basic subscription of national members (at the expense of subhegemons). It will also earn money on any loans made to subhegemons and from taxes imposed on surplus regions.

The major policy instrument of the Authority and its subhegemons is their ability to affect rates of exchange. There will exist specified rates of exchange (fixed in the short run) among the four units of account. Countries' currencies are defined in terms of their subhegemon's unit of account but can be changed by application to the subhegemon, which can endorse or deny the new proposed rate or, presumably, strike some common ground between the extremes. The mechanism by which rates of exchange are changed between currencies of members of the same region is, therefore fairly straightforward.

The determination of the rate of exchange of a currency (of A1 – Country 1 in region A) with another national currency belonging to B2: (the currency of Country 2 of region B) involves the product of four rates. The rate of exchange of currency A1 with its subhegemon's unit of account is multiplied by the rate of exchange between the sub-hegemon's unit of account with the Authority to get the currency's value in the unit of account of the Authority. This in turn is multiplied by the rate of exchange of B2's currency with the Authority to yield the rate of exchange between the two national currencies. Thus, intervening between two national currencies, whose rates of exchange may be affected by their local subhegemon, is a rate of exchange between two supernational institutions. This rate can be changed by the executive committee of the Authority. This power will be constrained as listed:

(1) The Authority will only be able to change a rate between two units of account by majority vote of its Executive Committee which comprises the president and vice-president of the Authority and the three presidents of the three regional subhegemons.[11]

(2) To appreciate a unit of account, a region must have been in surplus on current account for two years or for one year with a surplus in excess of 3 percent of gross regional domestic product. The Authority (or the president of another region) can propose an appreciation of a region's unit of account.

(3) The change shall not exceed a change of 0.5 percent per meeting. If meetings are held monthly, a national currency's rate of exchange can change by slightly more than 6 percent over a year.

Because of lags in obtaining information and the general inexactness of macrofinancial information, the conditions to warrant changes in rates of exchange will be based on a one-year lag and will require a surplus or a deficit to exceed 1 percent of gross regional product. Thus a change in January 2000, would be sanctioned by consecutive surpluses or deficits for the 8 quarters beginning in the first quarter of 1997 and ending in the fourth quarter of 1998.

This mechanism allows the Authority to confront chronic weaknesses or strength in the price competitiveness of a region. Because the initiative is in the hands of the authorities, this schema eliminates two of the great weaknesses of the Bretton Woods system – the IMF had to wait for a country to come to it for help and had no control over surplus nations. This schema allows the rates of exchange of countries within a specified region to appreciate against countries in other regions and would tend, over time, to reduce the region's surplus. A country running a deficit in a surplus region would have its currency strengthened against nations in the two other regions. However it would lie within the power of such a country to reduce the strength of its currency (subject to veto by its local subhegemon if it did not meet the criteria for depreciation – continuing deficits for two years). This national currency would be able to depreciate against its subhegemon's unit of account at just over 6 percent per annum (i.e. to hold steady in the short term, vis-à-vis foreign currencies in a different region).[12] With the approval of the Authority, the national currency could depreciate against national currencies in other regions by over 12 percent *per annum*. However, this rate of change could be reduced if the subhegemon deemed a rate of 12 percent *per annum* to be excessive and the exchange rate between the national currency and the subhegemon's unit of account would be allowed to offset the change between the two units of account. The advantage of having an incremental rate of change in nominal values is that it would allow the reallocation of resources required by the adjustment to be carried out smoothly.

The second policy weapon in the Authority's arsenal (and, by extension, in the arsenals of regional subhegemons) is the imposition of taxes on strings of current surpluses. This process, *supranational fiscal policy*, is described briefly in Chapter 8. Instead of confronting chronic international saving or dissaving at the national level, supranational fiscal policy addresses an insufficiency (or an excess) of global aggregate demand. Regions which have run current surpluses for more than 8 quarters in the immediate past can be taxed on their accumulation of INW.[13] This will discourage the accumulation of liquid liabilities at the regional level. The rate of tax would be variable depending on the degree of shortfall of global demand from global capacity. The way in which the regional subhegemon addresses the problem internally is intraregional. The subhegemon could be susceptible to policy suggestions by the Authority if the internal tax rate were deemed inadequate.

The remaining important task of the Authority is to create international liquidity as the system needs it. On a small scale, this could be done by balance-of-payments accommodation loans but the supply of funds for this purpose is finite. There are several ways in which this can be done but none is perfect. The obvious example would be to seek to create a mechanism similar to that put forward in the "Keynes Plan" (see Chapter 8 and Davidson, 1992–93). Using the organizational structure outlined here, another way would be for the Authority to appreciate its unit of account vis-à-vis those of the regions so that the value of all regional assets denominated in the Authority's unit of acount would increase in value in regional units of account and national currencies. The regional subhegemons could pass these gains on to member nations by appreciating their own units of account in terms of national currencies. In practical terms and depending on the composition of a nation's international reserves, this is more or less equivalent to a fiat increase in the price of gold. This procedure has the disadvantage that, unless modified, the appreciation of the regional units of account would increase the debt of a nation which has a balance-of-payments line of credit in its own national currency. Modification to eliminate the additional burden would be a simple matter.

This "broad-brush" system is not designed to operate a sensitive system but, rather, to avoid serious departures from tranquillity. So-called "fine tuning" is not feasible. In concrete terms, the system is designed to accomplish three things. The first is to maintain an adequate level of global aggregate demand and to reduce, over time, disparities in any shortfall of demand among regions. Second, the system will prevent events similar to the financial crisis in Bangkok in 1997 and reduce the probability of other, more isolated national crises both by exercising the power of the Authority and the subhegemons to intervene, under predetermined conditions, in the macrofinancial economies of members. Third, it will preclude the meltdown of an important world currency. All three functions involve the provision of international public goods on a more positive level than can take place in the existing dollar-reliant system.

The proposed system could be seen as implying reliance on a set of rules. The system must allow for the exercise of discretion by the executive committee of the Authority since there is always the possibility that exceptional circumstances will require a more flexible response. The system also implies the limited renunciation of the independence of nation states (e.g. a national economy can be "taxed" by the Authority or a currency can be appreciated or depreciated at slow rates by the (four) supranational institutions). This renunciation is made necessary by the much higher degree of international economic involvement in a globalized world and the new ways in which nation states interlock on many fronts (Langhorne, 2001, ch. 4).

III   Added detail

There exist details about the proposal outlined in the previous section, which can usefully be fleshed out.

Membership   Independent nations may prefer not to become members of an organization which has some potentially restrictive powers. Others might not consider themselves to be ready for membership in the global macrofinancial economy given the sophistication, which membership would require. Still others might choose not to be members for political reasons. Membership in the IMF was, in its early years, very large perhaps because membership was seen as offering advantages.[14] In 1955, the Fund had 58 members. *Inter alia*, membership offers the privilege of being able to hold reserves in a subhegemon's unit of account.

There is no need that all nations be members of regions. Some that are not easily included in a region, for geographic or cultural reasons, could have a special membership with the Authority, which would serve as a source of balance-of-payments accommodation loans. The major, indus-trialized nations and the industrializing nations would be members in part because they would expect the gain from membership to be worth the cost in terms of the independence surrendered. The major non-members would probably be the backward nations, largely identified in Boote and Thugge (1997) and those nations whose main reason for not joining, was political.

The most important possibility is that some nations would feel that the region to which they were allotted did not adequately represent them either geographically or culturally. The three regions can be seen as comprising: East Asia including some related APEC countries such as Australia and New Zealand; Europe and Africa; and the Western Hemisphere. This leaves, problems of coverage in Asian Russia and in the associated independent states, India, the major Asian Islamic coun-tries (from Pakistan in the east to Syria in the west) and the middle east-ern nations such as Israel, Jordan, Lebanon and Palestine. The Islamic nations would be capable of forming their own region or subregion with a headquarters in Bahrein.

The costs of a regional approach   It is important that any tendency by firms or national policies to discriminate among regions should be minimized. There is a possible danger that the three-region structure proposed earlier in this chapter, could contribute to such discrimina-tion. Precluding discrimination in current transactions, would be a responsibility of the WTO: for capital account transactions, including direct investments, the Authority would be responsible. There would exist what may be termed "natural" sources of discrimination in that a country within a region would face less uncertainty in transactions with a counterpart in the same region in terms of both exchange rates and cultural similarities.[15] Probably greater proximity within a region would tend to lower relative transportation costs on intra-regional exports and imports of goods and services.

Given the three identified sources of discrimination, only the greater financial uncertainty in "foreign regions" is specific to the proposal. There is, in fact, nothing that suggests that unequal financial uncer-tainty is a cost of the proposed system. The discrimination could be seen as a net gain in the sense that the financial uncertainty will be reduced within the region rather than increased for transactions with entities in "foreign regions".

Kobrin (1995) was concerned mainly with the creation, or enlarge-ment, of regional blocs within what was ostensibly a globalized system and the effects of such developments on global allocative efficiency.

There is some likelihood that currency blocs might form more easily given the regional construct of the proposal. Kobrin saw the spread of multinational corporations through direct investments and the transfer of proprietary technology among countries as helping to reduce any derivative inefficiencies in the globalized system. These gains would be reinforced by the transfer of improvements in managerial knowhow and the transfer of greater financial sophistication. In this, he offered a refreshing awareness of the multiple interlinked dimensions of international economic involvement.

The proposal is careful to define regions, which would contain a wide range of stages of development among members. Thus, poor countries in one region will still have access to more affluent trading partners in the same region. An inherited linkage with markets in a foreign region could conceivably be rendered less effective by new competitors under the proposed regional system. This danger also applies to the growth of regional blocs as the experience of Australia and New Zealand after British entry into the European Union, demonstrates.

IV   Conclusion

Two approaches must be excluded in both the transitional architecture and in the original long-term replacement architecture: complete reliance on full globalization, in which there is no discrimination among countries in the degree of involvement in the globalized system is permitted; and complete *laissez-faire*.[16] In the fullness of time, it may be possible for the system to evolve to increase the degree to which these approaches are utilized. What must be done is for recognition of the limitations of system management, particularly as the limitations affect the proposal that the idea presented first on the original Keynes Plan or what is termed here "supranational fiscal policy,"[17] be incorporated in the long-run system. In addition to problems of effective economic administration, the potential political difficulties may well prove insuperable.

The need of the long-run architecture for capacity to evolve is paramount. Changes in technology and in the ability of financial institutions (such as the development of hedge funds) to operate in foreign markets will continue to require that unsophisticated countries either adapt their economies to adjust to innovations in the global economy or shun full involvement in globalization. As information technologies mature, ongoing evolutionary change in the international financial architecture will prove necessary.

The idea of supranational fiscal policy recalls some of the more elaborate ideas of national fiscal policy. While data are much more accurate and much more detailed than in the 1930s, they are neither so accurate nor so reliable that they will form a reasonable basis for what came at one time to be called "fine tuning." What follows are some suggestions about limitations on the use of the mechanism.

Two limits should be recognized. The first derives from the margin for error in the data and suggests that the computation of the base should be net international saving in excess of 1 percent of GDP. The second concerns the duration of the base. Rather than use an accumulated stock measure, it will be more efficient to define the base in terms of a five-year period of time over which cumulative international dissaving (in excess of 1 percent of GDP) can be computed. The period would allow one full year for gathering the data and revising it so that the computation of the base in year t would use data $t-2$ through $t-6$.

Unilateral transfers (foreign aid) are usually included in the definition of the current account but where a transfer is provided in terms of a loan at a subsidized rate of interest, the value of the loan should be included in unilateral transfers for the purpose of computing the tax base.

The more serious the shortfall in global aggregate demand, the higher will the tax rate be. A similar latitude can be afforded to the taxing authority in terms of the rate of international saving of the country: the greater the excess over GDP, the higher the rate of tax to be imposed.

This exploratory proposal for a long-term international financial architecture can serve only as a basis for a first discussion. Probably the most important requirements of the new architecture are that:

(1) The conferees be avowedly concerned with the public (global) good rather than with narrow economic gain or self-aggrandisemen;
(2) that the transitional architecture have been a success;
(3) that the system have some built-in capacity for evolution as well as confronting both the possibilities of inadequate global aggregate demand and financial instability.

Part V
Concluding Assessment

11
The Grim Prospect
Ahead

I Introduction

This volume has painted a very foreboding picture. In this, it lives up to Carlyle's description of economics as a "dismal science."

The level of danger of and the necessary degree of concern for potential economic breakdown was seen as negligible in the "Preface" to the *Report* of the US Trade Deficit Review Commission (2000, p. ix–x):[1]

> Some witnesses believe that the most likely scenario is that reasonable adjustments in the exchange value of the dollar, together with economic recovery abroad will produce a "soft landing". In this case, the trade deficit comes down substantially in a normal adjustment process that would not generate significant adverse effects on the United States. Both American and foreign investors thus benefit. Indeed, this has been our experience in recent decades. This is a view that we share.

This benign summary of the Commission's findings followed the *Report's* main thrust with its failure to countenance the effect of continued current deficits on financial markets. Now, with three years more experience of ever higher annual amounts of international dissaving and a ratio of international dissaving to GDP of 4.8 percent in 2002, the *Economic Report of the President 2003*, (p. 63) concluded its brief consideration of the international position with:

> In the end, the key determinant of the sustainability of the U.S. international debt position is continued confidence in the economic policies of the United States. As long as the United States pursues its current market-oriented, pro-growth policies, there is no reason to

believe that the current account deficit represents a problem for continued economic growth.

Presumably, Mann's (1999) methodology notwithstanding, the United States is seen to "grow itself out of its deficit." But the necessary reduction in US absorption will, by itself, engender a recession. Given the lack of recognition of the basic problem by the authorities in the major nations, it would be a fervent optimist who would expect that the dollar can escape serious strain in international financial markets.

The monograph has stressed the importance for policymakers and analysts to be capable of casting off what has been taught and accepted for a lifetime.[2] Between the two world wars, the belief of those who harked back to the nineteenth century and the first decade of the twentieth century, was *the automaticity of full employment* without great reliance on proactive policies.[3] At the beginning of the twenty-first century, policymakers and analysts must realize that the resilience of the dollar has been used up in the course of almost sixty years as the macrofinancial (and the military) hegemon. In recent years, institutional evolution has made US liabilities both large and, predominantly, very easily encashable into the (private) owners' functional currency (Tables 5.1 and 5.2). The dollar is now prey to substantial depreciation and threatened with crisis.[4]

There is a second way of looking at the existing problem, which may be useful. A market system works effectively provided that there exists resilience in the economy. This resilience implies some organization capable of providing needed "public goods." The importance of the supply of (domestic) "macrofinancial public goods" is not stressed or explicitly identified in analyses that assume the existence of a natural tendency to return to the long-run growth path. The possibility that the resilience of the system can be run down if and/or when the supplying organization weakens, is not confronted.[5] The supply of international public goods is the duty of the hegemon. The great international wealth of the United States in 1945 was the source of resilience for the world economy. It has been used up.

According to this theory, the supply of international public goods (economic resilience) has the characteristics of a stock that can be "used up" over time as it contributes to the efficiency of the flow system.[6] Attention must be paid to ensuring that the stock of reserves is replenished (by flows) and, if need be, husbanded. This approach may help to explain the successes of increased reliance on decentralized (*laissez-faire*) economic systems in the United Kingdom and the United States in the late 1970s and early 1980s (under Prime Minister Thatcher and

President Reagan): the dollar had not then lost its power to provide resilience to the global economy. The outgrowth of the adoption of a more *laissez-faire* system contributed importantly to the globalization process and laid the basis for current problems. Yergin and Stanislaus (1998) suggest that the economic history of the years since the Second World War is largely based on the recognition that markets are more efficient than a system with heavy governmental interference and control. The danger with this philosophy is that the implications of using-up the stock of global resilience are not recognized so that the greater efficiency of *laissez-faire* may have a finite life.

II How we got here

While the preceding section offers an explanation of how the global macrofinancial system reached its current vulnerability, the explanation involves a rarified level of abstraction. This section provides a similar retrospective at a more pragmatic and mundane level.

There exist six major and inter-related explanations of the seeming lack of concern by the financial authorities in Washington with the ever-increasing net indebtedness to foreign holders of dollar-denominated assets: four are financial/economic and two predominantly political. Since the acceptance of the state of affairs requires only passive acceptance by other major nations, there is little value in attempting to explain this behavior, which was beneficial to these nations (by increasing global demand) as well as by increasing the price-competitiveness of their economies.

First is the conscientious awareness by the US Treasury and the Federal Reserve System of the country's leadership responsibilities towards the global economy. Such behavior prevents the collective economies of foreign countries sinking more deeply into recession with the inevitable negative feedbacks on the US economy.[7] Lack of concern with the United States running current deficits may have become built-in in Washington because of the many years when the net international investment position of the United States was so strong. Even during the concern with the problem of the resilience of the system at the end of the 1960s, the United States was saving internationally while it was losing reserves. The rate of acquisition of foreign assets, largely through foreign direct investment, simply exceeded the rate of international saving and reduced the US reserve position.[8]

Second, the attraction of foreign savings to the United States would be seen as warranted if the return on that capital exceeded the return available elsewhere. Received wisdom suggested that a system of free markets contributes to maximizing world income. This philosophy is also compatible with the belief that, the expansion of the US economy in the 1990s needed to attract capital from abroad and did so because the US saving rate was inadequate for the ongoing capital formation in the country. It followed that the foreign saving was put to better (global) use in the United States than in its home country. The zero household savings rate in the United States was ignored in Washington (Godley, 1999) (Velde, 1999).

The third reason must be the ingrained failure of mainstream economists to entertain the idea of financial instability emanating from a market-driven system without identifiable rigidities such as a gold standard or fixed rates of exchange. When major instabilities occur, they tend ultimately to become food for thought for economic historians. If the market system is self-balancing, no set of proactive policies is needed. This belief is more likely to hold for a small country than for the financial leader. A powerful leader can "use" its apparent strength to incur a huge measure of indebtedness before foreign creditors begin to worry over the possibility that a depreciation of the currency of denomination will impair the value of their investments.

A fourth, more rational belief is that the US economy performed so well in the last five or six years of the twentieth century that the current-account deficit was too small an item (as a percentage of total output) to warrant interference with the ongoing prosperity. It should be noted here that the deficits on current accounts did not increase to current proportions until 1999 when the current deficit (and the necessary increase in indebtedness) reached $344 billion. Economists do not immediately identify the full implications of new phenomena.[9] These four explanations provide, individually and/or collectively, a rationale for analytic neglect and a hands-off policy by the US authorities. They do not explain the current neglect: for that we have to rely on the inherited worldview and the two political reasons.

The two political reasons are only indirectly related to the financial/economic basis of the situation. In the present situation, complete passivity can be reconciled with a belief that there is no alternative to continued reliance on the US dollar as the global reference currency. To recognize the exhaustion of the dollar would be to admit the need for an international conference *among equals* and the mood in Washington did not and does not, after more than fifty years, lend itself to such an admission. This continuing "delusion of grandeur" has its historical precedent in the United Kingdom after the First World War.

A sixth explanation is of a different genus than the first five. Taking steps to reduce the strength of the dollar and to reduce the deficit on current transactions would inflict "economic pain" on the US economy.[10] As explained in Chapter 3, the reduction of a current deficit involves the implementation of two separate measures. To make US-made goods more competitive in world markets requires depreciation of the dollar (or equivalent). The release of domestic factors of production to supply foreign countries with exports and to substitute local products for imports requires a reduction in the amount of goods and services used up (absorbed) by the US economy. The depreciation will increase the cost of imports and expose the US economy to inflationary forces. Even in the absence of any instability in foreign exchange markets (so that a soft landing could, in principle, be engineered by a gradual weakening of the dollar), the US economy would need a large dose of higher taxes (preferably on consumers and therefore largely on rich consumers), lower high standards of living, and the provision of fewer governmental services. These circumstances provide a fertile setting for "political agency" (pp. 144–5, 148–9). Given the current high level of political antagonisms in Washington, DC, the problem of political agency may be expected to continue despite recognition of the depth of the economic problems.[11]

These six reasons for a lack of concern with the decline in the US INW hang together: it is impossible to assess their relative importance.

III   The problem is "built-in"

The present international financial system allows rates of exchange between (pairs of) currencies to adjust to the net flow of funds. This has important implications for the dollar's weakening. When foreign capital flows into the United States, the transfer of funds strengthens the dollar and reduces the price-competitiveness of the US economy.[12] In this way, the desire of non-residents to acquire US assets tends to finance itself since the strengthening of the dollar improves the price-competitiveness of the economies of the capital exporters. In addition, the relatively high rate of saving in those economies is likely to generate the necessary excess capacity to run a current surplus. Non-residents force the US economy to dissave by strengthening the dollar and making the US balance on goods and services decrease. If the United States takes its ability to finance the large amount of new "indebtedness" for granted, this will allow the country to disregard the problems until their very severity intrudes into the lack of concern.

The cost of indebtedness seems not to aggravate the decline in the US INW. Foreign investors have earned relatively small returns on financial assets in recent years. This low rate of return is responsible for the US balance on income on international assets not turning negative until 2002 (Table 3.2) even though the US INW turned negative in 1983 (Table 5.3). The *Economic Report of the President, 2003* (pp. 59–63) made much of the fact that the net income on international assets was still positive in 2001 and used the data to warrant a lack of concern with the large and rising INW (Godley and Izurieta, 2002).

IV   Recent initiatives

In the fall of 2003, the Bush Administration took some initiatives which had balance-of-payments implications. Negotiators addressed the severe undervaluation of both (Mainland) China and Japan and urged a strengthening of their currencies – preferably by the institution of a free float so that the exchange rate was determined by spontaenous flows of funds. While this initiative had the right direction, it was very narrow and did not address the broader problem. The protective tariffs on steel have been withdrawn because the WTO defined them as illegal and opened up the possibility of legitimate discrimination against US exports.

V   The long run

Langhorne (2001) describes the way in which globalization has sired the new institutional setting in which both international economic involvement and international (political) relations, to mention only two spheres of international interaction, are conducted. He attributes much of this development to the new technologies of communication. Langhorne's canvas is necessarily broader than that of this monograph but he sees globalization in its many dimensions continuing to require the generation of a new wave of procedural and institutional evolution in the world.[12] Langhorne (2001, p. 141) is on the same wavelength as this monograph when he expresses concern with both the lack of "machinery" to manage the new institutional setting and with the consequent threat of chaos. Such chaos will appear if policymakers in global organizations and national governments do not develop some means by which the new capabilities of individuals and groups can be "managed." The possibility of chaos "needs to be high on the agenda of global economic and financial organizations, national governments and, above all, the markets themselves." This monograph is essentially concerned with the difficulty of getting the problem of latent international financial collapse on the agenda of any supranational institution or of any major national government. The root of this stress is the dissonance between technology's impact on the required speed of institutional change and the inevitable desire of humans to hark back to the old approaches and solutions that accompanied national independence, and to ignore the implications of the new order.

The question is whether the nations of the world can unite to prevent the retrogression away from the globalized world that crisis will encourage. International financial crisis is only one of several sources of stress but it is probably the most imminent and the most devastating.

Notes

1 The Purpose and Three Propositions

1. The close, "contagious" interdependence between the two dimensions requires that the two sectors be analyzed jointly and the term "macrofinancial" has been coined to convey this close interdependence and to avoid the tendency in economic analysis to analyze the real and financial dimensions separately. See Chapter 5, pp. 108–10.

2. There exists no easily identifiable replacement for the US dollar as the key currency. While the euro is often thought of as a potential global key currency, the currency is not yet well enough established to perform such a task, and will not be, pending the successful accession to "Euroland" of ten new members from eastern Europe as well as, possibly, Denmark, Sweden and the United Kingdom. This assertion recognizes the potential stress put on a currency area when its "monetary mass" is increased by a substantial percentage (Mundell, 2003) and by any disparity between the sophistication of the macrofinancial systems of the new member nations and the existing members.

3. Traditional notation has seen the key-currency nation as the nth nation and the rest of the world as $n - 1$ nations. Of course, some currencies have key currency attributes: the French franc (and now the euro) for the Communeuté Financière Africaine (c.f.a.) franc area and sterling for the sterling area in the early years after the Second World War.

4. This neglect of a fundamental disequilibrium recalls the savings-and-loan débacle in the United States in the 1980s (White, 1991) in which an unsustainable macrofinancial condition was allowed to go on long enough to cause widespread collapse of thrift institutions.

5. The analysis must involve both stocks (of assets and liabilities) and flows of debits and credits. A preponderant part of economic analysis is defined in terms of flows. A flow analysis which disregards the implications of finite stocks is not acceptable.

6. Here the focus of this monograph parallels the concerns of Dunning (2003), which addresses the need for the world to ensure that the potential benefits of globalization are achieved.

7. Chapter 3 shows that the elimination of current deficits (and the international dissaving which they represent) requires both a weakening of the dollar and a restriction of US domestic aggregate demand, which, in the context of a deficit of about 4 percent of GDP, would almost certainly inflict a recession on both the US and the global economy.

8. In 2002, the dollar weakened substantially against the European currencies at the same time that the US economy slowed perceptibly. The deficit on current account (a first measure of the decrease in the dollar's negative net asset position) increased in that year both absolutely (in dollars) and relative to US GDP. The deficit also increased in 2003. However, current account imbalances have

historically adjusted to changes in the values of their major determinants only with a substantial lag.

9. Current transactions are distinguished from dealings in things which have lasting value, capital assets and liabilities. Of course, capital goods and consumer durables confound the simplicity of the distinction but most analyzes neglect the length of life of some goods, which change hands.

10. As will become clear, "claims" must include ownership of physical assets within a country as well as financial claims.

11. See the Appendix to this chapter, note 10.

12. In sequence, Secretaries Robert Rubin, Lawrence Summers and Paul O'Neill. The incumbent in the second half of the Bush Administration, Secretary Snow, announced unreserved support of the strong dollar policy during his confirmation hearings in February 2003. *The Economic Report of the President* (2003, pp. 59–63) shows no concern with either the negative stock or the flow.

13. "My own guess is that it will eventually simmer down because our propensity to import will continue to decline and eventually match the rest of the world. ... but I have been wrong on this for years. I have been waiting ... I expect to be waiting five years from now" Joint Economic Committee, *Proceedings* (November 13, 2002, p. 15). It should be noted, however, that this question of chronic deficits is the responsibility of the US Treasury and not of the Board of Governors of the Federal Reserve System.

14. Note that this comment does not address its potential implications.

15. As the string of deficits continues, the probability of depreciation will be expected to increase as will the expected magnitude of the depreciation itself.

16. As a parallel, one could note that a major sale of assets in 1931 was the final blow that forced the United Kingdom off the gold standard: the sale of £6 million late on a Saturday morning in New York by the Bank of France, which, until that time, had been supportive of British efforts to maintain the redemption of sterling in gold. The British government renounced the gold standard on the following day (Yeager, 1966, p. 297).

17. Cf. the preface to Keynes (1936, p. viii): "The difficulty lies, not in the new ideas, but in escaping from the old ones ... ." Here the problem is the built-in idea that the United States is financially invulnerable, which professional economists have taken as an item of faith for over fifty years. The proof of Keynes's observation is, in context, the difficulty that British policymakers had in recognizing the exhaustion of British capability to continue as hegemon in the years after the First World War (see pp. 17–19). There is no reason to suppose that the political appointees and senior civil servants in the United States are any more clear-sighted or any more willing to renounce their influence than their British counterparts in an earlier era.
This problem can be seen as a *leitmotif* for how the global economy got into its present predicament.

18. The term "dollar" will be taken here and throughout the monograph, to mean the US dollar and is the unit of measurement employed in the data in the absence of express identification of a different currency.

19. "Adjustment" to an imbalance on international transactions implies more than finding financing for a current deficit. It also implies the reallocation of resources and the reduction or elevation in living standards compatible with the elimination of any imbalance on current account.

20. Crockett's (1997) paper lays the basis for an understanding of the vulnerability of the real sector to instability in the financial sector. When the financial sector's international position is severely overextended, the reverse also holds and a deep recession can trigger a financial crisis.

21. The baht crisis in Thailand in July, 1997, could be attributed, in part, to the strengthening of the dollar: see pp. 24, 50, 83, 84–5. Equally, the restrictions on contracyclical fiscal policy in Europe caused by the need to set common practice on fiscal policy among those members of the European Union who committed themselves to the euro, will also have inhibited aggregate demand policies within the euro bloc. Global aggregate demand is the sum of national aggregate demands and the European restrictions will have increased the the necessary infusion of demand by the Keynesian locomotive required for adequate global aggregate demand.

22. INW measures the value of total claims on foreign residents plus the value of real assets abroad less the equivalent foreign-owned assets on US residents and in the United States. It is directly comparable to the accounting concept of net worth.

23. This data set runs only from 1976 (*Survey of Current Business*, July 2002, p. 18). As a percentage of GDP, earlier INW may well have been higher.

24. There are two ways of estimating the value of inward and outward foreign direct investment. The number given uses the more conservative approach.

25. See Table 5.2. What matters is not the *net* but the gross balance on foreign residents' private assets because there exists no authority for the US Government to require private US residents who own assets abroad, be they real or financial, to sell the assets and to repatriate the realized funds.

26. In 1988, Allen J. Wallis, Undersecretary of State for Economic Affairs and Agriculture, took strong issue with the term "debtor" asserting, unfortunately, that "our [so-called] debts are mostly in US dollars, not in foreign currencies that have to be earned in international trade." (Wallis, 1988) (Gray, 1992). That assertion was inappropriate both then and now in a world in which foreign-owned assets can be quickly withdrawn.

27. See Chapter 8.

28. See Chapter 3. For expository purposes, this can be seen as a current account that is in approximate balance – leaving the INW of the United States effectively constant. Clearly, once the United States has lost the aura of being the key-currency nation, it will be forced to run current surpluses and to increase its INW.

29. There were some cosmetic measures taken in the fall of 2003 at the G-7 meeting in September. These are discussed briefly in Chapter 11. For some possible explanations of the inaction in Washington also see Chapter 11. The US Congress did create a commission to investigate the sustainability of the current deficits: for a review of that Commission's work, see the Appendix to this chapter.

30. "Macrofinancial efficiency" is high when the rate of global capacity utilization is high and the danger of financial crisis is low. The rôle or responsibility of the hegemon is to assure that both requirements are met: the efficiency with which resources are allocated is also important but allocative efficiency can only be acceptably high when the global economy is operating at a satisfactory level of performance and a satisfactory level of performance requires that financial systems operate free from any threat of immediate instability.

31. The services provided by the hegemon *resemble those provided to a national economy by its "financial authorities"* (the treasury or exchequer and its central bank).
32. Crockett (1997, p. 9) identifies "financial stability" as a public good: this identification is quite compatible with Kindleberger's (1986) description of the responsibilities of the hegemon. The hegemon can only provide a "climate" (or setting) of financial stability and it cannot preclude instability afflicting a national financial system.
33. Kindleberger's concepts are described in greater detail in Chapter 2.
34. This double duty is one source of the danger of having a hegemon near exhaustion. This danger was addressed in Triffin (1961) when he addressed a weakening of the international reserve position of the United States. This aspect of the problem is discussed in Part III.
35. Holding assets denominated in a foreign currency does not automatically involve speculation which has been the terror of régimes of fixed rates of exchange. However, such holdings can imitate speculative flights when depreciation of the currency of denomination is perceived.
36. This fact leads many to assume that the dollar standard will continue well into the future. If all of the foreign-owned dollar-denominated assets were the international reserves of nations as distinct from assets of profit-seeking firms and wealth-maximizing individuals, this might be true – on the presumption that governments will be unwilling to precipitate any condition, which could trigger a crisis that would also disrupt their own economy (McKinnon, 2001).
37. The text uses the term "easily-encashable" in preference to "liquid" because the latter implies some range of price certainty. Assets are "easily-encashable" when they can be sold in secondary markets for dollars (for the currency of denomination) and the proceeds converted to the currency of choice very quickly. There is no assurance about the price which owners will receive when "easily-encashable" assets are sold nor about the prevailing rate of exchange.
38. For an analysis of the relationship between the rate of exchange of the dollar and the elimination of the current deficits, see Chapter 3; for a more detailed analysis of the relationship between the social costs of adjustment and the magnitude of the international dissaving and negative INW of the United States, see Chapter 6.
39. Under a full gold standard, the burden of hegemony required much greater financial strength.
40. Winch (1969) provides an excellent and readable account of the politics and economics of these events.
41. Note that the measures of inflation used to transpose a current financial exchange rate into an index of a so-called "real" exchange rate are neither precise nor good measures of the effect of price level changes on international price-competitiveness.
42. There is a parallel insofar as some "basic" US industries are concerned: these industries are being subjected to very damaging price-competition from foreign industries which benefit from the serious overvaluation of the dollar. See p. 32.
43. The conditions are very different but there is one unsettling thing in common: there exists substantial and possibly increasing antagonism among the

major parties concerned and it could play a role in the future in ways reminiscent of 1919 (Joffe, 2001).

44. This aspect of the problem is considered in greater detail in Chapter 8.

45. Joffe's (2001) description of the George W. Bush Administration's hard-nosed "orneriness" in international affairs is, in context, not encouraging nor are the strains in early 2003 between the so-called "Anglo-Saxon nations" and France, Germany, Belgium and Russia over the invasion of Iraq.

46. Adjustment involves the reallocation of assets and people among sectors and is therefore a process of substantial economic discomfort even for countries whose currencies are strengthening. The text assumes (with some confidence) that the greater the rate of economic change in resource allocations and incomes, the greater will be the dislocation and social costs of adaptation to the new conditions. Students of American politics will remember the expression "with all deliberate speed." It is important that the adjustment rate be kept close to the maximum feasible without generating serious dislocation likely to lead to a "crash landing."

47. The successful completion of the first task should provide a short-term solution to the problem of financing the system pending the creation of a new institutional framework.

48. One might suggest that the atmosphere in Washington has become one of supreme confidence unaffected by "outlandish events."

49. A formal model of an intricate system may require severely limiting assumptions, which can rob the model of operational value (Chick, 1998).

50. Paul Volcker, former chairman of the Federal Reserve System, has reported that there exists a saying in financial markets: "the trend is your friend" so that "the way to make money is to join, even to lead the herd" (Volcker, 2002, p. 17).

51. The late Hyman P. Minsky devoted much of his career to the problem of financial instability but his main focus was on a systemic failure of the system of intermediation (and the solvency of intermediaries) within a nation. For a summary of Minsky's views on the international economy, see Gray and Gray (1989).

52. So-called "euroland" presents definitional problems here or, more precisely, members of the European Union, which have not accepted the euro present problems. Tobin (1978) refers to inter-currency phenomena, but the important aspect is that countries with an individual currency are likely to make policy based on their own best interest. Making policy based on the collective interest is more difficult – the needs of the global system need to be taken into account (especially so after it absorbs several transition economies). This aspect has obvious implications for having the euro serve as the key currency.

53. The concept of contagion and its implications is described in detail by Crockett (1997). On currency crises, see Kaufman (2000).

54. For example, the CFA franc (the currency of fourteen African countries) is tied to the euro.

55. Little of the discussion of the collapse of the Thai baht has noted that the International Monetary Fund tied the baht to currency that was steadily gaining in foreign-exchange markets. This, by itself, would have imposed severe stress on the Thai economy and suggests that the key currency was being given a new role and a new responsibility (to maintain its value in foreign exchange markets *against both appreciation and depreciation*).

56. But see Blecker (1999b) and Blecker (2002).
57. For an example, see the discussion of the balance on income on international assets in Chapter 3.
58. In 2002, the weakening of the dollar was much less than its most obvious measure (its weakening against the euro). In December, 2001, to buy a euro required only 0.8912 dollars, but required 1.0194 dollars in December, 2002: the dollar had, therefore, weakened against the euro by about 14 percent. A broader measure of the value of the dollar in foreign exchange markets (based on 25 currencies including the euro) weakened by about 1.4 percent from an index number of 127.52 in December 2001, to 125.70 in December, 2002. Note that the dollar weakens as the index number declines. Source: *Federal Reserve Bulletin*, April 2003, p. A56.
59. This danger is recognized in Kissinger (2001) and Joffe (2001), but see also the report on the belligerently condescending addresses to the World Economic Forum by two senior cabinet members of the Bush administration in February 2002 (*The New York Times*, February 3, 2002, p. A3).
60. This implies that the latest available data were approximately those for, at most, the first half of 2000. The members of the Commission, if not those who made presentations before the Commission, were, therefore, aware of the very large increases in the current deficit (larger dissaving) in 1999 and in early 2000. (See Table 1.1.)
61. This asymmetry is described below. See also Greenspan's observation cited in n. 13.
62. Ozawa (2001b, p. 108) explains the link between capital inflows, the current deficit and the rate of exchange. See also pp. 36–7. The general attitude of the Commission and its witnesses emphasizes the wisdom contained in n.16, in Chapter 1.
63. The unequal rates of capacity utilization and economic growth in the United States and its overseas trading partners clearly influenced Mann's (1999) choice of analytic approach.
64. Deficits are also affected directly by such "real" factors as differences in growth rates, domestic rates of saving, the world price of imports which cannot be satisfied by home production (petroleum among other things). The latter goods are defined as non-competitive imports in Gray (1976, pp. 46–9).
65. This emphasis on Mann (1999) derives from the importance of her study while emphasizing its virtually complete reliance on asymmetric marginal propensities to import and export and disregarding the effect of capital flows on rates of exchange.
66. While expressing flows or stocks as a percentage of GDP has some advantages, it can bias perception. One of the problems is that the magnitude of a deficit should be seen in terms of those revenues which can be devoted to its reduction (in context, current foreign exchange revenues). Thus, a comparison of a deficit as a percentage of GDP for a small country with a high ratio of exports and imports to GDP, is not likely to exaggerate the difficulty of generating revenues for its reduction as much as in a country such as the United States where current international transactions account for only 0.3 percent of GDP and where, in 2000, the ratio of the deficit to current revenues from abroad was 30 percent (see Table 5.10).
67. This is not consistent with current data (see Table 3.2).

68. There is a danger that the relationship between international dissaving and capital formation will be misinterpreted. "Hard thinking about the trade deficit starts from the fact that [it] ... equals the difference between domestic investment and domestic saving" (U.S.T.D.R.C., 2000). It is quite probable that the recent excessive strength of the dollar could reduce the average propensity to save (Yeager, 1970). The US average propensity to save fall from 12.71 percent of disposable income in 1980 to 7.11 percent in 1993, to 5.58 percent in 1995 and to 2.63 percent in 2001. (Data from *The Economic Report of the President*, various issues). Also see Velde (1999).
69. See Chapter 5, Table 5.1.
70. Rates of exchange are determined in foreign-exchange markets by international flows of funds (see Chapter 3) (Gray and Gray, 1988/89) and it is incomplete to disregard the institutional changes and the importance of exchange rates to price-competitiveness.
71. The disposition of large sums in return for the sale of existing assets (mergers and acquisitions) can affect the validity of the equality generated by the national income and product account system: if these funds are used to fund new capital formation, the original model will come closer to holding.
72. Estimates of real rates of exchange should be seen as having some built-in margin of error (Leahy, 1998).
73. These pages of *The Report* are reported to draw heavily on Blecker's (1999b) *Economic Policy Institute Briefing Paper*, "The Ticking Debt Bomb."
74. The reasons mentioned in the second quotation include: the estimated growth in the ratio of the current deficit to forecast GDP; the weakening of the status and authority of the United States in the world as a result of the growing indebtedness; the likelihood that financial factors could become adverse for the US economy; there is no guarantee that this process will unfold in an orderly way.

2 Background Concepts and Relationships in a Globalized World

1. If the net capital inflow were completely indifferent to the rate of exchange, the deficit on current account would exactly offset the net capital inflow. FDI can affect the demand for goods and services in the year of the transaction as the multinational arranges to supply some capital goods (for a greenfield investment) from its home country (Reddaway *et al.*, 1968).
2. This question is foreign to theories of international trade because of the assumption of balanced trade (or current account).
3. The "other party" is "everybody else" and varies with the unit under scrutiny.
4. This apparatus applies to an individual family as much as to a country.
5. International net worth increases when a current-account surplus $(X > M)$ leads to the net acquisition of international assets.
6. This kind of effect is covered in detail in the annual Survey of Current Business article on the international investment position of the United States. The effect of a weakening in the dollar's financial rate of exchange can, of course, have a substantial impact on INW (measured in dollars) since all foreign assets will automatically increase in value in dollars.

7. Capital-account controls may be necessary to preclude financial instability in the short term but they are difficult to administer effectively and usually distort the allocation of investment both in and between nations. It is possible to conceive of changes being effected through the capital account if, for example, taxes on foreign-owned assets were introduced or increased and foreign-owned assets took every opportunity to seek safe havens elsewhere.

8. But not the standard of living of the global economy: allowing comparative advantage to allocate resources increases the efficiency of global output.

9. This is an example of how project-specific loans from industrialized countries to poorer nations (or foreign direct investment in a greenfield venture) will affect the distribution of aggregate demand. A similar outcome can be achieved without debt by financing a trade deficit by unilateral transfers and this summarizes the post-war policy of the United States (see Acheson's 1944 statement on post-war policy).

10. Note that this identifies the important point that the hegemon's INW can decrease because of either official capital movements or private profit-seeking capital movements.

11. For a review of the consequences of financial instability on the economic prosperity of a country see Crockett (1997). Even when the precipitating shock has been absorbed, lack of confidence in (Northian) institutions can continue to the detriment of the efficiency of the financial system and the recovery process.

12. This subsection draws on Gray (1997).

13. See Chapter 3, pp. 61–6.

14. The second term of the Clinton administration is an obvious example.

15. This can adversely affect the ability of the hegemon to impose its view of an efficient global economy on other nations: a point mentioned occasionally in the US Trade Deficit Review Commission (2000).

16. This is, of course, the focus of this monograph.

17. This condition was built into a full gold standard so that it was no concern of the United Kingdom. For the policies of the United States, see the report on the Roosevelt Administration's post-war economic policy in the next subsection of this chapter.

18. Leadership in the rôle of generating "foreign aid transfers" so that development may be stimulated in backward economies is unlikely to impose great burdens on the economic hegemon, if only because the US Congress has never given solid support to the program. It may be desirable to consider including this task in the list of hegemonic responsibilities when a replacement for the United States is designed.

19. Schwartz (1994a) reports that George Kennan could find no reason for US involvement in Vietnam other than the possibility that US military hegemony had become an end in itself. Recent events do not offer evidence to the contrary.

20. The invasion of Iraq took place after the problem of negative INW was well established. While that war may contribute to the difficulties of restoring an efficient global financial system, it was not a contributory cause.

21. The focus of this book is less on "how the problem arose" than on "what should and must be done." Similarly, the purpose is not to apportion blame at either the international level or the political level within the United States.

Possible reasons for the failure of the United States government to understand its progressive financial weakening are suggested in Chapter 8.

22. This section draws on Gray and Gray (1981, pp. 55–61) where the problem is covered in greater detail.

23. Crockett (1997) provides a good review of this problem.

24. Cooper and Little (2001, p. 33) note that the charge of the Federal Reserve System (its domain of responsibility) is purely domestic but that international concerns have played an increasing role since 1971 when the dollar's link to gold proved unsustainable.

25. The ability to perform as hegemon has, then, a stock dimension, similar to concern over the capital adequacy of commercial banks. The role of the hegemon cannot be adequately analyzed in terms of a theory that relies purely on flows. This aspect of the problem is taken up in Chapter 7.

26. Godley (1999) identifies the labor market effects as the major contributor to the loss of the political will to continue to fulfil the hegemonic duties.

27. The problem is confounded by the fact that inflows of capital strengthen the home currency and lead to current deficits as home-country economic units substitute relatively cheap foreign goods for domestic goods. Thus domestic investment will exceed the sum of domestic saving plus gross illiquid inflows of foreign saving (see p. 31).

3   A Theory of Balance-of-Payments Adjustment for the Hegemon

1. This was new ground for the international financial system. We assess its feasibility in Chapter 8 (p. 153).

2. World stocks of foreign direct investment have increased from $105.5 billion in 1973 to $495.2 billion in 1980, to $1,761.2 billion in 1990 and to $4,772.0 billion in 1999. (Source: UNCTAD, 2000, p. 294.)

3. Induced imports of capital goods and so on, tend to come more slowly after the merger or the acquisition than after a greenfields investment (Reddaway *et al.*, 1968, Tables XVII.2 and XVII.4) and Gray (1974, p. 144). Note that these data derive from a study conducted a long time ago but there is no logical reason to doubt the basic conclusion. Gray (1974, pp. 136–45) referred to the import component of greenfield investments as "induced international saving" because it directly financed a part of the capital outflow.

4. The functional currency of an economic unit is the currency in which it assesses its wealth or net worth or the currency in which it publishes its economic reports. The former can be seen as applying pre-eminently to individuals and families and the latter to public corporations.

5. Unfortunately, the argument has been extended to developing countries without recognition of the need for the existence of institutions of adequate sophistication if the developing economies are to become involved in the global financial system (Gray, 2002) (Shelburne, 2002).

6. The withdrawal of funds from the Thai baht in July 1997 is a very clear example of this capability (Rahman, 1998).

7. Reported international positions of US banks have increased from $81 billion (claims) and $53 billion (liabilities) in 1976 to $696 billion (claims) and

$633 billion (liabilities) in 1990 and to $1,416 billion (claims) and $1,298 billion liabilities in 2001. Source: *Survey of Current Business* (July 2002), pp. 18 and 19. (The 2001 data are "preliminary.")

8. This category of international capital movement is made much more complex by the rapid growth of multinational banks. This category also must contain large amounts of working capital of (non-bank) multinational corporations.

9. Like, the balance on unilateral transfers, this component of the current account is not included in the formal absorption theory. Both are discussed below in this chapter (pp. 66–9).

10. The idea of an equilibrium rate of exchange or terms of trade, implicit in reliance on a static equilibrium approach, can be misleading.

11. Once a pegged currency shows signs of not being able to maintain its pegged value, movements of financial capital become very sensitive to the exchange rate and to new perceptions about future exchange rates. In this way, the overvaluation of the host's currency is likely to be stripped away.

12. Competitive imports are those for which adequate substitutes can be produced domestically. Expenditure-switches were the sole policy measure of the earlier theories of payments adjustment for deficit elimination. These measures did incorporate an expenditure-reduction effect as the terms of trade worsened, but this was more than likely to be offset by the expansion induced by the increase in the balance on goods and services brought about by the change in price competitiveness.

13. Such high aggregate demand in the deficit country would also be likely to induce inflation and unwarranted improvement in the real rate of exchange. Thus, the absorption theory would address both dimensions of such a situation.

14. This is, of course, the problem facing the United States in the early years of the twenty-first century.

15. Thailand is the obvious example here: see Rahman (1998). This kind of activity becomes self-reinforcing as one person's sales become additional information and influence the expectations of other non-resident asset holders in the same market.

16. Divestment of earlier FDI is by no means unknown but, in most major countries, it has been small relative to inflows.

17. It is possible to refine the indicator given above (INW and S_l) by substituting the (gross) value of easily-encashable foreign-owned assets denominated in the currency of the debtor/deficit nation for INW. Obligations denominated in "strong" currencies are also important but for a different reason. If a financial crisis is perceived as probable, debt denominated in foreign currencies can lose value as and when the debtor is unable to meet its obligations: this reduction in outstanding liabilities by the deficit nation will not, except in very extreme cases, apply to sovereign (government) debt. In domestic currency, sovereign, strong currency-denominated debt will increase.

18. An excellent, albeit dated study (Dornbusch and Krugman, 1976) puts the minimum delay between the change in exchange rates and the full effect on the current account being achieved, at about six months.

19. While both genera are prone to instability, many economists believe that capital markets are more likely than goods markets to exhibit substantial instability. Keynes (1936, pp. 158–9) makes the argument, in terms of a

national equity market, that capital markets are capable of serious instability when what would now be called 'market-timing' (Keynes called it "speculation") dominates long-term investment. Post Keynesian economists would agree emphatically with this assertion.

20. Note that the absorption theory could easily be seen as a straightforward Keynesian construct adding fluctuations in rates of capacity utilization to the neoclassical model.

21. This asymmetry recalls Keynes's emphasis on a constructive role for surplus nations (paying interest on surplus balances in the same way that deficit nations would pay interest on borrowings) in *Proposals for an International Clearing Union* (1943). "Proposals" was largely Keynes's brainchild but is, officially, the plan put forward at Bretton Woods by the British delegation and was known as "The Keynes Plan." For the history of the origin of the Keynes Plan, see Harrod (1951, Chapter 13).

22. The major surplus countries, Japan and the Euro bloc ("Euroland") are essentially those which are in substantial recession brought about by domestic problems. See Table 5.1 below. For a contrary view see McKinnon (2001).

23. Economists used to be concerned with the possibility that a depreciation would be counterproductive because the elasticities were insufficiently large. This led to the development of the Marshall–Lerner condition which stipulated that, with perfectly elastic supply of tradable-goods and services in both (all) countries, the sum of home and foreign elasticity of demand should exceed unity for depreciation to increase the current balance.

24. Given unitary elasticities of demand, the arithmetic is relatively easy. When the currencies had changed relative values, foreign countries would buy as much in dollars (but more goods) from the United States while the United States would spend the same amount of foreign currency (on fewer goods) and this would amount to 10 percent fewer dollars. Thus, the global balance would increase by 10 percent of US imports (a saving of $1 billion).

25. Bearing in mind the assumed linearity of the elasticities, the percentage depreciation required for current balance would have to be increased from 25.64 percent to eliminate the 2000 deficit if all countries' currencies appreciated against the dollar to 47.39 if the western hemisphere countries and Japan offset the depreciation. The greater the necessary depreciation, the less likely is the assumption of unitary elasticities to be realistic.

26. This section draws on Gray (1998).

27. See Milberg and Gray (1992) and pp. 16–18 below for more detailed consideration.

28. Mann's (1999, Table 10.3) projections of BIA, using the "base case scenario" and based on a carrying cost of four percent of INW, are deficits of $177.6 billion for 2005 and $356.0 billion for 2010: these numbers will be shown to be overestimates because her assumptions do not take into account a substantial disparity in rates of return on US assets abroad and liabilities in the United States.

29. Receipts were $36.9 billion on assets of $421 billion and payments were $6.86 billion on assets of $266 billion (both asset figures were end-of-year data valued at current cost). Sources were *Survey of Current Business*, June 1993, p. 47 and July 2002, p. 51.

30. It is useful here to recall the steady appreciation of the dollar during the 1990s (Figure A1.2).

31. In 2001, trade in goods and services totaled $2.3 trillion and the sum of payments and receipts on (all) investments was $553 billion.
32. These revisions have been incorporated into Tables 1.1 and 5.1
33. The revisions are presented in Bach (2002) and the sources of the revisions given in some detail. Since most of the revision derives from a substantial reduction (20 percent or more than $100 billion in 2001) in net purchases of US securities by non-residents, there was no rate of exchange effect. The INW becomes less negative for each year of revision (1995–2000).
34. It took more than half a century for the strains of the key-currency rôle to come near exhausting the original positive INW of the United States and the inherent "line of credit," which the status affords the country.

4   A Model of Instability in Asset Markets

1. For a review of contagion, see Crockett (1997).
2. The flight from the Thai baht in July 1997, and its effects on Indonesia, Malaysia and the Philippines, is an example of instability being transmitted abroad.
3. This definition clearly makes "fragility" a function of the shocks to which the market is exposed.
4. The antonym of "fragility" is resilience, robustness or "stability efficiency." The latter, is defined in Gray and Gray (1988/89), as the size of an adverse shock which can be experienced by a market or system without generating a self-reinforcing decline in asset prices. Gray (2002) uses Taiwan's experience in the aftermath of the July 1997 meltdown in Thailand to provide an analysis of how a country can guard against serious international contagion.
5. Table 5.2 shows how changes in asset mix can increase the efficiency of conduits by increasing the ease of encashability of foreign-owned assets.
6. Note that the distance b is drawn to describe the "backfold" between the lowest price at which stability exists and the re-emergence of a stable price compatible with zero excess demand.
7. Keynes used a nonstandard meaning of "speculative" in this passage.
8. These factors also contribute to the change in the shape of the excess demand schedule.
9. Volcker (2002, p. 20) reminds the reader that in the, jargon of financial markets, "the trend is your friend" and that the way to make money is "to join, even lead the herd."
10. This section draws on Gray (1990) and (1992).
11. This is an excellent example of an adverse shock (a loss of confidence in sterling) which could trigger a currency crisis without generating a banking crisis. (Kaufman, 2000.)
12. This is the reason for emphasis being placed on the capital adequacy of financial institutions. In context in the present-day United States, the exposure of many intermediaries to families that are deeply indebted through credit card balances, is a cause for concern. For the recent US experience of family bankruptcies, see Table 5.8.
13. The concept of "excessive perceptions" used here is closely related to the state of euphoria in the Kindleberger-Minsky model of financial crisis (Minsky, 1972), (1977); (Kindleberger, 1978, Chapter 2).

14. "The unexpected happens: prepare for it." (see pp. 23–4).
15. In a country in a currency bloc, for example, a member of "Euroland", what matters is the percentage of foreign ownership by asset holders from outside the currency bloc (i.e. those with different functional currencies).
16. It is notoriously difficult for individuals and institutions accurately to quantify and to keep up-to-date with changes in political risk.
17. To the author's knowledge, no-one has proposed that the rate of the Tobin tax could be variable at the discretion of the host government so that, in a time of crisis, the tax could be raised steeply to reduce the outflow of funds. Such an arrangement would obviously reduce the inflow of funds.

5   The Data and the Danger: Assessing Proposition One

1. The fixed rate between the baht and the US dollar was disastrous for Thailand– not least because it created a spurious attractiveness for inflows of easily encashable foreign-owned assets but also because the dollar appreciated secularly through the 1990s (see Figure A1.1) so that the price-competitiveness of Thai value-added was being rapidly eroded by purely exogenous forces.
2. Godley and Izurieta (2002) and Mann (1999) see the domestic trigger being launched by the current deficit reaching unmanageable levels because of a failure of US trading partners to grow adequately. The trigger could also be launched by a spontaneous deep recession in the United States from any cause.
3. This dichotomy does not preclude the possibility of either a spontaneous economic shock, which heightens the identified stresses or a shock, which is not directly connected with economic phenomena but which will spillover onto economic relations. A natural disaster or a breakdown of diplomatic and economic relations among large blocs could be such a cause.
4. There would be substantial political difficulties in obtaining such legislation in the absence of great pressure and the international trigger, once activated, will act quickly. Without preplanning, or prior consensus, the requisite legislation could not be passed quickly enough to affect the outcome.
5. Recall that the freedom to invest abroad by US residents was inaugurated at a time when the reserves of the dollar far exceeded any possible claims on the dollar so that the currency was "better than gold."
6. McKinnon (2001) suggests that official assets would be actively used to counter any source of instability.
7. The second proposition is derivative from the first so that the same data set can be used to assess both propositions.
8. The data for the latest year in all data series are likely to be preliminary and subject to revision. Note *b* refers to the military-related basis for the transitory current surplus in 1991. For a discussion of the political background, see Yergin and Stanislaw (1998, 334–5).
9. This agrees with the usual definition of income but a case may be made for defining income as the difference in the net asset position at the beginning and end of the year plus current expenditures made during the year.

10. The sum of the two flows gives an estimated outside value of international saving/dissaving.

11. See Chapter 3 for the underlying theory.

12. Figure A1.1 shows the trade-weighted, real effective exchange rate over a slightly longer period.

13. This section draws on the work of Wynne Godley and his associates at the Levy Economics Institute. The Institute's Macro Modeling Team now consists of Dimitri Papadimitriou, Anwar Shaikh, Claudio dos Santos and Gennaro Zezzo. The essential underlying model is that of injections into and leakages out of the circular flow of expenditure: a net increase in injections will expand an economy and *vice versa*. The data derive mainly from estimates of the performance of the US economy made by Papadimitriou *et al.* (2002).

14. In principle, the key-currency nation might be required to reduce global aggregate demand but, given that it is the repository of international reserves of the rest of the world, this is unlikely.

15. The expenditures of the United States in pursuing its self-appointed rôle of military hegemon also played an important part in the steady erosion of the INW.

16. It is possible, in context, to see a limit to total government indebtedness setting a limit to contracyclical Keynesian policy even in a closed economy.

17. For a reverse view of this, see Velde (1999). Unfortunately, Velde neglected consideration of the effect of the composition of the marginal propensity to save by income class on aggregate saving. The very rich were inevitably destined to be net savers so that a zero average propensity implied large numbers of negative savers and the results, shown in Table 5.9, were inevitable if the consumption surge continued.

18. As Velde (1999) notes: the low saving rate of household was, given the behavior of the other sectors, a necessary offset to the high saving rate of the government sector if serious recession was to be avoided.

19. Failing a sudden boom in the market for corporate securities.

20. See also Godley and Izurieta (2002). After the great expansion that took place during the Clinton administrations, 8 percent unemployment would be considered unacceptable.

21. In the existing liberalized global economy, expansion of aggregate demand by the other industrialized nations would spread throughout the world and would not be confined to the economies in the expanding blocs.

22. Note that the bounds of the Godley model are confronted by the "dream scenario." First, the decision to depreciate the real rate of exchange of the dollar by about 25 percent does not address either the sourcing of the funds, which will be used to acquire the foreign assets needed to weaken the dollar nor the repercussions of raising those funds by the US authorities. The most obvious means would be for the government sector to run a surplus whose proceeds would be used to acquire foreign currencies or financial assets. The needed funds could also be raised by the sale of (new) federal debt: this debt would, of course, not add to the government's net debt because there would be offsetting foreign-exchange-denominated assets. Nor does the model allow for the effects of the policy shift on the willingness of foreign holders of dollar-denominated assets to continue to hold them. Explicit mention of the

inflation-adjusted ("real") rate of exchange recognizes the inflationary effects in the United States of the increase of the dollar price of imports.

23. Preliminary data for the first half of 2003 show that international dissaving is continuing at a higher rate than in 2002.

24. Effectively at a compound rate of interest of 3 percent.

25. Here, of course, it is the rate of the international leakage, which is most important. Note that the neoclassical assumption of the neutrality of money is rejected here.

26. For an account of Minsky's work in the international sector, see Gray and Gray (1994).

27. Keynes's multiplier involved an infinite series.

28. Depreciation of a currency can occur either as a result of the erosion of its domestic purchasing power or in foreign exchange markets when the currency loses value against other currencies. Domestic inflation is likely to bring about international depreciation.

29. The large banks may suffer from international financial upheaval but may be considered "too big to fail."

30. This conclusion assumes that the ongoing current deficit when the domestic trigger is activated is large enough to require a substantial weakening of the dollar (Chapter 6).

31. The source of these increases in efficiency is essentially the great strides in information technology during the 1990s.

6   Assessing Propositions One and Two

1. Proposition Two is examined later in this chapter.

2. "My suggestion is that [Political Economy]'s use should be revived as covering that part of our sphere of interest which essentially involves judgments of value. ... It depends upon the technical apparatus of Economics, but it applies this apparatus to the examination of schemes for the realisation of aims whose formulation lies outside of [Scientific] Economics and it does not abstain from appeal to the probabilities of political practice when such an appeal has seemed relevant" (Robbins, 1981, pp. 7–8).

3. US international dissaving in the first half of 2003 was higher than in the first half of 2002 (by $47 billion).

4. The data sources have, despite the undoubted conscientiousness and professionalism of the economists in the Bureau of Economic Analysis, all of the inevitable weaknesses of aggregate international data.

5. The dissaving in the first half of 2003 was over $47 billion larger than its equivalent in 2002. The data for the second quarter of 2003 are "preliminary": recent experience is that revisions reduce the deficit.

6. Table 5.9 can be thought of as offering something approaching a best-case scenario so that conclusions based on its estimates cannot be accused of biasing the conclusions in favor of crisis.

7. The erosion of the original financial depreciation can be offset by greater inflation in the depreciating country. This important problem is considered in detail in Chapter 7.

8. This is an assumption because, under the current system, no country can change its currency's rate of exchange by an announcement effect.

9. If the domestic trigger were to be activated, the initiative for dollar depreciation would come from the US economic authorities and this would require that the authorities generate funds to acquire assets denominated in foreign-exchange. These assets would be concentrated in the currencies of industrial nations running current surpluses – provided always that these nations would permit the implied large-scale interference by a foreign government in their country's financial markets.

10. Observations on the effect of the Iraqi war on the problem are given in Chapter 8.

11. This arithmetic computation does not allow for the increase in the deficit in income on assets. The series of current deficits is (in billions of dollars): 450; 400; 350; 315; 283; 255; 230 and 207 which sums to $2.49 trillion over eight years.

12. In fairness to members of the Commission, the reader should recall that the deficits to that point were much smaller than those of the last four years. Note, in context, that the meaning of "soft landing" was not precisely defined.

13. The term, *price-competitiveness*, is developed in detail in Chapter 7: here it is used as a shorthand expression for the relative prices of home-produced goods in home and foreign markets. It is, therefore, a composite of the exchange rate and the relative domestic price levels.

14. These firms and industries would have the worst of both worlds: buying steel produced at above the price available in a free-trade world but having to sell their products in foreign markets in which their costs were inflated by the strength of the US dollar.

15. This, of course, ties in with Keynes's comment on the difficulties of "unlearning" past history: see n.16 in Chapter 1.

16. If the years in Table 5.9 are included, the full period is 1983 through 2010 or 28 years.

17. This recalls the pessimism of Joffe (2001) with respect to future stress in international relations: see pp. 121–2.

18. This approach is responsible for the frequent allusion to the importance of high rates of foreign economic growth made by people discussing the future of the US current deficits.

19. This possibility of replaying the antagonisms of 1919 is probably enhanced by the "smugness" *et al.* of US foreign policy (Kissinger, 2001) and recent US irritation with some major industrialized allies.

20. The scheduled expansion of the European Community to allow the entry of many transition economies will make the adjustment process substantially more complex and more difficult to diagnose *ex ante*.

21. But see the text referenced by footnote 12 above in this chapter. One witness cited in the text of the US Trade Deficit Review Commission *Report* (2000, p. 26) referred to the ability of the United States to attract inflows of capital because "the U.S. economy is a good steady performer." This view abstracts from the importance of portfolio assets owned by non-residents (Tables 5.1 and 5.2) and the potential losses that would follow from a weakening of the dollar in foreign exchange markets.

22. This phenomenon was recognized in the early 1950s and gave rise to the concept of a dollar shortage whereby the US economy was so efficient that the European economies could not erase their bilateral deficits despite their best efforts. The European nations had a "shortage of dollars." Times have changed the word "shortage" for "surplus" but the stubbornness of the imbalance seems likely to remain if only because of the size of net US indebtedness.

23. This issue is considered briefly in Chapter 8.

24. Hyman P. Minsky, the leading authority on systemic financial instability, spent his last professionally active years at the Levy Economics Institute.

25. This statement can make no claim to omniscience of everything that has been written or spoken.

26. This issue and its potential consequences are taken up in greater detail in Chapter 8.

27. Always the problem of adjustment returns to the measures to change the price-competitiveness of the deficit nation and the level of global aggregate demand.

28. Here the unilateralist foreign policy of the George W. Bush Administration in the United States will prove a liability. This aspect of the problem is considered in Chapter 8.

29. Chapter 1, p. 17, identifies this as "the major goal of collective economic policy in the foreseeable future."

7   The Efficiency of Adjustment

1. Mann (1999) relied very heavily on the historical record of the marginal propensities to import in her estimates of the trend values of US current deficits. The historical record showed substantial asymmetry but there may be some small capacity to influence marginal propensities in nations with depreciating and appreciating currencies. The danger of adopting such policies is that it is likely to assume that policymakers know more than they, in fact, do. This possibility will be higher, the less the experience with the current conditions.

2. Mundell's (1961) (AER) famous concept of an optimum currency area was originally defined in terms of the characteristics which provided greatest sensitivity to currency depreciation and the lowest "real" costs of adjustment.

3. This sentence encapsulates the problems which beset the international macrofinancial system after the First World War. The erstwhile key-currency nation refused to effect an expenditure-switch but imposed a Draconian expenditure-reduction policy by depressing its domestic economy and no nation was willing to allow imports to become a larger share of absorption in a severely depressed world economy. For a history of those times, see Harrod (1951), Gardner (1969) and Winch (1969).

4. The difficulties in enforcing expenditure reductions cannot be neglected but they focus largely on political resistance and the ability of some units to draw down reserves rather than to reduce absorption.

5. The failure of some trading partners to allow the deficit country to depreciate its currency relative to their own can also be seen as a form of "contrary" slippage (see Chapter 3). Except as it affects the role of free trade areas in

adjustment, this aspect of a currency depreciation is not addressed in this chapter.

6. Alternative means of effecting an expenditure-switch can include such measures as higher tariffs on imports or excise-taxes on imported luxury goods. Such measures would be extremely difficult to legislate without retaliation under the existing set of global trade agreements and are therefore not detailed here.

7. The text assumes a tranquil world. An adverse exogenous shock will change the value of C needed for current balance so that with a constant value of C or real exchange rate, a deficit will ensue (Gray, 1974).

8. Subject to the cost accounting system used for goods in inventories.

9. Gray (1976, pp. 46–9) described goods which physically cannot be produced at home as "non-competitive imports." Such goods are likely to have very high per-unit gains from trade (Gray, 1986). The hegemon does not experience the effects of depreciation directly in commodities whose global price is defined in the key currency (Gray, 1999).

10. The British in 1948, when Sir Stafford Cripps was Chancellor of the Exchequer, did raise what is now called "pass through" to the national level when sterling was seriously devalued against the dollar. A message went to the distillers of Scotch whiskey suggesting that they maintain their price in dollars and substantially increase their mark-up in sales to the western hemisphere. In the same way, firms, which do not pass cost changes through to foreign markets may justify their policies in the national interest.

11. The number of yen per euro was: 1999, 121.55; 2000, 99.42; 2001, 108.9. The number of euros per US dollar was: 1999, 0.937; 2000, 1.082; 2001, 1.116. Source: IMF, *World Economic Outlook*, April 2002, p. 192.

12. The world price of oil rose from $3.39 in 1973 to $11.28 in 1974 and, with the Iranian crisis in 1979, soared further to $18.67 (per barrel) (Gray, 1981, 34).

13. The nominal wage lagged behind the c.p.i. in 1973 and 1974, despite an increase of 11.31 percent in the latter year. However, in the subsequent three years, the average annual increase in the nominal rate in manufacturing was 7.90 percent and the c.p.i. increased at an average rate of 6.32 percent (Gray, 1981, p. 65).

14. The importance of the efficiency of policy measures grow with the size of the needed adjustment. In terms of exhaustion of the key currency, the adjustment will be large enough for this to warrant serious consideration in all countries.

8   Policy Options and Constraints

1. Adelman (2000) suggests that there is no feasible alternative to a patchwork solution but her opinions preceded the large and chronic increases in the size of the US deficit.

2. The argument against a fundamentalist commitment to a *laissez-faire* system for the long-term system is made below in this chapter. The transition system cannot rely on *laissez-faire* (Chapter 9).

3. And severe currency overvaluation. Here the focus is not so much on employment and the domestic trigger as on the profitability and the future

competitiveness of its manufacturing industries when the net barter terms of trade become compatible with more-or-less balanced trade (Milberg and Gray, 1992). The lack of internally generated funds may not provide such a severe constraint for multinational corporations.

4. See, for example, Appendix 1A. Much of the blame for the 1997 crisis in Bangkok was laid at the door of the lack of sophistication of the Thai financial sector (Gray and Dilyard, 2002).

5. From July 11 2003 to August 23 2003, there was no substantial change in the euro/dollar rate indicating a lack of response to the proposal.

6. The constraint on the use of fiscal policy in a recession by members of the euro bloc is effectively the reverse of the idea of having nations with positive INW pay interest on their surpluses (as contained in the Keynes Plan in 1944). Under the Stability and Growth Pact, countries running fiscal deficits in excess of 3 percent of GDP are subject to fines. The limits on fiscal deficits also rules out the post-war strategy of the Roosevelt administration which was to make government-financed unilateral transfers to developing nations to finance an export surplus (Acheson, 1944). The pact was dissolved in 2002.

7. This raises the problem of how to expand aggregate demand and to supply the world with more international liquidity and recalls the problems of the late 1960s and early 1970s and some of the solutions proposed then. One favorite proposal at that time, to increase the price of gold, is now left to market forces.

8. If the multiplier were to build on the basis of the elimination of the US current deficit outside of the United States, without any discretionary fiscal policy offsets, the shortfall would be seriously enhanced. Of course, the complete elimination of the US current deficit could not be achieved in a single year and the induced recession would almost inevitably be partially countered by built-in stabilizers. (Leijonhufvud, 1973)

9. Creditor nations have to be aware of the dangers, which follow from a crisis lest they see no need to reduce their rate of international saving.

10. The United States is not playing a leadership role in this respect.

11. Crudely estimated, pp. 105–6, to exceed 30 percent in real terms.

12. These views are necessarily subjective.

13. In 2003, the federal ("domestic") deficit is likely to be of the same order of magnitude as the deficit on international current account.

14. According to Morgan Guaranty *World Financial Markets* (various issues), the real rate of exchange of the dollar increased monotonically from 100.8 in 1981 to 119.6 in 1984 and peaked at 122.5 in 1985.

15. Tourism is a major export for many developing countries and because of the need of these countries for so-called hard currencies, the leakage of tourists' expenditures from the global spending stream would be very small.

16. A quota could be built into the system so that foreign suppliers were allowed at predetermined shares of the market: such a program would eliminate the need for discrimination in the excise tax.

17. Given the withdrawal of the United States from the Kyoto Agreement and the country's reputation as a gas-guzzling major contributor to global pollution, this approach could substantially benefit the country's reputation as a

member of the global family of nations: a reputation which has sunk abysmally in recent years (Joffe, 2001).

18. The argument for renunciation of pure *laissez-faire* in the transition system could not be avoided.

19. Singh does not venture into questions of the morality and probity of executives of multinational corporations. Since the Enron bankruptcy, this concern has become very strong. Clearly, the supervision and regulation of large corporations must be tightened and this is the counterpart need for sophistication in host countries to that of a sophisticated financial system. In the light of these conditions, the proposal that developing countries would be unable to impose performance requirements on inward foreign direct investment needs to be reconsidered.

20. Bensel and Elmslie (1992) suggests that arguments that qualified the optimality of free trade were not acceptable to the profession. Even Tobin (1978, p. 159) felt some need to defend his proposal for a transactions tax on international capital movements: "I am aware of the distortions and allocational costs that can be attributed to tariffs, including tariffs on imports of foreign-currency assets. I don't deny their existence. I only say that they are small compared to the world macroeconomic costs of the present system."

21. See Chapter 6 for the problem of having private rather than public ownership of the hegemon's liabilities.

22. These intrusions may be partly traced to the encouragement of open markets by the International Monetary Fund in the 1990s. Here Thailand's meltdown in 1999 is a classic example. See also Galbraith's (2002) comments on Brazil.

23. Chapter 5 provides substantial support for a system with a hegemon which is prepared, even willing to dissave internationally.

24. The Keynes plan did not endorse freedom of international capital movements.

25. Davidson is the pre-eminent authority on this mechanism (1992–93), (1997) and (2000).

26. Recall that it is *not* the purpose of this monograph to allocate blame for current conditions – either to nations or individuals. A retrospective on "how the world got here" is undertaken in Chapter 11. Rather, the purpose is to show that recognition of the possibility of financial instability is a *sine qua non* of good political economic analysis.

9 The Transition Problem

1. Godley and Izurieta (2002, p. 12) recognize the lack of such conditions and co-operation: "But neither the institutions nor agreed principles that could carry out co-ordinated expansionary policies around the globe presently exist." In keeping with the Godley approach, the emphasis is on the unsustainability of the chronic current deficits and does not directly address the financial aspects.

2. Note that the transitional architecture is seen to involve both financial and non-financial dimensions. This will hold true for the post-transition, long-run architecture as well: see Chapter 10.

3. Unless the world and the United States are both prepared to institute Draconian controls over withdrawals of funds from the United States p. 150.

4. The terms on which assets owned by non-residents would be repurchased does not warrant consideration at this time. First, the terms will be very path-dependent and will require serious negotiation by experts in negotiations of this type.

5. Since the protected goods were a negligible measure in terms of the size of the ongoing deficit, the WTO could be forgiven for regarding the measure as a purely sectoral protectionist device.

6. While the text implies a virtually total reliance on an excise tax on gasoline, this strategy could be a major (or a minor) component of a package of measures. Of course, the affinity of both President Bush and his vice-president with oil industry interests suggests that little would be done prior to a change of the philosophy of the incumbent president. For a suggestion that such a measure would also serve the political, non-economic ends of the United States, see Thomas Friedman, *International Herald Tribune*, October 6, 2003, p. 4.

7. See Pryor (2002, p. 367).

8. It is interesting to note that what is the main duty of creditor countries, that is, to deliberately add to global aggregate demand to offset the US expenditure reduction, does not repudiate the *laissez-faire* system.

9. The expression "reducing the rate of international dissaving" does not preclude running a surplus on current account after a few years.

10. This would effectively require that the foreign governments create a line of credit for the US government. The schema suggests that any positive international saving would have some explicit portion earmarked for drawing down outstanding lines of credit.

10   A Proposed Agenda for Redesign

1. In the language of this monograph, the new system is "macrofinancial."

2. For recognition of the desirability of broad-based coherence among supranational institutions given the much wider range of interaction among nations in the modern world, see Lloyd (1999).

3. The idea of other regions following the European example gathers strength: see, for example (Mundell, 2003).

4. This premise raises an important issue in terms of the future of the Bretton Woods institutions. The proposal allows for the continuation of the World Bank in what is effectively its current rôle.

5. Note that this approach builds rationally on a definition of the purposes of the system. In contrast, the gold (or sterling) standard from before the First World War evolved naturally and its efficiency was assessed *ex-post* by historians. In contrast, there was no alternative to a dollar standard after the Second World War. Unfortunately, in its fifty plus years of successful operation, no one addressed the problem of what the main features of the international financial system should be (except to "patch up" the dollar-reliant system).

6. The main argument for having a regional system derives from assumption number 1. There is nothing sacrosanct about having three regions or about

restricting the layers of supranational hegemony to two. For example, a region which embraces areas with very distinctly different cultures and philosophies might create a separate subregion as a part of its organization.

7. This area of activity will trespass on the territory of the Bank for International Settlements. Since this organization dates from before the Second World War, it cannot be as easily "folded into" the new system as some other, UN-sponsored organizations. The Bank might very well prove to be the organization from which the Authority will emerge.

8. There has been a longstanding incompatibility between the partial analysis of certain types of activities and the general interdependence of the dimensions of international economic involvement (Gray, 1999).

9. Given the Fund's historical commitment to a purely *laissez-faire* régime, it will be necessary to impose a new world view and this may entail major changes in staff.

10. If a region's unit is appreciated by the Authority, then the reserves of its member nations increase in value in terms of the Authority's numeraire and in terms of the reserves of countries in other regions (see p. 168). The question of the status of gold is not considered here.

11. The president of the subhegemon whose unit of account is under consideration will not vote. In a three-region system, this opens up the possibility that the presidents of other regions will be able to block the Authority with a two-to-two vote. Since a strengthening or weakening of the unit of account under consideration will affect the economies of the other regions, a tie vote in the consecutive meeting will be considered to authorize the proposed change.

12. During a visit to Rutgers University in the 1970s, Sir Roy Harrod related the following summary of Keynes's views on the administration of the post-war international financial system. Keynes envisaged the president of the IMF of being a person of great insight, even genius, who would arrange for changes in exchange rates to take place as and when needed. From the 'centre of the universe', the president would tell national monetary authorities when, by how much and in which direction to change the value of their currency. Harrod also added that Keynes had no doubts as to who was capable of so difficult a task.

13. Note that tax is levied on the change in INW over a two-year period not on INW. Under such an arrangement, the United States would not have been subject to tax until at least two years after the inauguration of the post-Second World War system and then only if it were running chronic surpluses (as indeed it was because of the so-called "dollar gap").

14. For a thorough review of the experience of the IMF in its early years see Tew (1958).

15. These advantages echo the gains from membership in a system similar to "Imperial Preference" within the British Commonwealth in the first half or so of the twentieth century. Sterling was the key currency for member countries even after the time when the currency was no longer the key currency for the global system.

16. See Chapter 8 (pp. 151–4).

17. See in this chapter (p. 167).

11   The Grim Prospect Ahead

1. In fairness to members of the Commission, the reader should recall that the deficits to that point were much smaller than those of the last four years. Note, in context, that the meaning of "soft landing" was not precisely defined.
2. See Chapter 1, n. 17 (p. 183).
3. On this, see Leijonhufvud, 1973.
4. Kupchan (2002) suggests that the European nations are seeking to establish political parity with the United States. If this strategy spreads to exploiting the financial weakness, the probability of the dollar escaping serious strain is even smaller.
5. This assumption is far less serious in analyses of national economies than in analyses of a global system. Then the supply of public goods is "home grown" and is recognized as a part of the political fabric.
6. This relationship underlies the concern with the size of the debt of the federal government in the United States: the burden or cost of the debt which is the mechanism through which the supply of economic public goods would be curtailed. The size of the US federal debt is the value of the outstanding financial liabilities less the value of financial assets: measurement pays no attention to federal ownership of physical assets or of the contributions of these assets to the economy. It would be possible to combine the two arguments for the inability to provide economic public goods if federal debt instruments were widely held by non-residents.
7. John H. Makin, "Keep the Dollar Strong," *The Wall Street Journal*, July 11, 2001, p. A -16. Tom Redburn, "Strong Dollar Sustains the Imbalances in the World," *International Herald Tribune*, October 28, 2002, p. 13.
8. For a discussion of the linkage between foreign direct investment and the current account, see Gray (1972, ch. 6).
9. In this, Dr. Mann was well ahead of her time.
10. This reason also applies to the willingness of politicians to allow the size of the US federal debt to grow with only lip service to the danger of excessive debt (Figgie and Swanson, 1992). See n. 5 in this chapter.
11. This possibility is enhanced by the difficulty of conveying the need for restrictive policies to the electorate: see Pryor (2002, p. 367).
12. It is also possible that the stronger dollar reduces the average propensity to save. It would not be possible to establish or rebut this relationship econometrically because the saving rate has too many determinants.

References

Acheson, Dean, "Statement," *Hearings on Post-War Economic Policy and Planning*, Special Committee on Post-War Policy and Planning, House of Representatives, 78th Congress, Second Session, November 30, 1944.

Adelman, Irma, "Editor's Introduction," *World Development*, 28 (June 2000), pp. 1053–60.

Alexander, S.S., "The Effects of Devaluation on a Trade Balance," *I.M.F. Staff Papers II* (April 1952), pp. 263–78.

Bach, Christopher L., "Annual Revision of the U.S. International Accounts 1993–2001," *Survey of Current Business*, July 2002, pp. 33–40.

Bank for International Settlements, *73rd Annual Report 2003* (Basel, 2003).

Bank for International Settlements, *72nd Annual Report 2002* (Basel, 2002).

Bensel, Terrence and Bruce T. Elmslie, "Rethinking International Trade Theory: A Methodological Appraisal," *Weltwirtschaftliches Archiv*, Band 128, No. 2 (1992), pp. 249–65.

Blecker, Robert A., *Taming Global Finance* (Washington: Economic Policy Institute, 1999a).

Blecker, Robert A., "The Ticking Debt Bomb: Why the U.S. International Financial Position Is Not Sustainable," *Economic Policy Institute Working Paper* (1999b), pp. 1–22.

Blecker, Robert A., "Let it Fall: The Effects of the Overvalued Dollar on U.S. Manufacturing and the Steel Industry" (unpublished paper, Department of Economics, American University, Washington, DC, 2002).

Boote, Anthony R. and Kamau Thugge, *Debt Relief for Low-Income Countries: The HIPC Initiative* (Washington, DC: The International Monetary Fund, 1997).

Brigham, Eugene F. and Louis C. Gapenski, *Intermediate Financial Management* (New York: The Dryden Press, 1985).

Buch, Claudia M., "Chilean-Type Capital Controls: A Building Block of the New Financial Architecture?" *Kiel Discussion Papers*, No. 350 (July 1999).

Chick, Victoria, "On Knowing One's Place: The Role of Formalism in Economics," *Economic Journal*, 108 (November 1998), pp. 1859–69.

Cooper, Richard N., "Is the U.S. Current Account Deficit Sustainable? Will It Be Sustained?" *Brookings Papers on Economic Activity*, No. 1 (2001), pp. 217–26.

Cooper, Richard N. and Jane Sneddon Little, "U.S. Monetary Policy in an Integrating World," *New England Economic Review*, No. 3 (2001), pp. 33–56.

Crockett, Andrew (1997), "Why Is Financial Stability a Goal of Public Policy?" in *Maintaining Financial Stability in a Global Economy*, Federal Reserve Bank of Kansas City (August), pp. 7–36.

Davidson Paul, "Reforming the World's Money," *Journal of Post Keynesian Economics*, 15 (1992–93), pp. 153–79.

Davidson, Paul, "Are Grains of Sand in the Wheels of International Finance Sufficient to do the Job When Boulders are Often Required?" *The Economic Journal*, 107 (1997), pp. 671–86.

Davidson Paul, "Is a Plumber or a New Financial Architect Needed to End Global International Liquidity Problems?" *World Development*, 28 (June 2000), pp. 1117–32.

Despres, Emile, C.P. Kindleberger and Walter S. Salant, "The Dollar and World Liquidity A Minority View," *The Economist* 218, No. 6389 (February 5, 1966).

Dornbusch, Rudiger and Paul R. Krugman, "Flexible Exchange Rates in the Short-Run," *Brookings Papers on Economic Activity*, 3 (1976), p. 566.

Dunning, John H., Chang-Su Kim and Wonchon Ra, "Incorporating Trade into the Investment Development Path," in Rajneesh Narula (ed.), *Trade and Investment in a Globalizing World* (Oxford: Pergammon, 2001), pp. 135–55.

Dunning, John H., *Making Globalism Good: The Moral Challenges of Global Capitalism* (New York: Oxford University Press, 2003).

Economic Report of the President 2003 (Washington, DC: Government Printing Office, 2003).

Eichengreen, Barry and Richard Portes, "The Anatomy of Financial Crises," in Portes and Alexander Swobda (eds), *Threats to International Financial Stability* (Cambridge: Cambridge University Press, 1987).

Fama, Eugene F., "Agency Problems and the Theory of the Firm," *Journal of Political Economy* (April 1980), pp. 288–307.

Fetherston, T.A. and H. Peter Gray, "The Contribution of Financial Conditions to Successful Industrialization in East Asia," *Review of Pacific Basin Financial Markets and Policies* 1, No. 3 (1998), pp. 419–35.

Figgie, Harry E. Jr. and Gerald J. Swanson, *Bankruptcy 1995* (Boston: Little Brown, 1992).

Fischer, Stanley, "Financial Crisis and Reform of the International Financial System," *The Review of World Economics* 139, No. 1 (2003), pp. 1–37.

Fry, J. Maxwell, "How Foreign Direct Investment in Pacific Asia Improves the Current Account," *Journal of Asian Economics* 7, No. 3 (1996), pp. 459–86.

Galbraith, James K., "The Brazilian Swindle and the Larger International Monetary Problem," *The Levy Economics Institute, Policy Note* (2002), pp. 1–10.

Gardner, Richard, *Sterling – Dollar Diplomacy* 2nd edn (New York: McGraw-Hill, 1969).

Godley, Wynne, *Seven Unsustainable Processes* (Annandale-on-Hudson: The Levy Economics Institute of Bard College, 1999).

Godley, Wynne, *The U.S. Economy: A Changing Strategic Predicament* (Annandale-on-Hudson: The Levy Economics Institute of Bard College, 2003).

Godley, Wynne and Alex Izurieta, "Strategic Prospects and Policies for the U.S. Economy" (Annandale-on-Hudson, NY: *Strategic Analysis, The Levy Economics Institute of Bard College, 2002*).

Godley, Wynne and William S. Milberg, "U.S. Trade Deficits: The Recovery's Dark Side," *Challenge* (November/December 1994), pp. 40–7.

Gray, H. Peter, "A Keynesian Framework for the International Accounts," *Weltwirtschaftliches Archiv* (Fall 1969), pp. 1–22.

Gray, H. Peter, *The Economics of Business Investment Abroad* (London: Macmillan Press, l972).

Gray, H. Peter, *An Aggregate Theory of International Payments Adjustment* (London: Macmillan Press, 1974).

Gray, H. Peter, *A Generalized Theory of International Trade* (London: Macmillan Press, 1976).

Gary, H. Peter, "Oil-Push Inflation: A Broader View," *Banca Nazionale del Lavoro Quarterly Review* (March 1981), pp. 49–67.

Gray, H. Peter, "A Model of Depression," *Banca Nazionale del Lavoro Quarterly Review* (September 1990), pp. 269–88 (Correction in *Ibid.*, December 1990, p. 487).

Gray, H. Peter, "Dangers in the Reduction in U.S. International New Worth," *The International Trade Journal* VI (Summer 1992), pp. 427–42.

Gray, H. Peter, "The Ongoing Weakening of the International Financial System," *Banca Nazionale del Lavoro Quarterly Review* XLIX, No. 197 (June 1996), pp. 165–86.

Gray, H. Peter, "The Burdens of Global Leadership," in Khosrow Fatemi (ed.), *International Business in the 21st Century* (London: Pergammon Press, 1997), pp. 17–27.

Gray, H. Peter, "Dollar Depreciation and the Price of Gasoline," *International Trade Journal* XII (Spring 1998), pp. 119–28.

Gray, H. Peter, *Global Economic Involvement: A Synthesis of Modern International Economics* (Copenhagen: Copenhagen Business School Press, 1999).

Gray, H. Peter, "The Quality of Financial Infrastructure and Financial Resilience: Contrasting Taiwan and Thailand," *Review of Pacific Basin Financial Markets and Policies* 5, No. 2 (2002), pp. 1–14.

Gray, H. Peter, "The Dangerous Assumptions of the Theory of International Trade," Paper presented at the annual meeting of the Eastern Economic Association (Washington, DC: February 21, 2004).

Gray, H. Peter and John Dilyard, "Increasing the Contribution of Foreign Investment to Sustainable Development: Domestic and International Policy Measures," in *Finance for Sustainable Development: Testing New Policy Approaches* (New York: United Nations, 2002), pp. 135–57.

Gray, H. Peter and John R. Dilyard (eds), *Globalization and International Economic Instability* (Cheltenham: Edward Elgar Publishing Ltd., 2004).

Gray, H. Peter and Jean M. Gray, "Minskian Fragility in the International Financial System," in Gary Dymski and Robert Pollin (eds), *New Perspectives in Monetary Macroeconomics: Explorations in the Tradition of Hyman P. Minksy* (Ann Arbor: University of Michigan Press, 1994), pp. 143–68.

Gray, Jean M. and H. Peter Gray, "The Multinational Bank: A Financial MNC?" *Journal of Banking and Finance*, 5 (March 1981), pp. 33–64.

Gray, Jean M. and H. Peter Gray, "International Payments in a Flow-of-Funds Format," *Journal of Post Keynesian Economics* XI (Winter 1988–89), pp. 241–60.

Grubel, Herbert G., "The Benefits and Costs of Being the World Banker," *The National Banking Review*, 2 (December 1964), pp. 189–212.

Grubel, Herbert G., *World Monetary Reform* 4th edn (Palo Alto: Stanford University Press, 1984).

Harrod, R.F., *The Life of John Maynard Keynes* (London: Mamcillan, 1951).

Helliar, C.V., A.A. Lonie, D.M. Power and C.D. Sinclair (2000), "The Risks of Investing in Emerging Markets: Fund Managers' Perspectives," *Journal of European Financial Services*, 4, No. 1, pp. 7–30.

Herring, Richard J. and Robert E. Litan, *Financial Regulation in the Global Economy* (Washington, DC: The Brookings Institution, 1994).

Hicks, J.R., *Value and Capital* 2nd edn (Oxford: Oxford University Press, 1946).

Hicks, J.R., "An Inaugural Lecture," *Oxford Economic Papers*, 2 (June 1953), pp. 117–35.

Irwin, Gregor and David Vines (eds), *Financial Markets Integration and Capital Flows* (Cheltenham, UK: Edward Elgar Publishing Ltd., 2001 and Northampton, MA. USA, 2002).

Jensen, Michael C. and William H. Meckling, "Theory of the Firm: Managerial Behavior, Agency Costs and Ownership Structure," *Journal of Financial Economics* (October, 1976), pp. 350–60.

Joffe, Josef, "Who's Afraid of Mr. Big?" *The National Interest* (July 2001), pp. 41–52.

Johnson, Harry G., "Towards a General Theory of the Balance of Payments," in *International Trade and Economic Growth* (London: Geo. Allen and Unwin, 1958), pp. 153–68.

Kaufman, George G., "Banking and Currency Crises and Systemic Risk: Lessons from Recent Events," *Economic Perspectives*, Federal Reserve Bank of Chicago (2000), pp. 9–28.

Keynes, J.M., *The Economic Consequences of the Peace* (London: Macmillan, 1919).

Keynes, J.M., *The General Theory of Employment, Interest and Money* (London: Macmillan, 1936).

Kindleberger, Charles P., *Manias, Panics and Crashes: A History of Financial Crises* (New York: Basic Books, 1978).

Kindleberger, Charles P., "International Public Goods without International Government," *American Economic Review*, 76 (March 1986), pp. 1–13.

Kissinger, Henry, "America at the Apex: Empire or Leader," *The National Interest* (July 2001), pp. 9–17.

Kobrin, Stephen J., "An Empirical Analysis of the Determinants of Global Integration," *Strategic Management Journal*, 12 (1991), pp. 17–31.

Kobrin, Stephen J., "Regional Integration in a Globally-Networked Economy," *Transnational Corporations*, 4 (1995), pp. 15–33.

Kregel, Jan, "Economic Methodology in the Face of Uncertainty: The Modelling Methods of Keynes and the Post Keynesians," *Economic Journal* 86 (June 1976), pp. 209–25.

Kupchan, Charles A., "The End of the West," *The Atlantic Monthly* (November 2002), pp. 42–4.

Landefeld, J. Steven and Ann M. Lawson, "Valuation of the U.S. Net International Investment Position," *Survey of Current Business* (May 1991), pp. 40–9.

Langhorne, Richard, *The Coming of Globalisation* (Basingstoke: Palgrave, 2000).

Leahy, Michael P., "New Summary Measures of the Foreign Exchange Value of the Dollar," *Federal Reserve Bulletin*, 84 (October 1998), pp. 1811–18.

Leijonhufvud, Axel, "Effective Demand Failures," *Swedish Journal of Economics* (1973), pp. 27–48.

Lloyd, P.J., "Symposium: Economic Dynamics and the New Millenium: The Architecture of the Multinational Organizations," *Journal of Asian Economics*, 10 (1999), 211–36.

Machlup, Fritz, "Equilibrium and Disequilibrium: Misplaced Concreteness and Disguised Politics," *Economic Journal* LXVIII (March 1958), pp. 1–24.

Machlup, Fritz, "Adjustment, Compensatory Correction and Financing Imbalances in International Payments," in *Trade, Growth and the Balance of Payments*, R.E. Baldwin *et al.* (Chicago: Rand McNally, 1965), pp. 185–213.

Maehara, Yasuhiro, "Comming," in Herring and Litan (eds) *Financial Regulation in the Global Economy* (Washington: The Brookings Insstitution, 1995), pp. 153–62.

Makin, John H., "Keep the Dollar Strong," *Wall Street Journal*, July 11, 2001.

Mann, Catherine L., *Is the U.S. Trade Deficit Sustainable?* (Washington: The Institute for International Economics, 1999).

Mann, Catherine L., "Is the U.S. Trade Deficit Sustainable?" *Finance and Development*, 2000, pp. 42–5.

McKinnon Ronald I., "The International Dollar Standard and the Sustainability of the U.S. Current Deficit," *Brookings Papers on Economic Activity*, No. 1 (2001), pp. 227–40.

Milberg, William S. and H. Peter Gray, "International Competitiveness and Policy in Dynamic Industries," *Banca Nazionale del Lavoro Quarterly Review* (March 1992), pp. 59–80.

Minsky, Hyman P., "Financial Stability Revisited: The Economics of Disaster," in Board of Governors of the Federal Reserve System, *Reappraisal of the Federal Reserve Discount Mechanism*, 3 (Washington, DC: June 1972), pp. 93–136.

Minsky, Hyman P., "A Theory of Systemic Fragility," in Edward I. Altman and Arnold W. Sametz (eds), *Financial Crisis: Institutions and Markets in a Fragile Environment* (New York: Wiley International, 1977), pp. 138–52.

Minsky, Hyman P., *Stabilizing and Unstable Economy* (New Haven: Yale University Press, 1986).

Mundell, Robert A., "A Theory of Optimum Currency Areas," *American Economic Review* LI (November 1961), pp. 657–64.

Mundell, Robert, "Prospects for an Asian Currency Area," *Journal of Asian Economics*, 14 (February 2003), pp. 1–10.

Murray, Tracy, "How Helpful is the Generalized System of Preferences to the Developing Countries?," *Economic Journal*, 83, 1973, pp. 449–55.

North, Douglass C., *Institutions, Institutional Change and Economic Performance* (New York: Cambridge University Press, 1990).

Oberdorfer, Don, *Senator Mansfield: The Extraordinary Life of a Great American Statesman and Diplomat* (Washington: Smithsonian Books, 2003).

Olivei, Giovanni P., "Exchange Rates and Prices of Manufacturing Products Imported into the United States," *New England Economic Review* (First Quarter 2002), pp. 3–15.

Ozawa, Terutomo, "Putting the Pieces in Place for Japan's Economic Recovery," *Analysis from the East-West Center*, No. 57 (Honolulu, 2001a).

Ozawa, Terutomo, "Borrowed Growth: Current-account Deficit-based Development Finance," in K. Fatemi (ed.), *International Public Policy and Regionalism at the Turn of the Century* (Amsterdam: Pergamon, 2001b), pp. 95–113.

Papadimitriou, Dimitri, Anwar Shaikh, Claudio dos Santos and Gennaro Zezza, "Is Personal Debt Sustainable?" *Strategic Analysis* (Annandale-on-Hudson, N.Y.: The Levy Economics Institute.

Proposals for an International Clearing Union, Cmd 6437, 1943 (the "Keynes Plan").

Pryor, Frederic L. *The Future of U.S. Capitalism* (Cambridge: Cambridge University Press, 2002).

Rahman, M. Zubaidur, "The role of accounting in the East-Asian financial crisis: Lessons learned," *Transnational Corporations*, 7, No. 3, (1998), pp. 1–52.

Reddaway, W.B. and Associates, *Effects of U.K. Direct Investment Overseas: An Interim Report* and *A Final Report* (Cambridge: Cambridge University Press, 1967 and 1968).

Rehman, Scheherazade S., *The Path to European Economic and Monetary Union* (Boston: Kluwer Academic Publishers, 1997).

Robbins, Lionel, "Economics and Political Economy," *American Economic Review* LXXI (May 1981), pp. 1–10.

Robinson, Joan, "The Foreign Exchanges," in *Essays in the Theory of Employment*, 2nd edn (Oxford: Basil Blackwell, 1947).

Rugman, Alan, *The End of Globalization* (London: Random House Business Books, 2000).

Schwartz, B.C., "The Arcana of Empire and the Dilemma of American National Security," *Salmagundi* (Winter/Spring 1994a), pp. 182–211.

Schwartz, B.C., "Cold War Continuities: U.S. Economic and Security Strategy Towards Europe," *The Journal of Strategic Studies*, 17 (December 1994b).

Shelburne, Robert C., "Improving the Economic Performance of the Global Economy: The Challenge Ahead," Presidential Address to the International Trade and Finance Association, Bangkok, Thailand (May 2002).

Singh, Ajit, "Capital Account Liberalization, Free Long-term Capital Flows, Financial Crises and Economic Development," *Eastern Economic Journal*, 29 (June 2003), pp. 191–216.

Tew, Brian, *International Monetary Co-operation, 1945–1956*, 4th edn (London: Hutchinson University Library, 1958).

Tobin, James, "A Proposal for International Monetary Reform," *Eastern Economic Journal*, 4 (1978), pp. 153–9.

Triffin, Robert, *Gold and the Dollar Crisis* (New Haven: Yale University Press, 1961).

Tversky, Amos and Daniel Kahneman, "Judgement under Uncertainty: Heuristics and Biases," in Daniel Kahneman *et al.*, *Judgement under Uncertainty: Heuristics and Biases* (New York: Cambridge University Press, 1982), pp. 3–22.

UNCTAD, *World Investment Report 2000 (Geneva: United Nations, 2000)*.

US Trade Deficit Review Commission, *Report* (Washington, DC: Government Printing Office, 2000).

Velde, Francois R., "Americans are not Saving: Should we Worry?" *Federal Reserve Bank of Chicago Essays on Issues*, No. 141 (May 1999).

Volcker, Paul A. (2002), "Globalization and the World of Finance," *Eastern Economic Journal*, 28, No. 1, pp. 13–20.

Wallis, Allen J., Undersecretary of State for Economic Affairs and Agriculture, "American Leadership in International Trade," address before the President's Export Council (November 28 1988). (Bureau of Public Affairs, Office of Public Communication, US Department of State Washington, DC.

Walter, Ingo, *The Battle of the Systems: Control of Enterprises and the Global Economy* (Institut für Weltwirtschaft, Kieler Vorträge 122, Kiel, 1993).

White, Lawrence, J., *The S&L Débacle* (New York: Oxford University Press, 1991).

Winch, Donald, *Economics and Policy: A Historical Study* (London: Hodder and Stoughton, 1969).

Yeager, Leland B., *International Monetary Relations* (New York: Harper and Row, 1966).

Yeager, Leland B., "Absorption and Elasticity: A Fuller Reconciliation," *Economica*, n.s. 37, (February, 1970), pp. 68–77.

Yergin, Daniel and Joseph Stanislaw, *Commanding Heights: The Battle Between Government and the Marketplace that is Remaking the Modern World* (New York: Simon and Schuster Inc., 1998).

Index